Photographing the Holocaust

Janina Struk

PHOTOGRAPHING THE HOLOCAUST
Interpretations of the Evidence

I.B. TAURIS
LONDON · NEW YORK

in association with

European Jewish Publication Society

Published in 2004 by I.B.Tauris & Co. Ltd
6 Salem Road, London W2 4BU
175 Fifth Avenue, New York NY 10010
www.ibtauris.com

in association with the European Jewish Publication Society,
PO Box 19948, London N3 3ZJ
www.ejps.org.uk

In the United States of America and in Canada distributed by Palgrave
Macmillan, a division of St Martin's Press, 175 Fifth Avenue, New York
NY 10010

The European Jewish Publication Society is a registered charity which
gives grants to assist in the publication and distribution of books relevant to
Jewish literature, history, religion, philosophy, politics and culture.

ISBN 1 86064 546 1

A full CIP record for this book is available from the British Library
A full CIP record for this book is available from the Library of Congress
Library of Congress catalog card: available

Set in Monotype Fournier and Gill Sans Heavy by Ewan Smith, London
Printed and bound in Great Britain by MPG Books, Bodmin

Contents

Illustrations

All photographs have the captions allocated to them by the archives and libraries credited, indicated by quotation marks. If there was no caption I have offered a brief description and/or date.

Acknowledgements

I would like to thank the many people who have generously contributed their time and knowledge to my work. I am particularly indebted to Tim Gopsill for his invaluable criticism, comments and encouragement throughout the various stages of this book and to my editor Philippa Brewster for her skill and judgement; also to Joanna De Regibus for tirelessly working with me on the translations of Polish texts and documents; to Rosemarie Nief at the Wiener Library for both professional assistance and her continuing support for my work; to Arie ben-Menachem in Israel for trusting me with photographs from his precious photo album and his memories of the Łódź ghetto; to Wilhelm Brasse in Poland for sharing his memories as a photographer in Auschwitz concentration camp 1940–45; to Anna, Andrzej and Paweł Stefaniuk, for their friendship and for providing me with a home in Kraków during my research in Poland.

In the UK thanks go to the late Nick Anning; to Stanley Forman of ETV Films; to the Holocaust Educational Trust, London; to staff at the Imperial War Museum photo archive and department of printed books, and particularly James Taylor and Terry Charman; to Jadwiga Olszewska and staff at the Polish Underground Movement (1939–45) Study Trust; to staff at the Polish Institute and Sikorski Museum; to Dr Klaus Leist at the Wiener Library for assistance with translation of German texts; to staff at Novosti; to Jane Rosen at the Society for Co-operation in Russian and Soviet Studies; to Dorothy Sheridan and Joy Eldridge at the Mass-Observation archive in Sussex and to the Trustees; to author Rafael F. Scharf; to photographer Wolf Suschitzky.

In Poland thanks to the staff at Auschwitz-Birkenau State Museum, particularly to Dr Piotr Setkiewicz, Teresa Świebocka, Wojciech Płosa, Halina Żdziebko. At Majdanek State Museum to Janina Kiełboń and Krzysztof Tarkowski. To Feliks Forbert-Kaniewski, Janina Kęsek, Jerzy Lewczyński, Christine Rickards Rostworowska and Zbigniew and Zofia Zegan.

In Israel thanks to Linda Baharier and Zvi Reiter; to Zvi Oren, Marek Herman and Deborah Schwartz Jacobs at Ghetto Fighters' House photo archive for their professional assistance and hospitality; at Yad Vashem to Daniel Uziel and Nadia Kahan.

In Canada I thank Dr Hélène Mair, for sharing with me her personal archive and memories of her father Maurice Bolle; in Ukraine Victor Susak for his assistance in L'viv; at US Holocaust Memorial Museum, Judy Cohen, Ann Millin, Sharon Muller and Alexander B. Rossino, for making my visit to the photo archive fruitful and a real pleasure and to Leslie Swift. In Sweden I thank Nachman Zonabend for sharing his knowledge of the Łódź ghetto. Thanks also to Katia Forbert Petersen in Denmark.

Thanks also to Ruth Cherrington, Mimi Gealageas, Zara Huddleston, Roberta McGrath, Hazel Medd, Vaughan Melzer and Chris Struk.

I would also like to give acknowledgement to the late Sybil Milton whose essays on photographs of the Holocaust were a source of inspiration in the early days of my research for my MA in Visual Culture at Middlesex University. I thank Barry Curtis, my tutor at the time. I would also like to acknowledge the Polish embassy in London for awarding me a postgraduate scholarship to the Akademia Sztuk Pięknych in Kraków which enabled me to begin my research in Poland. I would like to thank the European Jewish Publication Society for financial assistance towards the reproduction of the photographs. Thanks also go to Ewan Smith for his work in designing this book and to copy-editor Janet Law and proofreader Chris Parker.

Every effort has been made to trace all the copyright holders, but if any have been inadvertently overlooked we will be pleased to make the necessary arrangements at the first opportunity.

Author's Note

I have used the German and Polish spelling of words throughout this book but have quoted authors in the form they have chosen to use. Since 1939 many place-names in Eastern Europe and the former Soviet Union have changed due to the shifting of territorial borders. I have endeavoured to make clear the different place-name spellings at different periods in history.

This book is dedicated
to all those who risked their lives
to make photographs as evidence
1939–45
and in memory of my father
Władysław Struk 1916–99

Śniatyń – znęcanie się na żydami
przed egzekucją. 11.V.1943.

1 · 'Śniatyń – tormenting Jews before their execution. 11.V.1943.'
(Courtesy Polish Institute and Sikorski Museum)

INTRODUCTION
A Photograph from the Archives

§ Three naked men stand on the edge of a pit. Another man and boy, also naked, are walking into the frame. Surrounding them are seven perpetrators, some armed, some in uniform, some not. A uniformed man in the far right-hand side of the picture is standing on a mound of earth, presumably dug from the pit, seemingly directing proceedings, and appears to be gesturing towards the camera. The text reads: 'Śniatyń – tormenting Jews before their execution. 11.V.1943.'

I first saw a copy of this image (Figure 1), without the caption, as I was filing through photographs in the Polish Underground Movement (1939–45) Study Trust (hereafter Study Trust) housed in a leafy suburb of west London. It was this photograph that marked the beginning of my research into photographs taken during the Holocaust – that is, photographs related to the persecution and extermination of European Jewry during the Second World War. At the time I did not understand what I was looking at. I had not encountered a scene quite like this before. The pitiful sight of the hunched figures thoroughly shocked me. The bowed heads of two men in the foreground are facing into the pit. The child is still wearing a hat and the elderly man to his right appears to be wearing a shoe or a sock, as though made to undress in a hurry. The majority of perpetrators are standing behind their victims and turn towards the camera. Was there a lull in the proceedings so that the photograph could be taken?

I felt ashamed to be examining this barbaric scene, voyeuristic for witnessing their nakedness and vulnerability, and disturbed because the act of looking at this photograph put me in the position of the possible assassin. But I was compelled to look, as if the more I looked the more information I could gain.

It was also difficult to know how to find a context for this photograph, in terms of either an historical event or a photographic genre. It was apparently taken during the Second World War, but could it be defined as a war photograph? It seemed to cut across the boundaries of what I perceived war photographs to be about – it did not show the dead strewn on battlefields, nor seemingly the devastating consequences of war on civilians. Instead it appears to show four men and a boy passively awaiting their execution. This I found profoundly disconcerting. There is no apparent struggle, no resistance and no fight. It is of course impossible to know the circumstances prior to this photograph being taken and what was happening outside the frame when the camera shutter was released. A photograph is a two-dimensional object, a fraction of a second framed and frozen in time. An image alone can tell us little about an event. As Susan Sontag points out, 'photographs do not explain, they acknowledge'.[1] In order to be able to interpret a photograph, there must be some knowledge of the event being photographed. And to be morally affected by a photograph, Sontag argues, there must be a 'relevant political consciousness' without which it 'will most likely be experienced as simply unreal or as a demoralizing emotional blow'.[2] Sometimes the horrific nature of a picture can prevent rational or critical thought being applied to it. It can be easier to recoil from it rather than confront it.

I asked the archivist if she knew who had taken the photograph. She said she didn't. I understood from her look that she regarded this question as irrelevant and somewhat morbid. Wasn't the existence of the image enough evidence of the barbarism of the Nazis? But were those in the photograph Nazis? The lack of clarity in the image makes it impossible to identify the uniforms and ascertain exactly who the perpetrators are.[3]

It was only as I came to understand some historical facts about the activities of Nazis and their collaborators that I was able to place the photograph in a historical context. In the early years of the Second World War, particularly in Eastern Europe and the Soviet Union, executions by Nazis and their collaborators of groups of people lined up on the edge of pits, which they had been made to dig themselves, were not unusual. Those being executed were often made to undress, presumably to humiliate and degrade them, but also so that their belongings could be confiscated or recycled. Although this information contributes towards understanding what the scene could be about, it still does not tell me anything more about the photograph itself. I presume the naked people are about to be shot, but the photograph does not tell me that.

I wanted to know where and why it was taken. Who were the people? Were they Jews? Or Gypsies or Poles, communists or homosexuals? Were they aware they were being photographed? Was it an official photograph for the files of the Reich or an unofficial photograph, a memento for the photo album of a Nazi or Nazi sympathizer? This photograph could not have been taken by anyone but a perpetrator or supporter of the crime, because no one else could have had this kind of access to the scene, given that the perpetrator in the uniform is looking directly towards the camera.

There is evidence to show that the photograph was distributed among the

German occupying forces in Poland. In 1990 Jacob Igra, about whom nothing else is known, donated an album of twenty-six photographs to the US Holocaust Memorial Museum in Washington, DC. The only information that Igra gave was that he had found the album, which had belonged to a German, in an apartment in the town of Sosnowiec in Silesia, south-west Poland, immediately after the Second World War. In the album was the 'death pit' photograph with no accompanying text.[4] It was placed on the same page as another photograph which showed a group of clothed men digging a grave surrounded by uniformed members of the Wehrmacht (German armed forces). On the back is written in Polish, 'from a series on Hitler's Crimes during the German occupation in Poland'. After the war had ended the latter photograph was identified as one of many that were taken during an execution of fifty-one civilians in Bochnia, south-west Poland, in December 1939. These photographs will be discussed further in Chapter 2.

It is not known when the 'death pit' photograph first reached Britain, or other allied countries, but the fact that it is in the Study Trust archive suggests that it was sent during the war by the Polish underground. The Polish government-in-exile, based in London from June 1940, reccived thousands of smuggled documents and photographs from occupied Poland which showed the terror of the occupation and the sufferings of the Polish and Jewish populations. After the German army invaded the Soviet Union in June 1941, the Soviet embassy in London received thousands more photographs of the crimes committed by the German army on Soviet territory. The images were of paramount importance as evidence. Who took them, where, when and why, were not matters of great consequence. What was important was what they showed, or seemed to show. How these photographs were received in the allied countries and the reaction of the press and government officials towards them will be analysed in Chapter 2.

Despite the fact that thousands of atrocity photographs were available in Britain and the USA during the war years, the British and American governments were reluctant to publish them, seeing them largely as propaganda from Poland, the Soviet Union or from Jewish sources. Consequently, Polish, Jewish and Soviet authorities published their own formidable documentation. In 1942 the Polish Ministry of Information in exile published a book, *The German New Order in Poland*, almost 600 pages of documents and photographs, as evidence of the brutality of the German occupation. In the same year, *Soviet Documents on Nazi Atrocities* was published by the press department of the Soviet embassy in London and contained '200 original photographs' of the barbarity of the German occupying forces on Soviet territory. In 1943 *The Black Book of Polish Jewry: An Account of the Martyrdom of Polish Jewry Under Nazi Occupation*, published by the American Federation of Polish Jews, contained over 300 pages of photographs and documents. The 'death pit' photograph was not in these books, presumably because it had either not then been taken or was not yet in circulation in the allied countries.

After the war ended, during 1945 and 1946, the documents that had been received by the Polish government-in-exile were shared out between the Study Trust and the Polish Institute and Sikorski Museum (hereafter Polish Institute). The former became a depository for documents relating to the underground Polish Home Army (Armia Krajowa, AK) and the latter for official documents of the government-in-exile. There appears to have been little logic as to how these photographs were divided between the two archives, as copies of some photographs can be found in both.

In the Study Trust archive the photographs are divided between the 'official' collection – those received from the underground in Poland – and the 'unofficial' collection – those donated by individuals after the war had ended. Prints of the 'death pit' photograph can be found in both. In the unofficial collection the photograph has no accompanying data but in the official collection, the first one I saw, it is mounted on the same sheet as a second photograph, which shows eight men standing in front of a car. This one is like a snapshot of a group on a day out. Most of the group are looking to camera; one is drinking from a bottle. The juxtaposition of the two photographs creates a narrative. Some of the same perpetrators are in both photographs. Was it taken on the same day, before or after the presumed execution? The caption for the two photographs reads in Polish: 'Execution in Śniatyń.' (The town of Śniatyń was in Galicia in eastern Poland until the war; currently it is in Ukraine.) There is another copy of the same photograph of the men in front of the car. This time it is mounted without the 'death pit' photograph and the handwritten caption in Polish reads: '20. III.1943 – Śniatyń – execution.'

A copy of the 'death pit' photograph is also in the files of the Polish Institute. In fact, they have several copies kept in different filing cabinets and boxes. After a number of visits I came across a fourth copy (the image printed here) but it was only when I located the negative in the archive that I found it also contained the caption (the entire negative is printed here). The photograph can be found in almost every archive I have visited – in Britain, the USA, Israel, Poland, Germany or Ukraine – and the accompanying information locates the scene in many different times and places, but in no other archive, nor in any published work, do we see the man on the right-hand side of the frame. Why not? Was the image printed here the 'master' copy from which all other copies were made? If so why was he cropped out of the photograph and by whom? Was it not considered important to include the perpetrators, only the victims?

Photographing the Holocaust

On the copy held at the Bildarchiv Preussischer Kulturbesitz in Berlin he is partially visible and the date and the place are the same as in Figure 1. It reads: 'Four naked men and one naked Jewish child with cap await execution. Śniatyń 11th May 1943, Photographer unknown.'[5]

This image has been widely used in books, films and exhibitions to the extent that it has become an icon of the barbarism of the Nazi regime. It is not unique in this respect. There are many others which have come to represent the Holocaust and which have suffered from contradictory interpretations, as will be discussed throughout this book. Where the 'death pit' photograph was taken and when and what exactly it shows will probably never be known, but this has not prevented its use. So why is it so widely used? Is it simply for its shock value? It has become a symbol of the Holocaust in its entirety; the people in the photograph are both individuals and universal symbols of suffering. It is used as evidence, but by different people towards different objectives.

To begin to understand why and how this and many thousands of other photographs were taken during the Second World War it is useful to consider both the technological and creative developments in photography during the 1920s and 1930s in Europe, the USA and the former USSR, and the relationship between this photographic culture and social and political expression. Chapter 1 begins by discussing the pre-war innovative practices of photography – realism, socialist realism, social-documentary, photojournalism – genres based on the assumption that a photograph was a true reflection of reality. This notion was exploited by the National Socialist government in Germany during the years 1933–39 for propaganda purposes.

In the early months of the Second World War all photographic production in the territories occupied by Germany came under the control of the Nazis. Throughout the war, thousands, possibly millions, of photographs were taken in Poland and the Soviet Union, officially and unofficially, by Nazis, their collaborators and by ordinary German soldiers. Photography was of equal importance for those who resisted the Nazi regime. But among the many different narratives that have been constructed from photographs taken during the war few take into account who took them and why. Consequently they are placed side by side without distinctions being made between them. Chapters 2 to 5 address this question and discuss photographs taken not only by the Nazis and collaborators but those taken by members of Polish and Jewish underground organizations, photojournalists, Jews in the ghettos, prisoners in concentration camps and anonymous individuals. Some of these photographers were amateurs, others had been professional photographers before the war. Some used their cameras as an act of resistance, recording the acts of terror committed by Nazis or collaborators. For others, taking photographs of family or friends, making family albums or recording the hardship of daily life were ways of resisting and surviving. The only common purpose that these different photographers had was that all sought to record their own truths. The idea that a camera recorded reality was a notion that everyone traded on.

Photographic creativity, which had flourished during the pre-war years, did not come to an abrupt end when the war began, as some histories of photography suggest, but was redirected. The surviving collection is unique and distinct as a photographic entity in that it comprises so many diverse types of photographs: studio portraiture, photojournalism, photomontage, social documentary and family photographs. Chapters 8 and 9 will discuss the photographic collection and its current uses in museums and exhibitions.

I have attempted to reflect the diversity of this collection, and thus broaden the perception of what Holocaust photographs are deemed to be, through the photographs I have chosen to include in this book. Some photographs are published here for the first time. For example, the Jewish ghettos are commonly represented in books, exhibitions and films by images of the poor and the dying in overcrowded streets; this type of image has become the iconography of the ghettos. But there are other photographs of the ghettos whose impact is less immediate. A range of remarkable images was produced in the Łódź ghetto, for instance, and for diverse and complex motives: propaganda albums were made for the Judenrat, the Jewish council that administered the ghetto for the Nazis; underground activists produced images critical of this collaboration; documentary photos were clandestinely taken by professional Jewish photographers to record the horrors of ghetto life; some of the world's earliest colour transparencies were taken in Łódź by a Nazi bureaucrat and amateur photographer; professional photo studios functioned; family albums were still compiled by ghetto residents; and Nazi 'ghetto tourists' took their own ghoulish snapshots. Photography in the ghettos will be discussed in Chapter 4.

In 1944 and 1945 it was the turn of the Soviet, British and American army photographers and photojournalists to record the horrific scenes they witnessed during and after the liberation of the camps – Majdanek and Auschwitz-Birkenau in Poland and, among others, Dachau, Buchenwald and Bergen-Belsen in Germany. The majority of photographs the public in the West saw were taken by American army photographers and photojournalists and carried the hallmark of the humanist documentary tradition popular in the USA during the 1930s. Those made by British and Soviet army photographers had their own particular character. Chapter 6 discusses the photographs made during the liberations and the attitudes towards them in Europe and the USA and in the Eastern Bloc countries. Written accounts and images of the Soviet liberation of Majdanek and Auschwitz-Birkenau, the two biggest and most notorious camps in Poland, were generally regarded in the West as Soviet propaganda and largely ignored. But in the months following the liberation of the camps in Germany, photographs of starved human forms behind the barbed wire and tangled skeletal bodies stacked in mass graves were widely published and exhibited throughout Europe and the USA. As Nazism was defeated and the allied armies swept across Europe, a large amount of visual material, some of which had been made by the Nazis, was collected by the allied armies and used in exhibitions, books and the press and as evidence in the war trials, notably at Nuremberg in 1945–49. For the purpose of this book, only the Nuremberg trials will be referred to in any detail. The complexity of the many other trials which took place over fifty years, and the use of visual material in them, warrants a separate study. At that point the images were interpreted as evidence of a universal suffering, not particularly a Jewish one. The fact that millions of Jews had been sent to their deaths, simply because they were Jews, was not in the late 1940s given any prominence in either the popular or the official history of the Second World War.

During that period, however, in Europe, Britain and the USA, the official attitude towards images of Nazi concentration camps and atrocities was to change. Chapter 7 discusses this change, the reasons why it occurred and how it affected the use of images for the next twenty years. The photographs of concentration camps, which had been seared into the imagination of the British and the American public, were gradually withdrawn. The world order was changing and there was a new enemy to consider and new images to construct. Following the Nuremberg trials, Germany's Nazi past was pushed aside for the sake of the Western alliance against the Soviet Union. In Israel where Holocaust survivors accounted for 40 per cent of the post-war population, the ethos of Zionism was to place emphasis on the martyrs and fighters who resisted Nazism in the ghettos. In the Soviet Union, atrocity photographs of Nazi barbarity were displayed and published as a general reminder of the barbarity of fascism and in memory of the 27 million Soviet civilians and members of the armed forces who had died. In Poland images of atrocities were used in publications as a memorial to the murdered 3 million non-Jewish Polish citizens. The memory of 3 million Polish Jews who had died was largely part of the national memory. The Cold War was beginning and would have a profound effect on how the extermination of European Jewry was remembered, or rather forgotten, in both the West and the East. Each nation had its own memory of the war to construct, and each claimed the photographic evidence to help tell its story.

The 'death pit' photograph is only one example of many which have been used to represent each nation's interpretation of the history of the Second World War. The earliest known publication of this photograph was in *Zagłada Żydostwa Polskiego, Album Zdjęć* (The Extermination of Polish Jews, an Album of

Photographs), a book published in 1945 by the Central Jewish Historical Committee in Łódź, Poland, which claimed to be the first publication of its kind in post-war Poland and included many other atrocity photographs. In this book the 'death pit' photograph is identified as having been taken in north-east Poland. The caption reads: 'Jews standing before a grave pit for mass burial, a moment before being shot down.' On the same page is a photograph of what appears to be some of the same perpetrators standing in front of a group of partially clothed women who are seated on the ground. Both photographs are said to have been taken in Śniadowo, in the district of Łomża, after the liquidation of the ghetto. The perpetrators in the latter photograph are said to be 'Germans and secret police agents'.[6]

In *1939–1945 Cierpienie i Walka Narodu Polskiego Zdjęcia – Dokumenty* (1939–1945 the Suffering and Struggle of the Polish Nation, Photographs – Documents) published in Poland in 1958, the photograph is flipped from left to right and is simply captioned, 'execution of Jews'. In the first two of three editions of *1939–1945, We Have Not Forgotten*, published in Poland in 1959, 1960 and 1961, the photograph is again flipped from left to right. The introduction to the 1960 edition explicitly warns against the rise of neo-Nazi activity in West Germany. In the third edition in 1961, the photograph is flipped back, right to left.[7]

In 1959 it was one of many atrocity photographs flashed on the screen without commentary in the East German documentary film *Action J*, which revealed the activities of the former high-ranking Nazi official, Dr Hans Globke, who at the time was Secretary of State in Chancellor Konrad Adenauer's government.[8] The same year author Jakub Poznański, a former manager of a workshop in the Łódź ghetto, used the photograph as an illustration to his ghetto diary, *Pamiętnik z Getta Łódźkiego* (Memories from the Łódź Ghetto), in an entry dated 1 October 1944. It had no caption.[9] In 1960 it appeared in *Męczeństwo, Walka, Zagłada Żydów w Polsce 1939–1945* (Martyrdom, Struggle and the Extermination of the Jews in Poland, 1939–1945), captioned as 'a group of Jews before their execution'.[10] In 1955 it appeared in French avant-garde film-maker Alain Resnais's film *Nuit et Brouillard* (Night and Fog) with no commentary. In 1967 it appeared in a book, *La Déportation*, published by Fédération Nationale des Déportés et Internés Résistants et Patriotes, with the caption '*Ces hommes, cachants leur nudité, vont être fusillés. La même fosse recevra le père et son enfant*' ('These men hiding their nudity are going to be shot. The same ditch will receive the father and his child').[11]

By the 1970s, in the West, the destruction of European Jewry was becoming central to the story of the Second World War. Chapter 8 will address this period from 1961 and the trial and execution in Israel of the high-ranking Nazi official Adolf Eichmann to the present day. From this point on, in the West and in Israel, awareness of the destruction of the European Jewry, as a uniquely Jewish event during the Second World War, began to take shape and became known as the Holocaust.[12] There are a number of frequently stated reasons that effected this change of interpretation, notably the American Civil Rights movement and the Six-Day War in Israel. By the 1980s, particularly in the USA, the number of Holocaust memorials and museums dramatically increased, as did the number of publications, films and exhibitions. Photographs which had hardly been seen for decades in the West became central to the memory of the Second World War. In historian Martin Gilbert's book *The Holocaust: Maps & Photographs*, published in 1978, the caption to the 'death pit' photographs reads: 'Four Jewish men and a boy about to be shot at Śniadowa, a village near to the Polish town of Łomża.'[13] In 1978 it was one of many Nazi atrocity photographs published in Gerhard Schoenberner's book *The Yellow Star: The Persecution of the Jews in Europe 1933–1945*, which raised the issues of 'German guilt', the collaboration of France and 'other occupied countries' during the war and the lack of action taken by the allies towards the refugee question and the Jews.[14] In the book *The World Must Know: The History of the Holocaust as Told in the United States Holocaust Memorial Museum*, the photograph is identified as having been taken in 'Poland/Lithuania c. 1941'.[15]

In the BBC's *World at War* documentary (1975), the photograph was flashed on the screen as a Polish Jew, Rivka Yosilevska, was telling her personal story of how during a massacre of around 500 people, she was made to undress and then shot and left for dead under a pile of corpses in a 'death pit'.[16] In 1991 it was published, not to accompany the story of a survivor, but to illustrate the war diary of a Nazi, Felix Landau. The entry made on 12 July 1941, during his stay in Drohobycz in eastern Poland (now in Ukraine), described how he and other colleagues took part in an execution of twenty-three people at a death pit. The caption to the photograph reads: 'Naked Jews, with a child on the right, just before their murder.'[17] In a video called *Executions*, the 'death pit' photograph was used as a backdrop overlaid with the number of Jews killed in Józefów and the Lublin district in the east of Poland.[18] The image, however, cannot belong to all these stories.

During the late 1980s the collapse of communism had a decided influence on the way in which the Holocaust was represented. The 'evil' which had pre-occupied the Western world for over half a century was no longer perceived to be relevant. The Western democracies needed a new symbolic evil to affirm their values and the spectre of Nazism was temporarily revived. A number of factors gave credence to this, notably the rising popularity in the USA of the Holocaust as a subject and the proliferating publicity about it. Steven Spielberg's 1993 film *Schindler's List* played a central role in popularizing knowledge of the

Holocaust, as did the changing political organization of the former Eastern Bloc countries. For the first time in fifty years these countries were able to reassess their recent histories, including the events of the Second World War. At the former concentration camp Auschwitz-Birkenau, historians assessed those who had died there and for the first time it was publicly acknowledged that the vast majority were Jews. The former Eastern Bloc countries also became more accessible to Western tourism and the phenomenon of 'Holocaust Tourism' arose, particularly in Poland. The site of Auschwitz-Birkenau was to become the central focus not only for Holocaust tourists, but for a bitter ideological battle over the memory of the Holocaust. Images played a central role in these changing representations and will be addressed in Chapter 8.

By 1995, a large number of television programmes, books and exhibitions had been produced on the theme of the Holocaust for the fiftieth anniversary of the liberation of the camps. A deluge of photographs, those showing atrocities committed by Nazis and collaborators, those made on liberation of the concentration camps and those made by opponents of the Nazi regime, were placed side by side to highlight the annihilation of European Jewry. In March 1995 an exhibition opened in Hamburg as a contribution to the anniversary. 'The German Army and Genocide', curated by the Hamburg Institute for Social Research, included the 'death pit' photograph which was identified as being taken 'presumably in Latvia, summer 1941'. The perpetrators were said to be 'members of the local auxiliary forces (presumably Latvians)'. In the exhibition catalogue the image shares a page with two others of men undressing apparently before their execution. Though the caption implies a connection, there is no evidence that the incidents were related.[19]

During the 1990s the internet became an increasingly popular way of disseminating information and thousands of websites were created on the theme of the Holocaust. Many of these use photographs, including the photograph of the 'death pit'. On one website, the image, which is credited to *The Pictorial History of the Holocaust*, identifies the photograph as a 'mass execution of Jews in Nazi occupied Soviet Union'.[20] The way in which other photographs are used on websites is addressed in Chapter 9.

Whether the 'death pit' scene was photographed at Śniatyń, Bochnia, Śniadowo, Łódź, Józefów, or Drohobycz – towns hundreds of kilometres apart – in Poland, Lithuania or Latvia, or somewhere else, and whether it was taken in 1939, 1941, 1943 or 1944, we do not know. It may be not surprising, then, that this, and other photographs which are used in a generalized and confused way, have been exploited by Holocaust deniers. The main aim of the book *Forged War Crimes Malign the German Nation*, written by Udo Walendy, is to discredit Holocaust photographs as 'falsified pictures'. The 'death pit' image is defined as such.[21] Reference is made, not so much to its many interpretations as to what is referred to as its 'unclarity'. The allegation, which is also directed at other photographs, is that the image is not a photograph at all but a drawing. This claim is based on the fact that two copies of the photograph published in *The Yellow Star: The Persecution of the Jews in Europe 1933–1945* and *1939–1945 Cierpienie i Walka Narodu Polskiego Zdjęcia – Dokumenty* are 'not the same' and have 'incorrect light and shadow portions'. These statements exploit the fact that the quality of a photographic print can vary tremendously depending on a number of technical factors. For example, poor-quality photographs were sometimes crudely retouched with pencil to enhance the detail lost in print enlargement or in their transmission. Additionally, smuggled atrocity photographs were frequently copied many times for distribution purposes, often unprofessionally, and as a consequence the sharpness and the tonal range of the images was reduced and details lost. It is these technical points that Walendy distorts in order to discredit this and other images. The Holocaust deniers' criticism of Holocaust photographs will be referred to in Chapter 9.

Chapter 9 will also discuss the photographic archives. As the photographs of the Holocaust are prolific and diverse, so are the archives which keep them. Within them, photographs are ordered, filed and categorized according to bureaucratic conventions. Archives are not neutral spaces; they impose their own meanings on photographs. The ways in which they are organized are determined not only by where they are and when and how they were established, but also by the political culture of the countries in which they are found. Their unity, photographer and historian Allan Sekula points out, 'is first and foremost that imposed by ownership'.[22] And no archive, of course, is ever complete. In recent years, for instance, Holocaust archives have been collecting pre-war snapshots from Jewish families, adding a sentimental dimension to their composition.

During my research I have visited archives in Britain, the USA, Israel, Poland and Ukraine. There are primarily two categories of archive which contain Holocaust photographs. Those specifically defined as Holocaust archives include Yad Vashem Martyrs' and Heroes' Remembrance Authority and the Ghetto Fighters' House Museum in Israel, the Wiener Library in London, and the US Holocaust Memorial Museum in Washington, DC. Then there are those which have a broader remit: national archives, government archives, regional archives, museum archives and the private archives of individuals. The distinctions between them are important because while many of the same photographs can be found in a cross-section of these archives they are not always imbued with the same interpretation or meaning. In Poland, for example, there are many archives with images of the Nazi occupation, which historically have not necessarily been viewed as examples of the Holocaust. The largest collection is held at the national government archive, Instytut Pamięci Narodowej (IPN, Institute of National Memory), which was established in 1945 as the Main Commission for Research into German Crimes in Poland to collect material relating to war crimes. In the same period the Jewish Historical Institute was also established in Warsaw to house documents and photographs specifically related to the destruction of Polish Jewry. In addition there are photographic archives at the former concentration camps of Auschwitz-Birkenau and Majdanek which specifically relate to the history of each camp. Collections of atrocity photographs taken during the occupation can also be found in local history museums where they are contextualized by local or regional history.[23] However in Ukraine, where the former Soviet archive system is still largely in place, local history museums were apparently prohibited from keeping original photographs; they were regarded as important sources of propaganda which, presumably, could be misused. The archives were centralized both regionally and nationally. I was able to gain access to the Regional State Archive in L'viv, where I came across three extraordinary photo albums. They were made in the late 1940s and contain images and documents collected by the Soviet authorities during their investigations into Nazi crimes committed in the L'viv region. In these albums, images of atrocities are presented as evidence of the crimes committed against the Soviet people. In Holocaust archives and publications, some of these images are used as evidence of the crimes committed against the Jews. Two of these albums are discussed in Chapter 7 and two pages from them are published here for the first time (see Figures 48 and 49).

In addition, there are archives which were established not by nations but through a personal or political commitment by those who suffered under the Nazi regime. The first 'guardians' of the Auschwitz concentration camp museum, for example, were a small group of former Polish prisoners who returned to the camp, shortly after the liberation, committed to letting the world know what had happened there. In 1949 Beit Lohamei Haghetaot Kibbutz (Ghetto Fighters' House Kibbutz) and the Ghetto Fighters' House Museum was founded in western Galilee by a small group of Jews who took part in the Warsaw Ghetto Uprising as a memorial to the heroes of that struggle. The Study Trust and the Polish Institute were both established after the communist government took power in Poland in 1946, to keep alive the spirit of a free and independent Poland and to preserve the memory of the Poles who resisted the Nazi occupation.

There is no way of knowing how so many of the same photographs came to be deposited in so many different archives in different countries. In the majority of cases there is no record as to how they were received or when. Even where the identity of the donor is known, there is often only a name. But the fact that many of the same photographs exist in different archives in different countries has connotations not only for how they are interpreted, but also for their ownership. While some archivists acknowledge the tenuousness of their ownership rights on photographs taken by anonymous photographers and which exist in any number of archives, others claim to own them, and require a fee for their reproduction. In the Byelorussian State Archive of Documentary Film and Photography, the 'death pit' photograph – which it claims was taken in Białystok, north-east Poland – is said to be in the public domain. But research carried out at the US Holocaust Memorial Museum photo archive has established that the Bildarchiv Preussischer Kulturbesitz, YIVO, the Institute for Jewish Research in New York (which state the location is Białystok), and the Centre de Documentation Juive Contemporaine in Paris (which state the location is Śniadowo) claim to own the copyright.[24] The photograph published here, courtesy of the Polish Institute, is considered to be in the public domain, as are the four copies at the Wiener Library, where one is said to have been taken in Poland and another in Byelorussia; the other two are not captioned.

To whom, then, does this photograph belong? And whose story does it tell? The photographic representation of the Holocaust does not give a comprehensive account of the historical events which photographic narratives generally lead us to believe; that is not possible. Photographs are fragments. They illustrate stories, they do not tell them. It has been left to curators, film-makers, historians and propagandists to determine how they are interpreted. This book is therefore about omission as well as inclusion; fiction as well as fact; and personal as well as political motivation. As author James E. Young has said: 'Memory is never shaped in a vacuum; the motives of memory are never pure.'[25] The photographs and their interpretations may not always give us a better understanding of the historical event we call the Holocaust; rather, they remind us how the world has been ordered since then. The present always has its own agenda for reconstructing the past.

ONE

Photography and National Socialism 1933–39

The authority of the photograph

When the National Socialists came to power in Germany in January 1933 they inherited the artistic legacy of the Weimar Republic (1919–33) and an unprecedented mass communications system that they refined for their own propaganda purposes. They were quick to recognize the role that photography could play as a medium through which to promote their propaganda.

The Weimar Republic was one of the most intense and innovative periods of artistic expression of the twentieth century. There were links between the German modernist movement and the revolutionary artistic movements in Soviet Russia, both of which shared a commitment to engage with the rebuilding of societies following the First World War.[1] Photography was seen as an ideal form of expression for these innovative and radical ideas. Hungarian-born László Moholy-Nagy, a lecturer at the Bauhaus, said: 'The limits of photography cannot yet be predicted. Everything to do with it is still so new that even initial exploration may yield strikingly creative results.'[2]

Technological advances in mass communications such as the 35mm camera made photography accessible and gave it a reputation as a democratic medium. Painters, poets, sculptors, political activists and workers' organizations turned to photography as a means of expression.[3] 'The illiterates of the future', wrote German-Jewish Marxist writer and critic Walter Benjamin, in 1928, 'will be the people who know nothing of photography rather than those who are ignorant of the art of writing.'[4] The National Socialists seized upon the new status of the photographic image. Three principal developments in photography made the medium appealing to them: first, the widespread belief in its ability to be objective, to reflect the truth and be tantamount to scientific evidence; second, the ability to mass produce images; and third, the development of documentary photography during the 1930s which consolidated these principles.

The belief in the photograph as scientific evidence had been established in the nineteenth century, when photography was utilized by the disciplinary institutions of the state and the new social sciences: anthropology, criminology, physiognomy and psychology. These disciplines embraced the idea that human physiognomy, accurately recorded in a photograph, could reveal the inner truth about an individual's character. The relationship between photography and the state gave the photograph a new authority. Those who came under the scrutiny of the camera were placed passively in a full frontal pose, emphasizing features, facial expressions and gestures. The poor and the colonized were frequently photographed rooted in their environments, synonymous respectively with dingy streets and exotic landscapes. These photographic records were used with physiological data for a series of discursive operations levelled at the body. They were used in association with written data or statistics as 'proof' or 'evidence'. This viewpoint, though essentially authoritarian, was interpreted as 'neutrality'.[5]

By the 1920s, the belief that a photograph alone could reflect the true character of an individual had become pivotal to an understanding of photography. 'Criminal photos' were included in the radical exhibition, 'Film und Foto', held in Stuttgart in 1929. In an exhibition review, A. Kraszna-Krausz categorized them as images that give 'an unfaked reproduction of situations' and 'vitally catch physiognomies'.[6] The influential and distinguished German photographer August Sander was an advocate of the scientific physiognomic image.[7] In a lecture given on German radio in 1931, he postulated the creation of a physiognomic image of a whole generation or a whole nation, suggesting that it would be possible to detect 'group-sentiments' in 'certain individuals' which, he said, 'we can designate by the term, the Type'.[8]

In the same year Walter Benjamin, in his essay 'A Short History of Photography', praised Sander's major photographic study of German society for which he had taken portraits of all classes and social groupings: workers, peasants, the middle classes, Jews, National Socialists, soldiers, students, the disabled and artists. He wrote: 'Sudden shifts of power such as are now overdue in our society can make the ability to read facial types a matter of vital importance. Whether one is of the left or right, one will have to get used to being looked at in terms of one's provenance. And one will have to look at others the same way. Sander's work is more than a picture book. It is a training manual.'[9]

Photographing 'types' was a popular concept throughout Europe. In Poland in 1937 the Warsaw Jewish monthly newspaper *Głos Gminy Żydowskiej* (Voice of the Jewish Community) published a page of photographs in four separate issues headlined: 'Small town typical Jews.' These pictures, almost entirely of men, showed individuals and vendors in the streets, placed squarely in front of the camera.[10]

The representation of 'types' and the theory on which Sander based his practice were fundamental to National Socialist propaganda, but the distinctions he portrayed in German society were not acceptable to their ideology. Whereas Sander's photographs had given his subjects a degree of dignity and had celebrated difference, the theory was appropriated by the Nazis to condemn difference. In 1934, while the plates of the first edition of Sander's book, *The Face of the Time*, were being seized and destroyed by the Nazis, Hans F. K. Günther's book, *Rassenkunde des deutschen Volks* (Racial Elements of the German People), first published in 1922, had become a best-seller in Germany. It contained photographic portraits to establish the physiognomic superiority of the Nordic 'race' over those considered 'inferior', including the Jews. By 1933 sixteen editions had been published, and by 1944, 420,000 copies had sold in Germany. The fact that some of the 'same faces' appeared in both Sander's and Günther's collections emphasized the point that, even though Sander's liberal project centred on social rather than racial distinctions, both collections traded on the principle of physiognomic truth.[11]

In the late 1920s this scientific approach to photography was further developed to meet the demands of the changing economic and political climate. In 1926 Scottish film-maker John Grierson coined the term 'documentary'. The destabilized economies of the USA and Europe, following the Wall Street crash, had prompted artists and photographers to look for a visual language to convey the social consequences of economic hardship. Author and critic John Tagg argues that documentary was not only 'a complex strategic response' to this economic and social crisis, but also to a crisis 'of representation itself'. It transformed the earlier scientific photography from what Tagg describes as 'the flat rhetoric of evidence', into 'an emotionalised drama of experience'. The scientific approach was no longer sufficient. This emotive element, Tagg argues, helped to seal the relationship between the photographer and the photographed, the viewer and the viewed, into the paternalistic relations of domination and subordination on which documentary truth depended.[12]

This development coincided with what Walter Benjamin called the age of photo-mechanical reproduction. Photojournalism and illustrated magazines flourished. The most successful German illustrated magazine was *Berliner Illustrierte Zeitung* which in 1929 had a circulation of approximately 1.5 million copies a week.[13] Other countries followed Germany's lead. In 1936 the USA's first mass circulation illustrated magazine, *Life*, was launched, followed in 1938 by *Picture Post* in Britain. According to Benjamin, the technological possibilities of reproducing and publishing photographs for mass consumption changed the role of photography and freed the work of art 'from its parasitical dependence on ritual'. Benjamin wrote that once 'authenticity' has ceased to be applicable to artistic production, then the function of art is reversed and it becomes not about

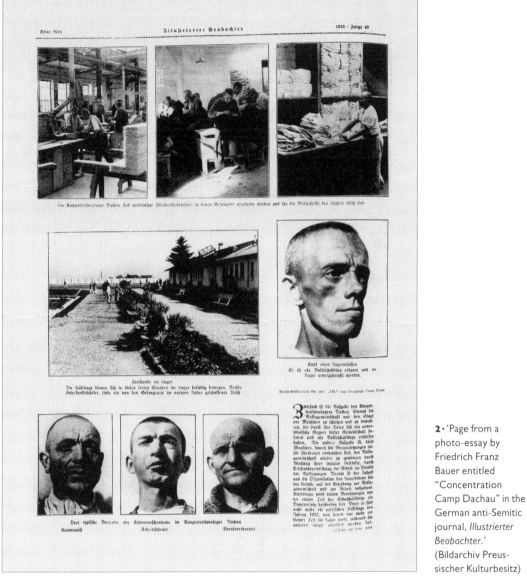

2 · 'Page from a photo-essay by Friedrich Franz Bauer entitled "Concentration Camp Dachau" in the German anti-Semitic journal, *Illustrierter Beobachter*.' (Bildarchiv Preussischer Kulturbesitz)

ritual but 'it begins to be based on another practice – politics'.[14] The politicization of the image, as Benjamin saw it, was not only applicable to those on the left, but also to the National Socialists. In 1926, an article in the pro-Nazi illustrated journal *Illustrierter Beobachter* expressed the idea that the 'vivid suggestiveness of photographs' could be 'more convincing than any text … The majority of readers would regard them as an authentic depiction of reality.' The article went further and suggested that the truth of the photograph could be improved on by 'shrewdly manipulating' the relationship between the image and text.[15]

Photography and National Socialism 19

The propaganda value of image and text was something the National Socialists exploited well. Documentary images and those which drew directly on human physiognomy were used widely. For example, in a four-page photo-essay by Friedrich Franz Bauer, entitled 'Concentration Camp Dachau', published in *Illustrierter Beobachter* on 3 December 1936, the majority of images show neat and orderly lines of marching prisoners and camp guards. On one page are eight photographs including 'prisoners at leisure by the pond in front of a barrack', workers in the 'interior of workshops' and four mug-shots of 'various types of criminals' (see Figure 2). In the latter the stark lighting, emphasizing the facial features, gives credence to the idea of the 'criminal type'. The contrast between the supposed tranquil and ordered environment of the camp and the harsh appearance of the men suggests betterment and rehabilitation. This typifies the way that concentration camps were represented by the National Socialists during the 1930s, as places of tranquillity and reform. Other examples will be discussed later in this chapter.

The Discredited Jew

Although all opponents of the Nazi regime were represented as 'undesirable', the primary target was the Jew, systematically portrayed as a parasite on the Aryan race, either as a communist conspirator or a capitalist rogue, an agent of either the Russian Revolution or British plutocracy. The Jew, according to Nazi doctrine, had many disguises and must be exposed for what he was: a carrier of disease, lacking in morality, and infecting all that was pure and good, that is, the Aryan sensibility. Visual 'evidence' of characterizations of the Jew was prolific throughout the Reich.[16]

These images were widely distributed on posters, in the Nazi press and in photographic exhibitions organized to mobilize photography for the National Socialist cause. The first of these was 'Die Kamera' which opened in 1933. On 8 November 1937 the most successful of all Reich exhibitions, 'Der ewige Jude' (The Eternal Jew), opened in Munich.[17] In August 1938 it opened in Vienna, and toured major cities in the occupied territories, including Paris in 1941. The exhibition drew together the diverse and often contradictory characterizations of the Jew, giving leverage to the idea that the Jew was inextricably linked to both capitalism and communism. This is exemplified in the exhibition poster (see Figure 3) in which the hunched bearded Jew is holding coins in his right hand, representing the capitalist, and in the other a knotted whip and map of Germany on which is drawn the hammer and sickle, denoting the Soviet threat. An anti-Soviet exhibition 'Bolschewismus ohne Maske' (Bolshevism Unmasked), shown throughout Germany in 1936–37 declared Bolshevism 'global enemy number one'.[18]

3 · Exhibition poster for 'Der ewige Jude' (The Eternal Jew), Deutsches Museum, Munich, 1937. (Wiener Library, London)

The image of the Jew in the National Socialist imagination was almost invariably a male one. Women presumably did not constitute the same threat, because in Jewish, as in National Socialist societies, they were first and foremost wives and mothers. They reproduced the race, but did not represent it. When women were subjected to humiliation and photographed, it was as sexual beings rather than as challenges to authority. This is a point I will return to in Chapter 3, but pre-war propaganda images that do show women are concerned with the public humiliation not of Jewish, but of German women, supposedly for fraternizing with male Jews. These images appeared on posters and in local newspapers.[19] One shows a woman being paraded through the streets with a large sign hung round her neck which reads: 'I have allowed myself to be defiled by a Jew!' Another shows a woman in the street standing next to a male Jew surrounded by Nazis in uniform. The placard around her neck is translated as: 'I am the biggest sow in town, I never on the Jew boys frown.'[20]

When the National Socialist boycott of Jewish shops began on 1 April 1933, only two months after Hitler took power, photographs which degraded and humiliated opponents were already commonplace. The authority of photography was drawn upon to intimidate those who did not obey the boycott. Street signs outside Jewish shops announced: 'Jewish Business! Whoever buys here will be photographed!'[21] Photography was so inextricably linked to the state that, as Rolf Sachsse, in his essay 'Photography as NS State Design/Power's Abuse of a Medium', points out, although no mention was made of the use to which these photographs would be put, 'the mere threat of having one's photograph taken was comparable to a police measure'.[22]

By the time the boycott was imposed, thousands of trade unionists, communists, socialists and political opponents of the regime had already been interned, tortured or murdered in Dachau, Esterwegen or Sachsenhausen concentration camps. There were Jews among these but they were a minority. It was not until late 1938 that Jews were interned in camps simply because they were Jews.[23] The stringent measures against opponents of the regime forced many into exile in other parts of Europe or the USA, including prominent photographers, journalists and editors. Among the exiled was Stefan Lorant who, in 1929, had become editor of the notable illustrated magazine *Münchner Illustrierte Presse*. In 1933 he was imprisoned for six months and fled to Britain later that year. In 1934 he became picture editor of *Weekly Illustrated* and in 1938 editor-in-chief of *Picture Post*. Three renowned German photographers, Tim Gidal, Kurt Hutton and Felix H. Mann, became the main contributing photographers to *Picture Post*. Political photomontagist John Heartfield also sought refuge in Britain, as did the founder of photo agency Dephot, Simon Guttmann.[24] Dr Erich Salomon, considered by some to be the founding father of modern photojournalism, fled to Holland but was later deported to Auschwitz-Birkenau where, in 1944, he died with his wife and son in the gas-chambers.[25]

A 'Pure' German Photography

By the end of 1933 the noose had tightened and all the media came under the control of the Reich Press Chamber, a sub-division of Josef Göbbels's Propaganda Ministry. From then on not only was propaganda well managed but so was the image of the party and its leaders. One of the most powerful figures in this organization was Heinrich Hoffmann, Nazi Party member and friend, confidant and personal photographer of Hitler. Hoffmann was given exclusive rights over Hitler's image by the Führer himself, and enjoyed the power to determine which photographs were suitable for publication. When the Second World War began, he set up a photographic agency in Berlin where all photographs destined for the German and world's press were sent for approval. As a result of his position he became immensely rich and powerful.[26]

As all forms of existing media were mobilized to further National Socialist ideals, new technological developments were taken up in the propaganda cause. From 1934–35 colour film, developed by I. G. Farben and Agfa, was used both as a source of foreign revenue and as a propaganda tool. It was seen as being more 'real' than black and white and therefore as potentially having more impact on the psychology of the masses. The first known successful colour photographic negative, made in 1935, contained the emblem of Nazi Germany, the swastika. It showed 'two female workers in front of the laboratory in Wolfen wrapped in colourful cloths; visible behind them is a colour chart for spectrometric analysis – and a swastika flag'.[27]

As the popularity of photography increased and developed into a mass consumer pursuit, so did the number of amateur photographers. The contribution the amateur could make to Reich photography was seen as crucial to the compliance of the German population towards National Socialism and anti-Semitism. In July 1933 the photographic magazine *Photofreund* defined the direction in which photography should develop.

> We ought and want to create a German photography ... The heart must speak in it, the German heart; the spirit must form it, the German spirit; sentiment must be tangible in it, German sentiment; and from this the new German photo will be born ... The German people have been rapidly united in the spirit of National Socialism ... All that seems in some way appropriate and good should and must be placed at the service of this tremendous idea, and thus photography too is called upon to help and contribute ... Photography should no longer distract from the struggle; no, it should lead into the midst of the fray and become a tool, a weapon in this struggle. The fact that it can be an explosive and powerful weapon is something the men of the new Germany have recognised clearly. Let the Führer determine the direction in which photography should develop.[28]

German families were encouraged to reflect on their racial superiority through family photographs and albums. Heiner Kurzbein wrote in *Photofreund* in 1933: 'Above and beyond its significance as a memento, the family photo can have an educational and affirmative effect with regard to race policy and can sharpen the eye of every comrade for the endeavours of race research.'[29] To educate the populace, amateur photography magazines published 'tips' on how to produce 'racially impeccable' photo albums.[30] In January 1939 a photo album containing sixty-eight photographs was made by a group of German students to present to their instructor as a memento of a visit to Poland the previous summer. It is a model of what a racially impeccable album should be. The photographs include scenic views, exotic indigenous people and their culture and details of Catholic, Orthodox and Jewish religious symbols. Orthodox Jews are pictured in the streets of Sosnowitz (Sosnowiec). Seven Polish peasants pose stiffly in front of the camera outside a wooden house, captioned 'Polish Types'.[31] Photo albums of this type became increasingly popular when the war began, and their contents became extraordinarily macabre. (These photo albums will be discussed in Chapter 3.)

As ordinary German families set about making their racially pure family photo albums, whether in Germany or abroad, so Reich officials made photo albums of their duties. Such albums offered an opportunity to elaborate on the accomplishments of the Reich and to lavish praise on high-ranking officials. Handwritten captions not only anchored the meaning of the photographs, but added a personal touch. Frequently they included personal dedications to superiors or Reich officials, including the Führer himself.

In 1935 a presentation album for Adolf Hitler, containing thirty-two photographs, was made by Arbeitsführer Ehrhardt of scenes in his work camp in Aue in Saxony.[32] The photographs, which are of a high technical quality, show a spotlessly clean, ordered environment. The inmates are photographed from a distance, portrayed as though a natural part of the camp landscape, reminiscent of the way in which workers were portrayed in landscape painting in the eighteenth century. In the same year, an SS Standartenführer (Colonel)[33] made an album containing 149 photographs of six work camps for political prisoners in the Emsland region of Germany, as a Christmas present for Hitler. The photographs skilfully use the genres of landscape, documentary and portraiture to portray the camps as if they were holiday camps in idyllic countryside. The precise, well-lit photographs again show empty and clean hut interiors, emphasizing orderliness, while landscapes, complete with grazing cows and farmyard ducks, capture the supposed tranquil surroundings. Orderly lines of prisoners in immaculate uniforms march to work. Others are photographed in workshops and on building sites. In heroic poses, reminiscent of the way in which socialist realism depicted hero workers in the Soviet Union, are prisoners at work and camp guards on duty, while uniformed Nazi bureaucrats are photographed sitting at desks in softly lit offices. The overall impression is that of workers and the rulers united in a common goal.[34] The comparison between the images in this album and those published in *Illustrierter Beobachter* (Figure 2) is an interesting one. Both the album and the journal contain images of orderly camp life, but in the album there are no 'criminal types', only heroic workers. Perhaps the Nazi hierarchy did not need to be convinced about their racial superiority, nor about the need for the camps, only that they functioned to perfection.

In 1936–37 approximately eighty photographs in a set of three albums were dedicated to Reichsmarschall Hermann Göring by photographer Eric von Rosen. They show him in hunting parties, in his lavish home and taking part in Nazi party ceremonials.[35] Another album, signed by Dr Lutz Herk, with the text 'Braunschweig 1936' on the cover, features photographs of Göring holding a kestrel on a hunting party and visiting a zoo.[36] According to a *Library of Congress Quarterly*, when Göring became Reichsmarschall, he ordered his office staff to collect and organize all the available photographs of himself into 'a series of super-albums'. The albums present a detailed chronological series of events from 1933 to 1942. At least forty-seven official albums were made, containing an estimated 18,500 photographs.[37] The number of photographs taken of the Nazi hierarchy and the meticulous attention to detail in the albums reflect the authoritative status bestowed on images by the Third Reich.

Photographs as Social Documents

While ordinary Germans and Reich officials were engaged in representing the triumph of National Socialism and the purity and superiority of the Aryan race in their photo albums, the Jewish population were becoming more and more excluded from the cultural and economic life of Germany. In September 1935, anti-Semitism was intensified with the introduction of the Nuremberg Laws which declared that 'Jews were to be allowed no further part in German life; no equality under the law; no further citizenship'.[38] In neighbouring countries, the popular support for pro-fascist parties encouraged discriminatory measures to be taken against the Jews. In Poland in August 1936, the Polish Ministry of Commerce ordered all shops throughout Poland to display the name of the owner, making it easier for those owned by Jews to be identified and as a consequence inciting anti-Semitic acts.[39] When on 12 March 1938 the German army entered Vienna, and Austria was absorbed into a greater Germany, almost overnight the 183,000 Jews of Austria were denied their civil rights.[40] Later that year, the night of 9 November, known as Kristallnacht, saw the widespread destruction of Jewish property and the round-up and murder of Jews throughout Germany. 'In twenty-four hours of street violence', wrote historian Martin Gilbert, 'ninety-one Jews were killed. More than thirty thousand – one in ten of those who remained – were arrested and sent to concentration camps.'[41]

4 · A photograph by Roman Vishniac: 'Warsaw, 1938.' (Collection of the International Center of Photography © Mara Vishniac Kohn, courtesy the International Center of Photography)

As the livelihoods of Eastern European Jewish communities looked increasingly under threat – in 1937 more than 35,000 European towns and villages had Jewish communities – there was an increasing desire to document their traditions and their plight.[42] In contrast to the pseudo-scientific image of the Jew in National Socialist propaganda, documentary photographers and film-makers saw the poetic and the picturesque in poverty-stricken Jewish communities. Józef Kiełsznia of Lublin and Mojżesz Worobiejczyk of Vilno documented the Jewish communities of their respective cities.[43] In the summer of 1939 two film-makers known as the Goskind Brothers were commissioned by a Yiddish film company in New York to document the daily lives of the Jewish communities in five Polish cities – Warsaw, Lwów, Vilno, Kraków and Białystok. The result was a fly-on-the-wall documentary showing the daily street life of Jewish communities in each city. In 1936 American film-maker and photographer Julien Bryan travelled to Poland to film Jews in the streets of the Jewish district of Kazimierz in Kraków.[44]

In 1935, the year the Nuremberg Laws were introduced, Russian-born photographer Dr Roman Vishniac, a specialist in micro-photography living in Berlin, was asked by American Joint Distribution Committee representatives in Berlin to document the daily life of the Jewish communities of Eastern Europe.[45] Between 1935 and 1939 Vishniac travelled thousands of kilometres with his Leica and Rolleiflex cameras and a movie camera, photographing and filming communities in Poland, Romania, Hungary, Czechoslovakia, Carpathia-Ruthenia and Lithuania, for evidence of their destitution. The man in Figure 4, according to Vishniac, was hiding from the Endecja (Polish National Party). Vishniac was arrested a number of times and many of his 16,000 negatives were confiscated. Some of his photographs were taken with a hidden camera, not only to avoid the eye of authorities but also because those he photographed were often suspicious of his motives. In *A Vanished World*, a book of his photographs published in 1983, Vishniac wrote: 'A man with a camera was always suspected of being a spy. Moreover, the Jews did not want to be photographed, due to a misunderstanding of the prohibition against making graven images (photography had not been invented when the Torah was written!). I was forced to use a hidden camera.'[46] The dilemma – whether or not to photograph people who did not wish to be photographed – did not seem to trouble Roman Vishniac. Indeed, he seemed to view their suspicions as backward. Vishniac felt it important to mention that the inhabitants of Upper Apsa, a village in the Carpathian mountains, knew nothing of photography: 'I felt myself transported several centuries back in time.'[47]

These images were some of the last documentary photographs taken of Jewish communities before the war began. Although some of Vishniac's images were distributed during the war as supposed examples of war-time ghettos, it wasn't until the 1980s that his images, and the documentary films made by the Goskind Brothers, were to re-emerge in the context of what had become known as the Holocaust, as compelling testimonies of those lost communities. These photographs of the Jewish communities were not widely seen in Britain or the USA before the war began, but other photographs, which showed the oppressive measures in operation in Germany, were published. Nevertheless, after the German invasion of Poland on 1 September 1939, Britain was unprepared for the deluge of photographs that followed. As the fighting in the Second World War began, so did the war of photographs.

TWO
Photographs as Evidence

The War of Propaganda

During the first six years of Hitler's rule many reports and photographs had been published in the British and American press about the increasingly barbarous measures adopted against Jews and opponents in the Reich, but British and other Western governments had been reluctant to comment.[1] The reason was not just the British government's policy of 'appeasement' towards Germany; there was also a fear that it would be discredited by the public, at home and in the USA, for spreading false atrocity stories about Germany, as it had done on an unprecedented scale during the First World War only twenty years earlier. According to historian Phillip Knightley, from 1914 to 1918 'more deliberate lies were told than in any other period in history', and so powerful was the atrocity campaign that it 'became the model on which Goebbels based that of the Germans some twenty years later'.[2]

Although in November 1939 the British government did publish a White Paper on German Atrocities, it did so reluctantly, not necessarily to publicize the persecution of the Jews and those who opposed the regime, but in response to increasing pressure to counter Nazi propaganda. In their defence of the concentration camps the Nazis were circulating material about the camps set up by the British in South Africa during the Boer War (1899–1902). Throughout 1939 these propaganda stories about Britain were gaining momentum; they were broadcast daily in South Africa by the Nazis, 'in an effort to stir up passions', urging Afrikaaners to revolt. So agitated was the British government about these allegations that a memorandum, dated 16 September 1939, from a Foreign Office official, Ivone Kirkpatrick, suggested that a White Paper be published 'immediately'. On 28 September a report in *The Times* criticized the British Ministry of Information for not countering what it referred to as the 'insidious Nazi propaganda'. The Foreign Office responded unequivocally: 'I think the time has come when we must publish something about German concentration camps ... We simply cannot afford to let the Germans get away with it like this.'[3]

The reports about German concentration camps which had accumulated in British government files had not been intended for public release. Kirkpatrick wrote that 'so long as there was the slightest prospect of reaching any settlement with Germany it would have been wrong to do anything to poison relations between the two countries'.[4] Now Britain was at war with Germany, this material could be utilized in the propaganda battle. While there was support for a White Paper, however, there was also caution. The first hurdle was how to deal with the fact that a large amount of information about German concentration camps had come from Jewish sources; Jews, in the opinion of a Foreign Office official, were 'not, perhaps, entirely reliable witnesses'. Equally problematic was the fact that public sympathy towards the Jews in Britain seemed, as one official put it, to have 'waned very considerably during the past twelve months'. Furthermore, it was thought that to show Jews sympathy would give the Germans 'further proof that the British Empire is run by International Jewry'. This was an accusation the government was keen to disprove.[5]

The second hurdle was how to prevent the public being reminded of the scurrilous First World War stories spread about Germany. This proved to be difficult. When the White Paper was published, many people believed that they were again being manipulated by the government. This, as Tony Kushner points out, was to have far-reaching consequences, as from then on 'all future Nazi crimes would be viewed through the prism of "atrocities" and thus ran the risk in war time of being dismissed as manipulative propaganda'.[6]

There was also public scepticism in the USA. A few weeks into the war, *Life* magazine wrote: 'This war's propaganda will have to be less crude, more credible than that of the last war.'[7] A report sent in January 1940, from the British embassy in Washington, DC to the Foreign Office, stated there was a widespread fear in the USA that they were going to be 'propaganded into the war'.[8]

The reports and photographs towards which this scepticism was directed came from a variety of sources: photojournalists, the Polish and Jewish underground, anonymous individuals and not least the Nazi propaganda machine. After June 1941, when Germany invaded the Soviet Union, a large number of atrocity photographs, received from the Soviet authorities, added to this glut of pictures and reports. It was not always clear who had taken the photographs, and for what purpose, but rarely was this considered significant.

Evidence from the Reich

While Britain was contemplating the pitfalls of an atrocity campaign, Hitler's Minister of Propaganda, Dr Josef Göbbels, had recognized the important role that images would play when the war began. From the start the Reich propaganda machine was busy flooding the USA with front-line documentary photographs taken by units of photographers and film-makers known as Propaganda Kompanien (PK) who were attached to every German division.[9] They had the latest photographic equipment and generous quantities of film, including colour film, which was still rare. According to the British Ministry of Information, 'the Germans send a flood of their hot photographs by radio to the USA or provide the facilities for the American agencies to send them at special rates'.[10] In mid-September 1939, *Life* magazine reported: 'On the propaganda front the Germans had definitely won the first week of the war.' *Life* described the German campaign as 'frankness', in comparison with what it called the 'secretiveness' of the British and French campaign. The article stated: 'most confusing to Americans was the total lack of visible evidence – in pictures – of any fighting at all on the western front ... Not only were two American correspondents permitted to report direct from the front but also, most convincingly, Berlin sent a steady stream of radio photos to America which left no doubt that there was fighting going on in Poland.'[11] The transmission of photographs by radio was another technological advance exploited by the Nazis, and indeed by the allies. The system, developed in the 1920s, allowed images to be scanned and transmitted on short-wave frequencies, making it possible to cover great distances.

In October *Life* congratulated Paramount on its 'great coup' in securing front-line photographs and films sent from Germany, and published a double-page spread of photographs under the headline 'Newsreel Camera Records a German Bombing Flight From Its Base in Poland'. 'The Germans', *Life* reported, 'collected everything taken by everybody, including their own photographers, and gave Paramount a complete reel before anyone else.'[12] A few months later, in April 1940, the Nazis were publishing their own illustrated magazine, *Signal*, an outlet for the front-line photographs of the PK as well as anti-Semitic and anti-communist propaganda. At the peak of its production *Signal* was printed in more than twenty languages, employed 150 translators and had a circulation of 2.5 million.[13]

The quality of the German photographs and their quick and efficient release impressed governments on both sides of the Atlantic. Even though in July 1939 a secret memorandum from a publicity division meeting at the British Ministry of Information had recognized that photography was one of the 'main forces in modern propaganda', little had materialized. In 1941 Cyril Radcliffe, director general of the ministry, was prompted to write a paper entitled 'Photographs as News', which attempted to analyse why American newspapers were generally filled with what he referred to as 'our enemies' photographs'. His conclusion was clear: German documentary photographs were 'immediate', 'alive' and depicted 'vivid and exciting incidents'. He cited those from the eastern campaign which had flooded the New York press and which showed German soldiers in action.

He criticized the British not only for their inability to make good documentary news photographs, but also for their failure to distribute those photographs they had. In similar circumstances, Radcliffe speculated, British official photographs would have probably shown 'British Tommies resting behind the lines, an Australian soldier washing his shirt or having a shave, a sailor being kind to a cat'. Even then, Radcliffe mused, they would have arrived 'some weeks after the event'.[14] This comparative lack of good British propaganda pictures was contributing to a decline in support for the allies in the USA. During the first three months of the war, according to a confidential report based on a survey of American press opinion sent to the Foreign Office, support for Britain had steadily declined.[15] The ineptitude of the British government in failing to produce photographs to counter the effective Nazi propaganda was to plague Britain's campaign throughout the war.

'The Heroic Battle of the Poles'

In 1939 the National Socialists were fabricating perhaps their most chilling propaganda to date, by using atrocity images to justify the invasion of Poland. Stories of attacks and appalling atrocities allegedly committed by the Poles on the German minority in Poland were widely distributed. According to a report in *Life* magazine in August 1939, 'in Germany the press churned itself up into a frenzy over "atrocities … provocations … waves of 'terror'" committed by Poles against Germans'.[16] To back up these allegations, photographs were widely distributed. According to author Andrew Mollo, some of the dead were taken from German concentration camps, dressed in Polish uniforms and then photographed.[17] When German troops occupied Bydgoszcz (Bromberg) on 5 September 1939, hundreds of Poles were arrested and executed.[18] A report from an English woman living in Bydgoszcz at the time recalled the revenge of the German army and how photographs were used as 'evidence' to inflame the situation. She said: 'Stories were spread of how hundreds of mutilated German corpses had been found in the forest, with eyes put out and tongues torn out, and photographs of the victims were shown to foreign newspaper correspondents.'[19]

In October 1939 a full-page photograph of a group of dead civilians, the majority of them women, was published by *Life* magazine under the heading 'WAR BY PROPAGANDA' with the caption: 'Who killed these civilians? Germany released this picture of "a Polish Atrocity" supposedly showing Germans in Bromberg massacred by Poles. They are really dead but who they were or who killed them is for the present anybody's guess. They may have been Poles executed for sniping at the German Army or they may have been Germans executed for sniping at the Polish Army. Whoever they were, they are now the stuff that propaganda is made of, the "proof" of some atrocity story.'[20]

5 · 'Polish women
executed in
Bydgoszcz during
the "pacification"
of the city'.
(Instytut Pamięci
Narodowej/
Institute of National
Memory, courtesy
of USHMM photo
archives)

The photograph appears staged, as if the bodies and the 'props' surrounding
them had been arranged for aesthetic effect. The woman in the foreground has
fallen in an unconvincing pose. Broken branches lie across two bodies behind
her, and between them stands a tea cup (see Figure 5). In 1940 this and dozens

Photographing the Holocaust

of other photographs were included in two editions of an expensively produced hardback book of documents, eyewitness accounts and photographs, to support German claims of Polish atrocities. The first edition, sarcastically entitled *The Heroic Battle of the Poles: Poland's Fight for Civilisation and Democracy*, was published in Geneva by the German government under the supposed auspices of the Ligue pour la Défense des Droits de l'Homme; the second, *Polish Acts of Atrocity Against the German Minority in Poland*, was published by the German Library of Information in New York and Berlin. Both editions claimed to have been published as a result of an initial 'investigation of 5,437 murders of minority Germans in Poland'.[21]

Polish Acts of Atrocity makes a calculating reference to the British 'atrocity' campaign during the First World War. It applauded *Falsehoods in War Time*, a book published in Britain in 1928 by Lord Arthur Ponsonby which had established that the majority of British propaganda had been made up of lies.[22] Emphasis is placed on the 'truth' of the pictures which, it stated, 'speak for themselves'. In addition to atrocity photographs, *The Heroic Battle of the Poles*, included a thirty-three-page section headed 'Medico-Legal Photographic Records', consisting entirely of grotesque autopsy photographs to illustrate the brutal ways in which the victims had been murdered. These images were excluded from the second edition on the supposed basis that they were 'too shocking to be reproduced in a volume intended for general circulation'. Instead, they were published in a separate volume, *Pictorial Report of Polish Atrocities*, which was apparently available on application to the German Library of Information in New York.[23]

There is no evidence that any applications were made, or that the books made much impact at the time, or that they were regarded as anything more than ferocious Nazi propaganda. The Polish Ambassador in London, Count Edward Raczyński, was incensed by the publications. He wrote in a letter to *The Times* that *The Heroic Battle of the Poles* 'is nothing but a most scurrilously slanderous pamphlet against Poland'. Raczyński claimed that the printers in Geneva, Imprimerie F. Vautier & Fils, were imaginary, and the Ligue pour la Défense des Droits de l'Homme, which he pointed out was an anti-Nazi institution, 'had taken steps to indict as a forgery this audacious German attempt to use its authority'.[24] Nevertheless, it was most probably the Geneva edition that impressed David Kelly, the British press attaché in Bern, who, in a letter to the Ministry of Information, referred to the 'splendid produced books which are distributed gratis'. In the face of what he called the 'deluge of propaganda', Kelly urged the British government to respond: 'It really is a bit startling … with a few negligible exceptions, there is no anti-Nazi propaganda material in German published here, and this situation is apparently accepted as though it were an act of God, like an earthquake.'[25]

Scurrilous as these publications were, they provided a chillingly accurate prediction of the crimes the Nazis themselves were to commit in occupied Europe and the Soviet Union, particularly against the Jews. The text stated that the atrocities were 'systematically planned and ordered' and described in detail the way in which the victims were murdered. Germans were being murdered by Poles, the book claimed, for no other reason than that they were German. The victims were subjected to 'mass arrests', forced on to 'deportation transports' to 'the dreaded concentration camp' or beaten, mutilated, tortured or murdered. Some were taken to 'the edge of a field or forest' and killed 'by shots in the neck'. Victims were made to 'dig their own graves with their bare hands before being killed'. Whole families and entire villages were obliterated and some were found 'horribly mutilated'. The perpetrators celebrated these crimes and bodies of the dead were put on 'commercial exhibition' to be 'loudly applauded by leering mobs'. The crimes were said to have been committed due to 'a political mass psychosis' which made the perpetrators capable of any action against Germans, who had to be annihilated. These atrocities, the book concluded, are 'among the worst disgraces in the bloody annals of racial discrimination' and are 'in a class by themselves in the history of twentieth century political murders'.[26] This was the precise conclusion the allies were to come to on discovery of the Nazi concentration and death camps five years later.

Evidence from the Occupied Territories

While the Nazis were distributing images of these alleged attacks, photographers in Poland were taking pictures of the devastation precipitated by the German invasion. Julien Bryan, an American photographer and film-maker, became known for his photographs of the Siege of Warsaw. Bryan had been in Poland in 1936 filming in Kazimierz, the Jewish district of Kraków, and was returning to Europe in 1939 for what he thought would be a summer in 'tranquil surroundings'. For years he had taken long summer trips to make 'documentary motion pictures' of what he defined as 'strange places and people all over the world'. At the end of August 1939, after completing filming in Holland and Switzerland, he decided to travel to Poland to obtain a few 'behind-the-lines photographs.'[27] When he arrived in Warsaw on 7 September the city was already suffering severe damage from the continual bombardment from German war planes. Bryan wrote: 'Here was a photographer's dream come true. I was in a city about to face, perhaps, the worst siege of all modern history, and I was lucky enough to be on hand to record these events with my camera. Not only that, but I had no competition. I had the siege of Warsaw all to myself.' For Bryan it was 'the kind of scoop every photographer and newspaper man dreams about'.[28]

With the official sanction of the mayor of Warsaw, Stefan Starzyński, he continued to photograph and film the devastation in and around the city until 21 September. Mayor Starzyński hoped that as a foreigner Bryan might be able to take documentary evidence of the destruction of Warsaw to the outside world. 'Your pictures may prove to be of real importance', he said, 'so that the world may know what has happened here.' Bryan felt that once back in America people might not believe his story in words but, he said, 'everyone would believe my pictures'.[29] The world generally did believe his pictures: Bryan's photographs were widely distributed in Britain and the USA. On 23 October 1939, *Life* magazine published five pages of his photographs under the heading 'Documentary Record of the Last Days of Once Proud Warsaw'.[30] One of these photographs showed a young girl kneeling over her dead sister. Bryan photographed this scene during a bombing raid: 'While I was photographing the bodies, a little ten-year-old girl came running up and stood transfixed by one of the dead. The woman was her older sister. The child had apparently never before seen death and couldn't understand why her sister would not speak to her.'[31] This photograph was widely used in British and American publications throughout the war, including British propaganda leaflets dropped over Germany in 1943–44.[32] It was a photograph that fitted many stories about the human cost of war.

In September 1958 Bryan returned to Warsaw to try to find some of those he had photographed in 1939. He had no names or current addresses but carried his book, *Siege*, and copies of his photographs, including that of the young girl kneeling over her dead sister. Leon Bielski, the editor of the evening newspaper *Express Wieczorny*, agreed to publish an article and photographs, headlined 'Do you see yourself, your closest, your home or street!' Some of those he had photographed in 1939 responded, including the 'little girl'. She was then thirty-two-year-old Kazimiera Mika.[33]

Bryan wrote that in 1939 all correspondents, photographers and film-makers had left Warsaw before the siege began, but in fact Polish photographers were still working. In the first days of the German invasion, the Polish army film unit, Sekcja Filmowo-Fotograficzna, accompanied the Polish army to the front line, but by 28 September Warsaw had capitulated to the German army, and on 26 October the German-controlled General Government was formed in Kraków.[34] Immediately, throughout Poland newspaper and publishing houses were closed down, photographic processing laboratories and photographic materials factories were commandeered by the Germans and severe restrictions were put in place curtailing unofficial photography and the ownership of cameras and photographic equipment.

Despite the prohibitions a few photo studios continued to function, including the Jewish-owned Foto-Forbert, one of the most fashionable in Warsaw. This

6 · Two frames of a strip of film smuggled from Poland. (Courtesy Polish Underground Movement [1939–45] Study Trust)

studio would continue to operate throughout the war, but without its owners. The two Forbert brothers, Adolf and Władysław, who were established photographers and film-makers, left Warsaw in September 1939 for eastern Poland. On 17 September 1939, the day of the Soviet occupation under the Molotov–Ribbentrop pact, they were captured by the Soviet army at the then Russian–Polish border town of Zaleszczyki (now in Ukraine) while filming for French Pathé news.[35] The brothers would not return to Poland until July 1944 when cameraman Adolf Forbert would record the liberation of Majdanek and later of Auschwitz-Birkenau. The work of Foto-Forbert is discussed in Chapter 4 and Adolf Forbert's memoirs of the liberations are referred to in Chapter 6.

Apart from the few photo studios, a vast and efficient Polish underground photography network was formed. In Warsaw, the Main Command Office for Information and Propaganda operated from various locations, including the Institute of Physics at Warsaw Polytechnic, and from the homes of individual photographers and underground workers. Among these were Zdzisław Marcinkowski and Janusz Podoski. There was also a 'school' for photographers run by, among others, Wacław Żdżarski and Władysław Bala.[36] Photography became a crucial weapon for the resistance movement whose aim it was to capture on film the devastating consequences of the occupation: Nazi persecution, German posters which announced increasingly stringent measures against Poles and Jews, arrests and public executions. The objective was to smuggle them abroad to allied governments and to the Polish government-in-exile established under the leadership of the Polish General Władysław Sikorski in France. Following the capitulation of France in mid-1940, the government-in-exile moved to London. From its London offices, throughout the war, it received enormous amounts of information and photographs via a network of Polish underground liaison bases in Europe, which in turn involved hundreds if not thousand of couriers.[37] In 1945, one of the best-known couriers, Jan Karski, wrote in his book, *Story of a Secret State*, of how he was captured crossing to Hungary carrying a roll of Leica film concealed in the handle of a razor.[38] In addition to Polish sources, photographs and documents came from individuals who managed to escape the occupied territories or from Jewish sources, through Geneva, Slovakia, Hungary, Constantinople and wherever representatives of Jewish news agencies or newspaper organizations were based.[39]

Many of these images were taken and distributed under extremely difficult circumstances, with the consequence that the technical quality varied. Some, for example, were copied on to strips of thin microfilm so they could be smuggled more easily. Figure 6 is an example of two frames from a thin strip of film (approximately half the size of a 35mm film), showing two bodies in rags and a cross on a grave, probably taken in the autumn of 1939.

Images such as these would often be of a poor technical quality when blown up and would be 'retouched'. At that time retouching methods were generally crude: figures, buildings or other details in the photograph were often outlined with what appeared to be a thick pencil, which sometimes made photographs look like drawings. In addition, the 'master copy' had sometimes been cropped, or sections of it blown up to emphasize or omit parts of the image, depending on what those distributing or publishing the photographs wanted the image to convey. Enlarging sections of the photograph also increased the lack of definition.

With a large number of individuals and organizations smuggling photographs, it was not uncommon for the same image to be widely distributed by more than one agency or organization, and for any number of copies to be circulating at any one time, often with different interpretations of what the image was supposed to show. Some photographs were received without data. Caption writers and editors would often add their own. When photographs *were* received with captions they were not always used, depending on the context and the story being told. There were no hard rules about the use of photographs; the only consideration was what they *appeared* to show. Photographs of the specific were used as examples of the general and vice versa. For example, on 5 April 1940, *The War Illustrated* published German propaganda photographs of British prisoners of war. The caption read: 'British soldiers, captured by a German patrol but still not down hearted, are being taken to the rear by an escort along a railway track on their way to an internment camp.'[40] The photograph was credited to Associated Press, Wide World and Planet News. Another photograph of the same British POWs, taken from a different angle, was distributed by Keystone, but this time the subjects were said to be Jews.[41]

One photograph which was, and still is, used to tell different stories was taken by Julien Bryan in Warsaw in 1939 (see Figure 7). In the centre of the image are two elderly Orthodox Jews hunched over the shovels they are digging with. In the far left of the frame is a hand holding a gun, in the right of the frame a civilian wielding a pick. In Bryan's book *Siege*, published in 1940, it is captioned: 'EVERYBODY HELPING: Orthodox Jews, Like Others, Dig Trenches Under the Direction of Soldiers.'[42] In 1942 it was published in *The German New Order in Poland*, but here the man wielding a pick had been cropped out. The caption read: 'Two elderly Jews forced to dig earth under the supervision of a German soldier', and added that it had appeared in *Illustrierter Beobachter* on 9 November 1939.[43] This indicates it had been copied from the Nazi publication. In 1943 this same version of the photograph was published in *The Black Book of Polish Jewry* captioned, 'Aged Jews At Forced Labour'.[44] This is a photograph which could be interpreted to suit everyone's purpose. For Bryan, the author, it was an example of the bravery of the people of Warsaw who helped defend their city; to the Nazis it was 'evidence' of their supremacy over the Jews; for those who opposed the Nazi regime, accepting the 'truth' of the Nazi propaganda version, it was 'evidence' of Nazi persecution of the Jews.

The fate of this photograph was not, however, unusual. The practice of copying photographs for propaganda purposes had been common on all sides

7·Credited by photographer Julien Bryan in his book *Siege* as: 'EVERYBODY HELPING: Orthodox Jews, Like Others, Dig Trenches Under the Direction of Soldiers'. (Wiener Library, London)

even before the war began. In 1936 Victor Gollancz published a substantial book, *The Yellow Spot: The Extermination of the Jews in Germany*. To back up accounts of the persecution of Jews, Gollancz used photographs, the majority of which had been copied from the official Nazi illustrated press, including *Der Stürmer*. The Nazis had published them as propaganda, and Gollancz had used them as 'evidence' of the oppression of the Jews.

In Poland, copying German newspapers, magazines and other propaganda material and images on to film or microfilm was a major part of the work of the underground photo-duplication operation.[45] It is probable that this is what happened to Bryan's photograph of the Orthodox Jews, as the print in the Polish Institute and Sikorski Museum and the Polish Underground Movement (1939–45) Study Trust exactly corresponds with the 'Nazi' version. What is surprising is that this interpretation of the photograph is still used in exhibitions, museums and books about the Holocaust to illustrate the oppressive measures taken against the Jews in Poland.[46]

The British press also saw the propaganda value of using images from Nazi publications, which was no doubt partly a response to the lack of 'good' British photographs in circulation. The Ministry of Information seemed unsure how to

Photographs as Evidence

respond to this practice. When in 1941 some members of the British press made official applications to the ministry to import German newspapers and magazines, it was unable to decide on an official response.[47] The primary concern of the ministry was whether they should make copies of German copyright photographs without a licence from the Patent Office. The question of copyright had preoccupied the photographic division since their first meeting in July 1939. Then they had mused on the troubles caused by the fact that during the First World War the government had distributed pictures and paid virtually no copyright fees to the press agencies.[48] The director of the photographic division, H. R. Francis, was concerned that this might be the case again, but more importantly he worried that disregarding photographic copyright could be exploited by enemy agents 'who might', he said, 'use the copyright infringement to cause embarrassment'. In March 1942 the executive board of the ministry finally decided to take the 'risk' of using enemy photographs.[49] But this decision was a technicality. Numerous photographs of German origin were already being used by the press in Britain and the USA, and indeed by the ministry itself.[50]

By early 1940 photographs taken by resistance photographers and individuals in Poland were beginning to be widely circulated and published in Britain and the USA. The fact that many pictures could be reported as having been 'smuggled' became integral to newspaper and magazine stories. The implication of risk gave photographs an extra credibility, authority and an added drama which they might not otherwise have had.

In February 1940 *The War Illustrated* published a double-page spread entitled 'Helpless Poles Caught in Hitler's Trap'. The report described Poland as 'a land of darkness and the shadow of death', and one of the four photographs showed crosses on graves in the streets of Warsaw, as the cemeteries, the caption stated, were 'filled to overflowing'. Another showed three people walking in the road away from the camera with yellow triangles in the centre of their backs, captioned: 'Pitiable in the extreme is the plight of the Jews in Poland under Nazi rule. On their backs they must wear a triangle of yellow cloth to show that their faith is abominable to the Nazi, and they must walk in the gutter, for the pavement is for Aryans only.' The photograph had, according to the caption, been 'smuggled out of Poland by a neutral'.[51] The following week *Life* magazine published this photograph as 'the first evidence of the most terrible story in the world today – the death of the Polish people'. The 'amazing' picture, reported *Life*, had been taken in Warsaw 'by a ruined nobleman who hid a tiny camera in his rags' and managed to escape.[52]

In March 1940 the *Daily Telegraph* published a front-page picture which it reported had been 'smuggled out of Poland', captioned: 'A group of Jews being escorted by a Gestapo man from Warsaw to a concentration camp.'[53] In April,

Life published what it referred to as a 'gruesome picture' of three men hanging in the streets of Warsaw which it claimed had been 'recently smuggled'.[54]

By early 1941 another batch of photographs, apparently smuggled into Switzerland by a Swiss journalist, was being distributed by Interphoto News Pictures Inc. in New York. In addition to the images of street arrests, graves in the streets, hangings and executions, there were now pictures which showed the formation of the ghettos and the deportation of Jews. In February 1941 *PM* published fourteen of these photographs over five pages with the headline: 'Inside Poland: Smuggled Pictures Show Nazi Persecution.'[55] The photographs, which reportedly had been taken in 1940, showed German posters in the streets announcing stringent measures against Jews, the 'ghetto wall in Warsaw', Jews 'fleeing Cracow' and 'Labor Battalions of Polish men and women' repairing roads.[56] In March the Fox photo agency distributed some of these photographs in Britain with the caption: 'SMUGGLED PICTURES: SHOW INSIDE POLAND: These remarkable pictures were taken behind the backs of the Nazi authorities in Warsaw, Lublin and Cracow, and are the first to be smuggled out of Poland ... Just received in this country, they make the first comprehensive picture story of Nazi Poland.'[57]

In November 1941 this batch of photographs, with the same captions, were sent to the British Ministry of Information from the British Press Service in New York at the request of H. R. Francis. In September 1941, when the request was made, he had apparently been unaware of their precise nature but had heard that pictures, which showed 'the horrors of the Nazi regime', were in circulation in the USA.[58] When the ministry received them, some doubted their authenticity. The image of the Warsaw ghetto wall, which had been published in *PM* nine months earlier, was received with suspicion. An official noted 'to the best of my recollection this is no more the ghetto than Malet Street' (the location of the headquarters of the Ministry of Information in central London).[59] As a general point, Francis noted that the photographs 'owe what interest they had to the very exaggerated style of the captions'.[60] The ministry's scepticism was fuelled by the fact they already regarded Interphoto with the 'gravest suspicion' and as an 'active distributor of pro-Nazi pictures'.[61]

In 1941 another set of photographs which showed men being rounded up by German soldiers, men digging a grave, an execution and a public hanging were in wide circulation in Britain and the USA. The captions on each were identical and headlined: NAZI MASS EXECUTION IN POLAND. THESE PICTURES WILL SHOCK THE WORLD. Figures 8 and 9 show the image of the hanging and the original caption which is pasted on to the back of the photograph. Both the *Illustrated London News* and *The War Illustrated* printed a full-page spread of these photographs.[62] The former used the headline: 'WHERE GERMANS RULE: DEATH DANCE BEFORE POLISH EXECUTION' (see Figure 10).

8 · One of the prints in wide circulation in 1941. Part of the original caption reads: 'Two of the victims hang from a litter box post. Germans on the right gaze at the spectacle.' (Imperial War Museum, KY440521)

After the war, these and other pictures were discovered in a photo album entitled 'Retaliation in Bochnia', which was found in the home of an SS man in Bavaria. The album contained a detailed chronological police report of the 'course of action' taken as a response to an assault by members of the conspiratorial organization 'Orzeł Biały' (White Eagle) on a German police station on 16 December 1939 in Bochnia. The day after, in revenge for the attack, the conspirators were hanged and on 18 December 1939, fifty-one inhabitants of Bochnia were taken outside the town to the Uzbornia forest and executed.[63] The nocities.

NAZI MASS EXECUTION IN POLAND
THESE PICTURES WILL SHOCK THE WORLD.

The most sensational pictures of the war,
this series of Photographs just reached us
from America shows the almost incredible
brutality of Germans in Poland. They are
the first pictures ever to show the
workings of Nazi justice in the Ravaged
Land. Violent German protests were raised
to have the pictures stopped when it was
learned that they had been smuggled through
to America, and the successful agent
issueing them appended a request that no
credit should be mentioned.

Story is that in revenge for the death of
a German soldier, one hundred Polish Males
were rounded, Jews being prominently among
them. They were marched through the Town,
hands crossed behind their heads. The men
were then ordered to dig their own graves.
Methods of execution were varied, numbers
of the men being shot, others hanged and
stoned on posts. One picture, revolting in
its revelation of the depths of Nazi
sadism shows how the tortured men, ringed
by armed German Troops were forced to perform
for the Nazi's ammusement a "dance of death"
before their end.

Two of the Victims hang from a litter
box Post. Germans on the right gaze at
the spectacle. 4/Keystone.440521.

9·The original
caption pasted on
the back of the print
(Figure 8). (Imperial
War Museum,
KY440521)

photographs, which showed the different stages of the execution, were included
in the album alongside the detailed report. Exceptionally, these images *can* be
verified as evidence.

It is not known how these photographs were smuggled to the allied countries,
although the original heavily retouched 'master copy' of the men digging a grave
can be found in the Polish Institute and Sikorski Museum, indicating that it
came to Britain via the Polish underground. Janina Kęsek, curator at the history
museum in Bochnia, told me that it was possible that they were secretly copied

WHERE GERMANS RULE: DEATH DANCE BEFORE POLISH MASS EXECUTION.

A GHETTO SCENE IN POLAND, WHERE, UNDER NAZI RULE, THE HORRORS OF THE MIDDLE AGES HAVE REAPPEARED. THE JEWS ARE WEARING ARM-BANDS.

REVENGE FOR THE DEATH OF A GERMAN SOLDIER: HANDS TIED BEHIND THEIR HEADS, ONE HUNDRED POLES MARCH THROUGH THE STREETS TO THEIR EXECUTION.

THE LINE OF VICTIMS DIMINISHES AS THE RIFLES CRACK. THE NAZIS PICK OFF THE MEN SEPARATELY, WHILE AN OFFICER NONCHALANTLY SURVEYS THE SCENE.

UNDER THE EYE OF NAZI SOLDIERS, AND BEFORE THEIR OWN EXECUTION: DOOMED POLES DIG THEIR OWN GRAVES AND THOSE OF OTHERS ALREADY MURDERED.

A SAMPLE OF HITLER'S NEW ORDER: AT THE POINT OF THE BAYONET THE VICTIMS ARE FORCED—TO AMUSE THE GERMANS—TO PERFORM A DANCE OF DEATH BEFORE EXECUTION.

JEWISH WOMEN AND MEN TOO OLD OR WEAK FOR OTHER WORK ARE COMPELLED TO PULL ROLLERS TO REPAIR ROAD DAMAGE.

The above sensational pictures, received from America, are the first published to show the workings of German "justice" in Poland. Showing as they do the cold-blooded and well-nigh incredible brutality of Hitler's New Order, strenuous protests were made by the Germans to prevent their publication once it was known that they had been smuggled through to America. Behind these pictures is a story of cold-blooded horror reminiscent of the Middle Ages. Following the death of a German soldier, one hundred Polish men were rounded up—amongst them many Jews—and were marched through the streets with their hands tied behind their heads. They were then ordered to dig their own graves and, to gratify the barbaric sadism of the soldiers, forced at the point of the bayonet to perform for the Germans' amusement a "Dance of Death." Methods of execution varied, some of the men being shot, some hanged, and others tied to posts and stoned to death.

10 · A page from the *Illustrated London News*, 22 March 1941, entitled: 'WHERE GERMANS RULE: DEATH DANCE BEFORE POLISH MASS EXECUTION'. (Copyright Illustrated London News Picture Library)

and distributed by Stanisław Broszkewicz, a photo laboratory worker working for the Germans in Bochnia, who was known to have made copies of other photographs to smuggle to the underground.[64] Although these photographs are still among some of the most widely used in Holocaust museums, books and exhibitions, Bochnia is rarely mentioned. Kęsek, who sees these photographs as significant evidence of Bochnia's war-time history, is concerned about their frequent incorrect use. She made a point of showing me a copy of a page from *Life* magazine dated 24 February 1941 in which the photograph of men being marched down a street in Bochnia was captioned 'a Silesian town'. Shortly after the war, Jacob Igra (who is referred to in the Introduction) had found a photo album in Silesia which included the photograph of the men digging a grave placed alongside the 'death pit' photograph.[65]

In 1942 and 1943 the extensive reports and photographs received from the occupied territories in the first years of the war were published in two significant books. The first, *The German New Order in Poland*, published in London, consists of eyewitness accounts, reports on massacres, executions, concentration camps and the persecution of the Jews. The vast majority of the 187 photographs were copied from Nazi publications; one was Bryan's photograph of the two Orthodox Jews. Three of the Bochnia photographs are included though without specific data. In 1943 the first comprehensive account of the tragedy of the Jews of Poland was published: *The Black Book of Polish Jewry: An Account of the Martyrdom of Polish Jewry Under Nazi Occupation* included reports and eyewitness accounts of deportations, ghettos, massacres and gassings at the extermination camps of Chełmno (Kulmhof) and Treblinka. There were photographs of the Warsaw ghetto, the majority taken from Nazi publications. Dr Ignacy Schwarzbart, a member of the National Council of the Polish Republic, began his Introduction: 'On my table as I write these lines are a score of photographs of the Polish Ghettos. Children – more like tormented wraiths. Heaps of naked corpses piled for burial in a common grave. The hunger-swollen body of a child. Gangster Gestapo men looking on cynically at a mass burial. Bodies, covered with rags, huddled against a Ghetto wall. A Jewish woman lying unconscious on the ground, and nearby a screaming child with an expression of indescribable pain on its contorted face.' Schwarzbart ended his Introduction: 'May this *Black Book of Polish Jewry* serve to awaken the hearts and conscience of the nations of the world.'[66] There is no evidence that either of these books made much impact at the time outside the Polish and Jewish communities.

In October 1942, the underground courier Jan Karski made his last perilous journey from Poland with microfilmed documents prepared both by Poles and Jews, and with an account of his visit to the Warsaw ghetto.[67] It was given extensive coverage in *The Black Book of Polish Jewry*. Throughout 1943 Karski personally delivered his reports to officials and heads of state in Britain and the USA, among them General Sikorski, Szmul Zygelbojm and Dr Schwarzbart of the National Council of the Polish Republic, British Foreign Secretary Anthony Eden and Members of Parliament, President Roosevelt and leaders of the United Nations War Crimes Commission.[68] A few weeks after meeting Karski, Zygelbojm committed suicide. He left a note pleading for action to be taken on behalf of the Jews who were being massacred. To Karski his death represented the 'sharpest revelation of the extent to which the world has become cold and unfriendly, nations and individuals separated by immense gulfs of indifference, selfishness, and convenience'.[69] In January 1943 Count Raczyński, then Acting Polish Minister for Foreign Affairs, wrote to Anthony Eden pleading for the allies to act in light of the intensifying 'harrowing reports' arriving from Poland concerning concentration camps, including 'the most notorious', Oświęcim (Auschwitz), mass arrests, public executions and deportations.[70]

The British Foreign Office resented this request. In its judgement a good deal of help had already been given to the Poles and, besides, there was fear that an active publicity campaign might stir up a demand that more should be done. This, according to the Foreign Office, would be 'unfortunate and embarrassing', given that there was little they could do to help the Poles short of winning the war.[71] American journalist Vernon McKenzie apportioned some of the blame for this indifference to the effect of British First World War propaganda. In an article in *Journalism Quarterly*, he expressed his shock at the 'hangover of skepticism' and the 'seeming callousness' with which his friends and acquaintances were dismissing reported atrocities from Nazi-controlled areas.[72]

In August 1943, reports that 'Poles are being systematically put to death in gas chambers' were received by the government with incredulity. In a Foreign Office memorandum one official said that it reminded him of a story during the previous war which claimed that the Germans were using human corpses to manufacture fat which, he said, had been a 'grotesque lie'. The Foreign Office acknowledged that although this was not the first report which made reference to gas-chambers, there was insufficient evidence to substantiate these claims, given that they 'usually emanated from Jewish sources' and that neither Jewish nor Polish sources were considered 'trustworthy'. 'The Poles,' the memorandum continued, 'and to a far greater extent the Jews, tend to exaggerate German atrocities in order to stoke us up. They seem to have succeeded.'[73]

Soviet Evidence

After Germany invaded the Soviet Union on 22 June 1941 there were more photographs of Nazi atrocities to be added to those from Poland; but the Soviet photographs were quite different. The majority were taken by profes-

sional Soviet army photographers and did not have to be smuggled. The Soviet Union had an efficient news service operating from Moscow and from 1942 had the facilities to transmit photographs by radio around the world to governments, newspapers and picture agencies. Figure 11 is an example of a photograph transmitted by radio from Moscow to Britain.

There were also more Nazi propaganda pictures. As photographs had been misused by the Nazis to justify the invasion of Poland and inspire hatred towards the Poles, now they were used in exactly the same way to inspire hatred towards the Jews in the Soviet Union. When the German army reached Lvov (Lemberg in German, Lwów in Polish), occupied by the Soviet Union in September 1939, photographs of massacred civilians in the city were released, allegedly by Germany as propaganda. According to historian Gerald Reitlinger, when the Nazis occupied the city, they exhibited large photographs of what they called 'Jewish killing' in the shops.[74] A letter from a non-commissioned Wehrmacht officer made reference to photographs he had seen in *Der Stürmer* of what he referred to as the 'crimes committed here by the Jews', adding that the reality of the murders was much worse.[75] But according to photographs approved by the Nazi censor for release in Britain and the USA, the victims were said to be 'chiefly Ukrainians, who were murdered in the cells of the Soviet prisons just

11 · A photograph transmitted by radio from Moscow to Britain captioned: 'Hitlerite Atrocities in Kerch. Bodies of Residents Shot by Germans.' (Imperial War Museum, RR304)

Photographs as Evidence

prior to the occupation of the town by the Nazis'.[76] There was general scepticism about the German version of events. An article in the *Daily Mirror* quoted Sir Stafford Cripps, then British Ambassador in Russia, as saying that the prisoners had been murdered by the 'Huns', 'just to make propaganda pictures'. The *Daily Mirror* accompanied the article with what it called two 'grim pictures', one of lines of dead bodies and the other of a weeping woman. It reported that it was the *Mirror*'s duty to publish them so that the public 'may not be deceived'.[77]

Initially neither the British press nor the public were sympathetic towards the Soviet Union. In July 1941 Mass-Observation made an analysis of newspaper editorials and concluded that the overall impression was a 'lack of praise for the Russians, either as fighters, or as an army' and that the Red Army's chief value would be 'occupying the Germans for a time'.[78]

The invasion of the Soviet Union caused the Ministry of Information what a leading MP, Harold Nicolson, had predicted would be a 'grave publicity problem both at home and abroad': how could public support be shown towards the Soviet Union without the population becoming sympathetic to communism? The government policy which resulted from this dilemma was called 'Stealing Thunder from the Left', an initiative to publicize the Soviet war effort and '"safe" aspects of Russian life in order to forestall the more dangerous propaganda of the British Communists'. With the co-operation of the Soviet embassy in London, public meetings and a large number of exhibitions were organized. Any offers of support from the British Communist Party were 'steadfastly refused'.[79]

In the autumn of 1941 the British government seized the opportunity to use atrocity films captured from the Germans, showing fighting in the Soviet Union, which they released to newsreel companies. Their primary motive was not so much concern about the plight of the Soviet people as worry about apathy towards the war at home. In February 1941 a Mass-Observation report on British morale concluded that since the beginning of 1941 there had been a loss in 'dynamic momentum' which was 'strongest among munition workers and in the Army'. General apathy, it stated, 'is a danger to the whole national effort'.[80]

A great deal of publicity preceded the newsreel shows and Mass-Observation carried out a survey to assist the Home Intelligence Division of the ministry, which wanted evidence of the public's reaction to the films to pass on to the Film Division. In September a poster advertised the films in London: 'WAR IN THE EAST, Actual Pictures of captured German Films of Invasion of Russia. Sensational! Dramatic!! True!!' The newsreels, which showed burning houses, weeping victims, mutilated bodies, piles of dead Russians, and 'Jew-baiting', were preceded by a British propaganda film which showed images from home of 'slackers, lying on beaches, shop window gazing and lounging at street corners'. The commentary asked: 'Can you do better than this? Ask yourself if you want Germans here in this country as in this Nazi propaganda film prepared by Goebbels to terrify.' It concluded: 'We have got to win.'[81]

The newsreels drew mixed reactions from the British public. The extensive publicity left some feeling that they were not as 'horrible' as they had anticipated; they had expected to 'see more'. Others thought them 'terrible' and felt a general disgust with the Germans and pity for the Russians, although a majority felt that they had become used to seeing horror and that the images were nothing out of the ordinary.[82] Some commented on the poor quality of the films, rousing suspicion that they could have been faked.[83] Although the government publicly affirmed their authenticity, in truth they themselves were not entirely convinced.

From the beginning of 1942 Vyacheslav Molotov, the Soviet Foreign Minister, issued regular statements to all governments with which the USSR had diplomatic relations, outlining the 'appalling atrocities' being committed by the German army on Soviet territory.[84] The same year, two illustrated books, *Soviet Documents on Nazi Atrocities*, published in London by the press department of the Soviet embassy, and *We Shall Not Forgive: The Horrors of the German Invasion in Documents and Photographs*, published in Moscow, included hundreds of atrocity photographs.[85] The Foreign Office distrusted atrocity material emanating from the Soviet Union as much as that from Polish and Jewish sources. Although officials thought there was little doubt that the German army was committing atrocities, as they had done in Poland and other occupied territories, they felt certain that the Soviet authorities had deliberately played up atrocities in order to enrage the population and the Red Army and cause them to fight back with 'corresponding savagery'.[86]

Nevertheless, the Foreign Office was uncertain how to respond to these atrocity stories, and opinions varied.[87] There was an inherent feeling that a saturation point had been reached. One official said the constant repetition of horror 'is apt to produce mere boredom rather than active sympathy'.[88] Another simply thought that atrocity photographs were becoming 'all too common'.[89]

The British press were less cautious and saw it as their duty to publish atrocity photographs. In February 1942 the *Daily Sketch* published three photographs of a public hanging of five men, under the headline, 'War Pictures We Have to Print', and called their publication 'imperative'.[90] The following week *Soviet War News Weekly*, an English-language newspaper launched in January 1942, published six photographs of the different stages of the same hanging, under the headline 'This page shows why Germans must revolt: SIX PHOTOGRAPHS' by Ilya Ehrenburg. In the article Ehrenburg questions both the motives of the 'hangmen' and of the photographer who, although anonymous, he imagines to be 'a glassy-eyed German officer with a cold, dull face' who 'carefully recorded

12 · A page from *Soviet War News Weekly*, 19 February 1942, entitled: 'SIX PHOTOGRAPHS' by Ilya Ehrenburg. (Society for Co-operation in Russian and Soviet Studies, London)

the stages of the execution of five Soviet citizens'. He also points out that the pictures were intended as a present for his 'girlfriend' and had been found 'on his body after a Soviet attack' (see Figure 12). In an attempt to counter what Ehrenburg calls these 'successful pictures', two other photographs are printed on the same page to illustrate that 'not all Germans are hangmen'. These photographs, under the headline 'TWO PHOTOGRAPHS that Hitler Will Not Like', show, according to the caption, German POWs in a Soviet camp protesting against the 'German Government's treatment of Red Army prisoners'.[91] Throughout 1942, with increasing regularity, *Soviet War News Weekly* published atrocity photographs that it claimed had been found among the personal possessions of dead German soldiers.

In June 1942 *Picture Post* published a compelling three-page picture story about the atrocities committed by the German army on Soviet territory, which, it pointed out, 'are not exaggerated'. Under the headline 'What the Advancing Russians Found ... in honour of the men and women who have suffered or are still suffering', five striking images included the discovery of eight Soviet citizens publicly hanged, a mother searching for her son among a landscape strewn with corpses and three young men kneeling over the body of their brother.[92]

By late 1942 British public opinion towards the Soviet Union was changing. A Mass-Observation survey on 'political attitudes' showed that the majority of those interviewed were full of admiration and praise for the Soviet Union and the resistance shown to the German army. Many attributed the Soviet success and determination to the communist system; the general opinion seemed to be that Britain could learn a lot from the Russian way of life.[93] Not only was public opinion towards the Soviet Union positive but images of the war on Soviet territory were having an impact and requests were made, from the public and the press, for more. By late 1942 pictures from the Soviet Union and those from the other occupied territories which had accumulated in Britain and the USA were displayed in exhibitions which directly addressed the destruction not only of the Nazi occupied territories but of the Jews.

Exhibiting Evidence

When in August 1942 an exhibition entitled 'War Photographs' was held in the West End of London, it was the 'Russian atrocity section' which according to a Mass-Observation survey captured the imagination of the large majority of visitors. The most frequent suggestion from members of the public was that there should have been more photographs of the 'Russian type' so that more people would realize 'what's going on out there'. Another interviewee said that they were the 'most powerful photographs I've seen'.[94]

A month earlier, a north of England evening newspaper, the *Doncaster Gazette*, had made an appeal for more Russian atrocity photographs to be exhibited. It called for an end to what it saw as 'middle-class apathy'. The article, which quoted a *Gazette* commentator, stated, 'should not the sentimentalists be made to study photographs of Russian atrocities? If a series were offered for public exhibition in Doncaster would it not be refused because "The public would be shocked"? The complacency of the comfortable citizen can weaken a nation.' The article suggested that Doncaster's MP, Evelyn Walkden, might be interested in staging an exhibition of 'photographs of atrocities committed by the Nazis in Russia' and that 'it would be fitting if he could promote it'.[95]

By December 1942 an exhibition called 'The Nazi Way' was on the Ministry of Information future exhibitions list with the brief explanation: 'Done as an experiment but at the suggestion of an MP and staged under the auspices of a newspaper at Doncaster.' Andrew Ker, director of the exhibitions and display division at the ministry, explained in a memorandum that 'anonymity of presentation' was necessary for the ministry because the *Doncaster Gazette* had made 'a strong editorial plea for frankness and the information could not otherwise be made available to this paper because of the ruling against the featuring of atrocities as a subject'.[96]

The exhibition, finally called 'This Evil We Fight', was officially opened in Doncaster by the then Polish Minister of Information, Professor Stanisław Stroński, on 12 February 1943. A large banner above the entrance read: 'Doncaster Gazette EXHIBITION: THIS EVIL WE FIGHT: presenting in VIVID PHOTOGRAPHS The story of Nazi terror from Childhood to War: OFFI-CIAL PHOTOGRAPHS OF NAZI ATROCITIES IN OCCUPIED COUNTRIES.'[97] On 11 February the *Gazette* had advertised the opening with a front-page story headlined '"This Evil We Fight": *Gazette* Exhibition Turns Searchlight on Nazi Germany'. The story put responsibility for the atrocities on almost the 'entire German nation', a view opposed by Reverend R. Williams, from the Ministry of Information religious division, on the basis that the 'evil philosophy' should be attributed to the Nazis and not the whole German people. Neither Andrew Ker nor the *Doncaster Gazette* agreed.[98] As far as the newspaper was concerned, the exhibition was not propaganda but presented 'photographs of Germany's own actions' as 'unprejudiced fact'. 'It is high time', declared the article, 'that this material was made public.'[99]

Many of the photographs in the 'atrocity section' of the exhibition had already been published in the British press, in *The German New Order in Poland*, *The Black Book of Polish Jewry* or in *Soviet Documents on Nazi Atrocities*. Three exhibition boards focused on the plight of the Jews, highlighting 'Mass Extermination' and the '3,000 Polish Jews' who were being 'deported daily' from the Warsaw ghetto. Alongside this text was the photograph of the Warsaw ghetto wall which a few months earlier had been dismissed by a Ministry of Information official as looking like 'Malet Street'.

A section on the Soviet Union followed. Under the heading '7,000 civilians and children were butchered at Kerch' were two photographs which had been published in *Picture Post* in June 1942: the three young men identifying the body of their brother at Kerch and the mother searching for her son. A further nine photographs, said to have been found on 'German dead and prisoners', included three from the series of the public hanging published in the *Daily Sketch* and *Soviet War News Weekly* (see Figure 12).[100]

The *Doncaster Gazette* reported the exhibition an 'amazing success'. In eight days, 54,000 out of the town's population of 72,000 had visited it. Throughout 1943 and 1944 it toured to more than a hundred other towns in Britain.[101] This was the last large exhibition of atrocity photographs shown throughout Britain before the spring of 1945, when photographs of the liberation of the German camps would grip the public's imagination.

Three months after the opening of the Doncaster exhibition, on 17 May 1943 thousands flocked to the opening of an exhibition at the Rockefeller Center in New York City. 'The Nature of the Enemy', sponsored by the American Office of War Information, highlighted atrocities committed not only by the Nazis, but also by the Japanese.[102]

Meanwhile in Britain the exiled Polish Ministry of Information was bolstering Poland's cultural heritage in an exhibition, called simply 'Poland', which opened in Edinburgh in 1942. The Poles were anxious to prove that Poland was a civilized and cultured society and it was only as a result of the Nazi occupation that such barbarity had been unleashed. In March 1943 the exhibition toured England, opening at the Society of British Artists in Pall Mall, London. It was, said one review, 'one of the most impressive exhibitions London has had for some time'.[103] By 1944, statements issued by Polish government officials about the exhibition increasingly emphasized Poland's strong links with the allies and the 'whole of western culture'. As the German defeat now seemed imminent and the Red Army approached, the Polish government-in-exile was looking to the future and for Western allied support. It may have been as a consequence of this concern that the text on two panels of twenty-one photographs, under the heading 'The German New Order', which featured photographs published in *The German New Order in Poland*, relegated the Nazi destruction of Poland and the Jews to the past. It read: 'The monuments of Poland's culture were destroyed, her scientists and artists murdered. The Jews, who centuries ago had sought sanctuary in Poland when fleeing the persecutions raging throughout Europe, were shut in ghettos by the Germans, later to be ruthlessly exterminated.'[104]

Other events and exhibitions were beginning to draw attention to the annihilation of the Jews. In December 1942, 500,000 Jews in New York stopped work for ten minutes to draw attention to the massacres in Europe. In March 1943 'We Will Never Die', a 'stirring spectacle', was presented at Madison Square Gardens in New York. On a monumental scale, it included two 30-metre inscribed gravestones surrounded by American soldiers bearing American flags, as

Her crime was race. This poor little blonde Jewish girl should be enjoying the blessings of childhood, yet she is doomed to a lingering death through malnutrition and privation, *living in a dank cellar, her emaciated limbs covered with rags. Fear is the only emotion of which this poor mite is capable. Yet Hitler denounces her as a "devilish Jewish enemy"*

they believe that Continental reports about the massacres are exaggerated, let them look at the pictorial evidence which is now available.

The Nazis have not been squeamish about this evidence. Photographs of hundreds of murdered Jews have been found in the pockets of German prisoners of war who took part in the outrages and kept the pictures as souvenirs.

And if these pictures of the dead Jews do not speak an unmistakable language there are the photographic records of those who still survive. They show how Hitler is "solving the Jewish problem." They depict human misery such as has never before descended on a whole people.

Every one of these Jewish men, women and children have death written on their faces, slow death by starvation. Children of three look careworn and aged.

Many of them are too feeble to walk. Others,

according to the photographer who took these pictures, cried for food until they fell asleep and began to cry again as soon as they woke up.

The adults are not better off. Starving men roam the ghetto streets in a state of fatalistic semi-consciousness. Women are too weak to weep.

Yet the fate which Hitler prepares for the Jews is but a symbol of the attitude to all his enemies. Tens of thousands of Europeans in occupied countries are subjected to cruelties similar to those inflicted on the Jews by their Nazi torturers.

Wherever he succeeded in reducing a people, in occupying a country, his thugs practise what they have been taught to do to the Jews. They have done it everywhere on the Continent. They were already visualizing themselves doing it in Britain.

To help these hapless Jews, and indeed, all the heroic but equally persecuted Continental patriots, whatever race or creed, is the essence of this war of liberation.

DESPAIR

OVER

The camera of Roman Vishniac brings photographic evidence from the Ghettoes of Europe of Hitler's ruthless persecution of a race

13 · A page from a photo-essay in *Illustrated*, 24 April 1943, entitled: 'Murder of a People', featuring Roman Vishniac's photographs.

a memorial to the 'murdered two million Jewish civilians of Europe'.[105] In April 1943 an exhibition of Roman Vishniac's photographs, taken during the 1930s as documentation of the Jewish communities of Eastern Europe, was held at the Library of Congress in Washington, DC. In Britain, *Illustrated* publicized the exhibition and published nineteen of Vishniac's photographs over five pages under the headline 'Murder of a People' (see Figure 13). In a plea that the remaining Jews of Europe be saved from extermination, *Illustrated* presented Vishniac's photographs as evidence of how 'Hitler is "solving the Jewish problem"'. These photographs taken *before the war* were now used as evidence of the Nazi persecution during the war. Here Figure 4 is captioned as, 'Europe's Ghettos. A Jew peers anxiously from behind his door as he hears the sounds of Nazi boots.'[106] The article was also keen to point out that 'photographs of hundreds of murdered Jews have been found in the pockets of German prisoners of war who took part in the outrages and kept the pictures as souvenirs'.

In January 1945 an extraordinary exhibition opened at 60 Oxford Street in central London. 'The War in Wax – The World's Most Modern Waxworks' included a section on 'The Horrors of the Concentration Camp'. An exhibition leaflet advertised the 'Camp' section alongside 'A Fascinating and Delightful Children's Section of mechanical moving figures including CINDERELLA, SNOW WHITE, etc'. A Mass-Observation observer reported that a notice prominently displayed on the stairway leading to the children's section read: 'DO NOT MISS THE HORRORS OF THE GERMAN CONCENTRATION CAMP.' The bizarre array of exhibits included Nazi atrocities at Kharkov, in the form of a peasant hanging from a tree, and, in the Camp section, 'The Arrest', 'The Round-up', 'The Stone Quarry at Buchenwald' and 'The Sealed Wagon ... packed to capacity with doomed people', together with statements taken from the British government's White Paper on German Atrocities published in 1939. Also included was a panel of Nazi atrocity photographs, supplied by the Ministry of Information and Keystone. The report described the Camp section as a place where the lighting was 'very dull and subdued' to enhance 'the creepiness of the place'. It also stated that the exhibitions were 'putrid affairs', except for the Camp section, which was so effective that public feeling had reached 'fever pitch'. The report concluded: 'It's an excellent piece of propaganda, and conveys far more eloquently, far more graphically, far more forcibly, the 3rd Reich's interpretation of the "New Order" and provides the perfect answer to the question "What are we fighting for?"'[107]

Apart from the Mass-Observers' report, and the exhibition leaflet, I am not aware of any other information regarding this exhibition. I came across the photograph printed here (Figure 14) in 2001 at an exhibition in the National Portrait Gallery in Edinburgh of the work of Austrian-Jewish photographer and film cameraman Wolfgang Suschitzky, who had arrived in Britain after leaving 'fascist Austria' in 1935. When I asked him over fifty years later if he had any recollections of the exhibition he said: 'I was so disgusted when I came across it that I did not go inside.'[108] Perhaps it was an inconsequential show but it had a significance that could not have been realized at the time as the first example of the type of 'museum experience' which would become popular four decades later as a way of representing the events of what would then be known as the Holocaust. This will be discussed in Chapter 8. But in 1945 the collection of photographs which would be used to enhance this 'experience' in the 1980s was not yet complete.

Despite the extraordinary amount of photographic evidence which accumulated in the allied countries during the Second World War, there was more to

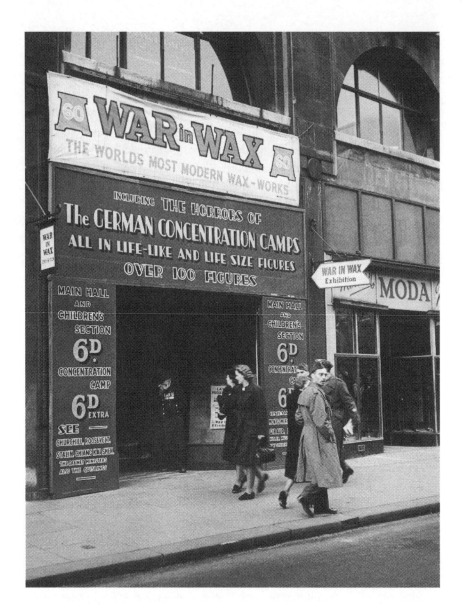

14 · The 'War in Wax' exhibition in Oxford Street, London, January 1945. (Copyright Wolfgang Suschitzky)

surface. The references that Soviet reports and the article in *Illustrated* had made to atrocity photographs being found among the possessions of dead German soldiers was a clue to the fact that photographing crimes was widespread among Nazis and ordinary German soldiers, but their sheer quantity was not realized until long after the war had ended. The overwhelming majority of photographs of Nazi crimes were taken by the Nazis and their collaborators themselves.

Photographing the Holocaust

THREE
Armed with a Camera

A Camera as Weapon

The enthusiasm with which photography had been appropriated for the National Socialist cause before the war continued after 1939. When the German army entered Poland they carried not only their guns but also their cameras, important weapons in war. In Eastern Europe photographs were taken, officially and unofficially, of the humiliation of the people and their culture, the Slavs as well as the Jews. Executions and hangings and carefully constructed sequences of 'actions' – a Nazi euphemism for the round-up of civilians for execution – were carefully and obsessively recorded on film. Many of these harrowing photographs were included in the personal photo albums of ordinary soldiers and Nazi officials.

In an essay 'Ordinary Men, Extraordinary Photographs', Judith Levin and Daniel Uziel, archivists at Yad Vashem in Israel, attribute the obsession with taking photographs in Eastern Europe to the deluge of pre-war propaganda directed at the Eastern European Jew,[1] but this view does not fully take into account the barbarity unleashed against the Slavs and the fact that demeaning photographs were also taken of Poles and the Roma and Sinti (Gypsies of Europe). Alexander B. Rossino suggests rather that the prejudice shown towards the people of Eastern Europe was 'a cultural phenomenon with a deep historical basis, not simply a by-product of Nazi-racism'.[2]

Rossino refers to letters sent home by German soldiers, which frequently referred to the Poles as 'inhuman' or 'sub-human' and commented on their inferior homes and lifestyles. One writer described the 'horrendous' Polish streets, the 'dirty, dilapidated' and 'simply wretched' houses. 'The people', he added, 'are about the same.' 'Civilisation to these men', writes Rossino, 'meant rule by culturally superior Germans who deserved to dominate the inferior Poles and Jews, whom they considered incapable of creating either a rational state or meaningful culture.' Attitudes towards the Russian people were to be equally derogatory.[3]

Photographs of harassment or brutality in the Western European occupied territories are significantly absent, even though the Netherlands, Belgium and France had large Jewish populations. As Levin and Uziel point out, 'it is very difficult to find a similar visual attitude towards West European Jews, who did not conform with the image reflected in the anti-semitic propaganda'.[4] This point is supported by two photo albums, made as a present for the commander of Westerbork camp in the Netherlands.[5] The photographs were taken by the official camp photographer Ruud Werner Breslauer, a Jewish inmate, which was unusual in itself, but even more extraordinary was that some photographs show Jewish festivals in the camp and Jewish prisoners addressing a dinner of Nazi officials. Here it would appear that Jewish culture and religion were tolerated. Western Jews were considered civilized, educated and middle class, and were treated accordingly. Their ultimate fate, however, did not differ. Most inmates at Westerbork were eventually deported to Auschwitz-Birkenau.[6] The Nazis' own distinction between Jews in Western and Eastern Europe was firmly established in the notorious Nazi propaganda film *Der ewige Jude* (1940) (The Eternal Jew) directed by Dr Franz Hippler which refers to 'better Jews' (German) and 'bad Jews' (Polish). It was promoted as an 'educational documentary', which addressed 'the problems of world Jewry' and is, according to Furhammar and Isaksson, 'probably the most evil film ever made'.[7] The opening commentary stated: 'The civilised Jews such as those we know in Germany provide an incomplete picture of their racial characteristics. This film shows original material shot in the Polish ghettos, shows us the Jews as they really looked before they concealed themselves behind the mask of civilised Europeans.'[8]

The image of the Eastern European male Jew had been repeatedly impressed on the imagination of German soldiers, and for many Poland and the Soviet Union would have been their first encounter not only with Eastern Europe but also with Orthodox Jews. For some German soldiers on the eastern front there would have been no contradiction between the enemy they were fighting and what Omer Bartov, in his book *Hitler's Army: Soldiers, Nazis, and War in the Third Reich*, calls the 'Judeo-Bolshevik Asiatic hordes' who belonged to 'the propagandists' imagination'. In encounters with Eastern European Jews, Bartov argues, rather than disproving the propaganda myth, the 'real' Jew was moulded to fit in within it.[9]

If German troops believed that they were being confronted with real-life manifestations of the mythical Jew, then Daniel Jonah Goldhagen's suggestion that their photographs of harassment and atrocities reflected an attitude of those who were 'entirely comfortable with their environment' is not wholly convincing.[10] It seems more likely that at least some of these photographs would have been made for the opposite reason. In the propaganda myth the Eastern

NOCHMALS
POLNISCHE JUDEN

15 · A page from an unidentified German photo album captioned: 'Nochmals polnische Juden' ('Polish Jews again'). (Wiener Library, London)

European Jew was depicted as a manifestation of everything evil in the world and a threat to the health and morality of every good Aryan. It is likely, therefore, that the ordinary German soldier felt a certain amount of trepidation entering Poland. Letters written by German soldiers to their families and friends at home refer to 'their shocking encounter with "real life" manifestations of the Jews'.[11] They were not only confronted by the physical threat of the enemy but with a psychological threat. In the opinion of Rossino, German soldiers had an irrational, 'even manic fear of Polish Jews'.[12] Photography could have been a way of alleviating that fear. Susan Sontag's general point, that a tourist who feels insecure in a foreign environment may take a photograph as a way of taking control and possessing it, is significant here. Taking a photograph, she argues, can become a 'defence against anxiety'.[13]

This would partially explain the German troops' obsession with taking pictures

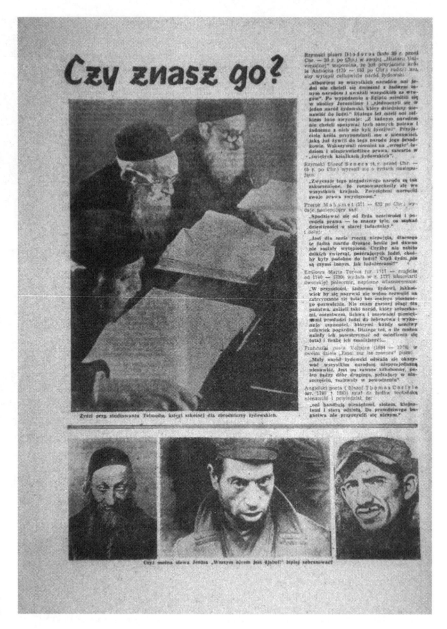

Czy znasz go?

of 'types', not only of Eastern European Jews but, to a lesser extent, Poles and
Gypsies. But the popularity of the 'truth-telling' physiognomic image of 'types'
firmly established during the 1920s, as discussed in Chapter 1, would have been
enormously influential as a way of representing the Jew. In Poland the Jewish
'type', frequently captioned as such, was commonly pictured in extreme poverty, framed in dingy, poor outdoor environments, staring into the camera lens,
rendered inferior and pacified. These kinds of images, including those which

showed Polish and Gypsy 'types', regularly featured in German photo albums. Two pages of an unidentified album show groups of men and women on snow-covered streets dressed in makeshift rag boots and coats tied with string. All are lined up facing the camera. The handwritten caption on one page reads, 'Lublin Jewish Types', on the other page, 'Polish Jews again' (see Figure 15). Another album made by a soldier from the 1st Mountain Division includes a photograph of a group of barefoot women and children posed for the camera captioned 'Gypsy types'; another of a group of shabby-looking Polish POWs is captioned 'Polish types'.[14]

Images of Eastern European Jewish 'types' were frequently published in the extensive German- and Polish-language press established in occupied Poland. Two notable publications were the daily *Krakauer Zeitung*, published from 12 November 1939, and *Ilustrowany Kurjer Polski* (*IKP*), a Polish-language maga-zine, illustrated in full colour, originally published fortnightly, but weekly from October 1940. There were other publications devoted entirely to discrediting Jews. A fourteen-page Polish-language news sheet, entitled, *Czy Znasz Go?* ('Do You Know Him?') was aimed at humiliating Judaism, and associating Jews with communism, criminal activity and the devil. On one page, using the publica-tion's title 'Do You Know Him?', are four photographs (see Figure 16). The caption to the top image reads: 'Jews studying the Talmud, a school text book for criminal Jews.' The other three photographs show criminal Jewish 'types' and, as the text states, the Jew as the devil himself.

In addition to anti-Semitism, there was propaganda aimed at convincing the Poles under occupation of the advantages of complying with it. Throughout 1940 *IKP* published photo-stories about the benefits to Poles of working in Germany. In March, a front-cover colour photograph of a group of six smiling women looking out from a railway carriage was captioned, 'We're Going to Germany' (see Figure 17). Inside were photographs of supposedly happy groups of workers on their way.[15] The reality was, of course, different.

Thousands of Poles were forcibly deported to Germany as slave labour. In contrast to the brutality of the occupation, the front cover of *IKP* regularly featured colour photographs of glamorous women or Poles dressed in tradi-tional costumes. Throughout the four years *IKP* was published, references were consistently made to photography. On 30 June 1940 the magazine began a regular feature inviting amateur photographers to contribute to the illusion that life was normal under the Nazi occupation and submit their photographs for publication, exhibition or competitions. Until mid-1943, *IKP* published amateur photographs which showed children with pets, flowers, landscapes and tranquil country scenes.

While *IKP* was circulating idealized images of life under the occupation,

17 · The front cover (in colour) of *Ilustrowany Kurjer Polski*, 10 March 1940. The box caption reads: 'We are going to Germany.' (Author's collection)

marauding German troops were taking photographs of their crimes. From the first days of the invasion, churches, synagogues, national monuments, shrines and public institutions were destroyed, Polish and Jewish citizens murdered, hanged, humiliated, tortured and shot and their homes looted.[16] In the town of Końskie, in the Kielce region, during the first two weeks of the campaign, a sequence of photographs was taken documenting the beating and shooting of twenty-two Jews.[17] One picture shows the renowned film-maker Leni Riefenstahl, who witnessed this event with her film crew, looking distressed amid the German troops. Riefenstahl has often been described as a Nazi propagandist herself, but according to the caption she had been physically threatened by the troops for attempting to stop the beating of the Jews. Her best-known films are characterized by an idealist approach to National Socialism. Perhaps the brutal reality was more than she could bear.

A few unofficial photographs were taken near the village of Ciepielów in the Iłża region in September 1939 where 300 Polish POWs were executed by Wehrmacht soldiers. In 1950 the German soldier who had taken the photographs anonymously sent five of them to the Polish consulate in Munich with a covering letter describing the incident. He recalled running towards the machine-gun fire and seeing 300 Polish prisoners shot and lying in the ditch by the side of the road. 'I risked taking two photographs,' he said, 'and then one of the motorized riflemen, who had carried out this exploit on Colonel Wessel's orders, placed himself proudly in front of my camera.'[18]

Not all photographs were taken clandestinely. It is apparent from extant photographs that some photographers not only had unrestricted access to the crimes, but also had the skills required to produce a narrative sequence of images.[19] In September 1939 a photographic narrative was constructed showing the stages of a massacre in Częstochowa.[20] The images show a round-up, men waiting to be executed, bodies strewn around the streets and bodies piled in a public square. After the war they were found by an American serviceman in a photo album which had belonged to a member of a German machine-gunners' unit. In the foreground of Figure 18 is a soldier looking directly at the camera. Behind him a group of men, some of them Orthodox Jews, are being rounded up. A man in civilian clothing and a trilby hat seems also to be taking photographs. Why this and other detailed photographic records of executions were taken is not known. They could have been intended as evidence that orders were being carried out with efficiency, to supplement a written report – as were those taken of the execution of fifty-one civilians in Bochnia in December 1939 – or as a personal record.

Besides photographing round-ups and executions, for some German soldiers, police or SS men, to be photographed mocking or humiliating Jews was a popular activity. A frequently photographed humiliation scene was of soldiers, police or SS officers cutting the beards or the sidelocks of Orthodox Jews. Figure 19 shows eight German police and SS men grouped around an Orthodox Jew who is stiffly posed looking at the camera. Those cutting his sidelocks are poised with their scissors at either side and others are smiling or laughing. This was not a clandestine photograph. The scene had been organized, considered and set up. The perpetrators had proudly arranged themselves in front of the camera in the same way friends on a holiday might pose for a group picture. Photographing the enemy was equal to possessing or conquering it. Publicly to humiliate,

degrade and possibly kill the 'real' Jew was metaphorically to destroy the image
of the mythical Jew. Taking photographs was an integral part of the humiliation
process; in a sense it completed the violation.

In the US Holocaust Memorial Museum the caption on this photograph
claims that it was taken in Sieradz, near Łódź, and that it shows a local rabbi
who was 'reportedly hanged along with eight others soon after' the photograph
was taken. However, in 1961 a copy of this photograph and a covering letter
were sent from a company in London to the Wiener Library. The letter said
that the photograph had been handed to the company office in Porto Alegre,
Brazil, by a female 'client' who claimed that it had been taken by a member
of the SS in camp Vapnearca, Romania. The letter named two of the SS men
in the photograph, whom the woman had apparently known. She had identified
the Jew as Moische Weintraub who came from Focşani in Romania, and said
that she had seen a second photograph (not in her possession) 'which depicted
the same man lying on the floor in a pool of blood'.[21]

Just as the image of the Jew in pre-war Nazi propaganda had been almost
exclusively male, so photographs taken in Eastern Europe which demeaned
Jewish culture and religion were taken of men. Goldhagen argues that humiliation
photographs represent the 'absolute mastery' of the German over the Jew and

19 · 'German police
and SS officers cut
the sidelocks of the
son of a local rabbi.
The father and son
were reportedly
hanged along with
eight others soon
after, Sieradz,
1939–40.' (Instytut
Pamięci Narodowej/
Institute of National
Memory, courtesy
of USHMM photo
archives)

the destruction of manhood.[22] The humiliation of the enemy was a male group
activity; it is unlikely that a soldier would have behaved in such a way on his
own. Encouraged by the reassurance of the mob, the perpetrators taunted and
played with their victims, as an animal might. Some images of public hangings
are 'trophy' pictures, with Nazis or their collaborators photographed alongside
the hanged person, smiling to camera, touching a leg or a foot as a hunter might
touch his recently killed prey, in order to boast about the catch. Susan Sontag

Armed with a Camera

argues that there is 'something predatory about taking a picture'. She writes, 'to photograph people is to violate them, by seeing them as they never see themselves, by having knowledge of them they can never have; it turns people into objects that can be symbolically possessed. Just as the camera is a sublimation of the gun, to photograph someone is a sublimated murder – a soft murder, appropriate to a sad, frightened time.'[23] The Jew had been humiliated and the photograph offered indisputable evidence that it had happened. The camera was a reliable witness. It captured the moment and preserved it. It was a photograph of a proud moment to send home or to include in a photo album.

The Reich Family Album

The practice of making photo albums was so popular among all military ranks that it seemed tantamount to a duty. By way of an introduction, many begin with uniformed portraits of their creators who preside over, approve of and identify with the bizarre collection of photographs that follow. The photographs shift seamlessly from picture-postcard views, drinks parties and social occasions, to poverty-stricken indigenous peoples in destroyed towns and cities, deportations, hangings, murders and executions. It was as though the atrocities were just another sight along the way, all part of the foreign adventure. Depending on the rank of the individuals, albums could be simple affairs or elaborately decorated and bound. In 1940, a German amateur photography magazine explained the role that photography could play in the armed forces: 'Photography in its widespread popularity has become one of the means of forging links and creating personal contact immediately … On the one hand, it records the experiences, landscapes and war effort on the front, while on the other hand creating a unique link between the front and home.'[24] The photo album was a way of providing those links. Albums which traditionally had been made to depict an idealized version of family life now became a way of creating a much greater family ideal; that of the nation-state itself.

A well preserved and executed example of this type of photo album was made by an Obersturmführer (Lieutenant) stationed in Łódź. It is now kept at the Ghetto Fighters' House, though it is not known when or by whom it was deposited there. The design of the album indicates the extraordinary amount of care and attention bestowed on it. It is finely bound with a woodcut cover in yellow, blue and green. Inside are 259 photographs stuck on black pages with neat handwritten captions in white ink. Among photographs which show the Obersturmführer at home and at work and among friends and colleagues are others of Catholic churches and graveyards, synagogues and Jewish graveyards, including their destruction. An entire page of photographs, dated 11 November 1939, shows the various stages of the destruction of the Łódź monument to

20a· The woodcut (coloured) cover of an Obersturmführer's photo album. (Ghetto Fighters' House)

General Tadeusz Kościuszko, which the album points out was being prepared for 'detonation by Jews'. This action symbolized not only the destruction of Poland but, as Kościuszko led the 1794 Polish Uprising, also its independence and freedom. A few photographs make reference to photography itself. A German soldier is pictured photographing a Jew in the street, standing to attention in front of the camera. In another photograph a man is pictured indoors with his camera on a tripod. There is even a reference to the album itself (see Figure 20 a and b). The Obersturmführer thought it appropriate to include a photograph of himself, captioned 'Arbeit am Album' ('Working on the album'). He is sitting at a table writing, in neat white capital letters, the captions to accompany three photographs of three men being publicly hanged in a square in Łódź. The text he is writing reads: 'EXECUTED FOR CRIMES AGAINST THE NATION, ONE JEW, TWO POLES ON THE BAŁUCKI RYNECK.' The text on the right-hand side of the page reads: 'Hanged in a sacrificial place and exhibited for 24 hours. They had murdered a badly wounded Lieutenant in a bestial manner' (see Figure 20b).[25]

Photographs of this hanging in Łódź and other public hangings were widely circulated and regularly featured in German photo albums, possibly because large numbers of hangings would have been accessible to photograph.[26] It is possible that some had been exchanged with colleagues, which was not an uncommon practice. Goldhagen writes of how photographs of the humiliation of the Jews

WEGEN VERBRECHEN
AM VOLKE
HINGERICHTET
EIN JUDE, ZWEI POLEN

AM SCHAECHTBOCK
GEHENKT UND 24 STD
ZUR SCHAU GESTELLT.
SIE HATTEN EINEN
SCHWER VERWUNDETEN
OBERLEUTNANT AUF
BESTIALISCHE WEISE
ERMORDET.

AUF DEM BAŁUCKI RYNECK

20b· A page
from the same
Obersturmführer's
photo album
showing a public
hanging. (Ghetto
Fighters' House)

and of atrocities taken in Poland by members of German Police Battalion 101 were 'generously shared among the entire battalion'. The photographs were apparently hung on the walls of the barracks so that comrades could order copies.[27] Kurt Wafner, who served in a territorial defence battalion in Minsk, claimed that none of the photographs which he included in his personal photo album, of hangings, dead bodies and the camp where he worked, was taken by him. He exchanged them, he said, 'usually for a little tobacco'.[28]

Although making albums was a personal activity, it was part of a wider collective responsibility. It gave individuals an opportunity not only to order their own experiences and decide how the past should be remembered and preserved, but also to express a commitment to National Socialist ideals. Organizing photographs and handwriting captions was a way of combining these aims and an opportunity to give a personal interpretation to a photograph and to direct the viewer in how to read it. Walter Benjamin argued that without captions photographs must 'remain arrested in the approximate'. They have no precise meaning.[29] In other words, Nazi ideology is not necessarily implicit in

Photographing the Holocaust

photographs of hangings or executions. Ulrich Keller makes this point in his essay about ghetto photographs, and wrote that photographs are not the best medium to show 'ideological bias'. They must, he said, rely on 'poisonous captions' to carry a prejudiced message.[30] This point is exemplified by a page of an album which shows four photographs of a round-up of a group of Jews. Under one of the photographs is the text: '*Jüdengesindel*' ('Jewish riff-raff').[31]

Macabre as some albums were, it would appear that the captions were not always derogatory. One has survived which apparently belonged to a German policeman, containing some photographs thought to have been taken at the ghetto at Szydłowiec. Photographs of dilapidated and poverty-stricken streets are captioned 'Misery of the Jews!' Others showing groups of people with bundles of belongings are captioned 'resettlements'. Under two photographs of the body of a murdered woman the caption reads: 'The end.' Finally, on the last page, under a photograph of Jews with their belongings on horses and carts, and a photograph of a public hanging, is the caption: 'And something else! Some lives ended like this.'[32] Levin and Uziel cite this photo album, along with others, in their essay as an example of an album that directly reflects Nazi ideology. However, according to the observations of a German translator whom I consulted, the tone of the captions is benign. The translator suggests that rather than reflecting Nazi ideology the captions express the curiosity of a tourist in a macabre and foreign landscape. It cannot be assumed that all albums which contain atrocity photographs were made to condone the crimes depicted on their pages.

In the Ghetto Fighters' House are two large albums of atrocity photographs crudely pasted on to the pages. They include a photograph of the same hanging in Łódź which featured in the Obersturmführer's album, pictures of deportations, harassment, naked corpses and the liberation of Dachau and Mauthausen concentration camps, and photographs from the series taken in Bochnia in 1939. On one page are three photographs: two show smartly-dressed groups of people smiling and posed for the camera, the other image is of the hanging of two people (see Figure 8). The handwritten captions are in Yiddish, indicating that they were made by Jews, to condemn the crimes, not to condone them.[33]

For some soldiers, the motive may well have been little more than curiosity. In the First World War, for example, photo albums containing images of the enemy dead had been made by soldiers on all sides.[34] And during the Second World War British troops also made photo albums.[35] In war-time, photographs are commonly taken of the dead, and they can include 'trophy' photographs, showing troops photographed alongside their dead enemies. There was a recent example of Israeli soldiers in Gaza posing for a photograph standing over a dead Palestinian.[36]

Focus on Genocide

The German invasion of the Soviet Union on 22 June 1941 began what Omer Bartov describes as a 'war of annihilation'. Over the next three years millions of Jews, Soviet POWs, communists, partisans and civilians were massacred. According to Rossino, it was the apparent willingness of ordinary soldiers to collude in the brutality in Poland before 1941 that provided 'a fertile psychological landscape into which the regime eventually sowed the seeds of genocide'.[37] Within months of the invasion, tens of thousands of Jews and those who resisted the Nazi regime were being executed at mass shootings and large numbers of photographs were taken. For example, a photograph taken in July in Slarow in the Soviet Union shows dozens of Jews digging their own graves before their execution. Near Kamenets-Podolsk, Ukraine, where over a two-day period 23,600 Jews were murdered, two photographs show a round-up.[38] A photograph taken near Ponary, in the region of Vilno, shows a column of Jews being herded to a place of execution where approximately 35,000 Jews were murdered.[39]

These large-scale executions became a kind of spectator sport for Nazis and their collaborators. When Reinhard Wiener, a German photographer of the Einsatzgruppenaktion, went to the site of the Liepaja massacre in Latvia, where in December 1941 approximately 2,700 Jews were murdered, specifically to film with his 8mm Kinekodak camera, he found, he said, 'German soldiers standing as spectators all around'.[40]

So widespread did photographing and filming at executions become that at times it was too much even for the Nazi high command. Chief of General Staff, Otto Woehler, wrote to the 11th Army Command on 22 July 1941, setting restrictions on photography:

> It goes without saying for any normal human being, that no photographs will be made of such abominable excesses, and no report of them will be given in letters home. The production and distribution of such photographs and reports on such incidents are looked upon as undermining the decency and discipline in the armed forces and will be severely punished. All existing photographs and reports on such accesses are to be confiscated together with the negatives and are to be sent to the Ic/counter intelligence officer of the army giving the name of the producer or distributor. It is beneath the dignity of a German soldier to watch such incidents out of curiosity.[41]

The following month Field Marshal von Reichenau, Head of Army High Command 6, issued an order prohibiting the voluntary participation of Wehrmacht soldiers in mass executions of Jews and the taking of photographs.[42] On 11 November 1941 and 16 April 1942 Reinhard Heydrich, Head of the Reichssicherheitshauptamt (RSHA – the Reich Security Head Office) reiterated the orders given by Woehler and 'forbade the taking of pictures at mass executions'. He requested that 'the commanders of the Order Police hunt for pictures, films, or plates circulating among their own men'.[43] However, Reinhard Wiener said that he had no problem filming at Liepaja. The ban, 'confined to the shootings which took place in the east', was not, he said, imposed until the end of 1941.[44]

There is little evidence that many soldiers were punished for taking photographs at the scenes of crimes, although the book *'The Good Old Days'* contains an account of the trial of SS-Untersturmführer (2nd Lieutenant) Max Taubner who was sentenced by an SS and police Supreme Court to three years' imprisonment for taking photographs at a number of executions of Jews, even though he knew that such a practice was forbidden. He had apparently taken the films to be processed in a photographic laboratory in Germany and then shown them to his wife and friends. This, it was considered, could have posed 'the gravest risk to the security of the Reich if they fell into the wrong hands'. The court made clear that the killing of Jews was perfectly acceptable, but taking photographs, pronounced as 'deplorable excesses ... shameless and utterly revolting', was not. The 'shameless' photographs referred to apparently showed an 'almost completely naked' Jewish woman. The court considered that for men to act out of 'self-seeking, sadistic or sexual motives' was unacceptable and a sign of 'inferior character'.[45]

Although the Nazi ideologues were keen to make a distinction between the extermination processes which were a matter of policy, and the 'sadistic impulses' of individuals which undermined military efficiency and discipline,[46] it is difficult to ascertain where the line was drawn; there are a number of photographs of partially-clothed and naked women which seem to have been officially sanctioned. Taubner's decision to photograph the Jewish woman in the way he did was unlikely to have been entirely a self-motivated act. It is apparent that while the Nazis exploited the male Jew in terms of his culture and religion, women were humiliated and exploited entirely in terms of their gender, and sometimes these deeds were photographed.

Reports from the occupied territories claimed that both Polish and Jewish women were not only commonly raped by German troops, but their sexuality was exploited for amusement.[47] This was reflected in a page of a German soldier's album which shows four photographs of Gypsy men and women and children. The majority of women are baring their breasts for the camera and smiling. In one photograph a German airman has placed himself alongside the group to pose for the photograph. The handwritten text on this page reads: 'Pictures from the Gypsy cemetery.'[48] Women were also subjected to sexual humiliation for Nazi propaganda films made in the Polish ghettos (this will be discussed in Chapter 4).

Armed with a Camera   71

One controversial set of pictures showing a savage public assault on women is thought to have been taken in Lvov in 1941. These are images of half-clad women with torn clothes and terrified expressions, sitting in the road or running through the crowded streets. These photographs have been used in contemporary exhibitions, articles and books about the Holocaust – an issue I will take up in Chapter 9.

Cruel and humiliating photographs of women were also taken before their execution. Many of the women in photographs of mass executions in the Eastern territories and in the Soviet Union are partially clothed or naked. The image referred to in the Introduction, of the partially clothed women seated on the ground, presumed to be taken at Śniatyń, is a case in point. Others were taken at the executions in Liepaja, apparently to prove that the massacre had been carried out primarily by Latvian collaborators. In a landscape strewn with clothes and other people undressing, four women and a girl, dressed only in their underclothes, are huddled together and photographed.[49] In 1942 at Mizocz, in the region of Rovno in Ukraine, approximately 1,700 Jews were executed. The photographs show large numbers of people being herded into a ravine, women and children undressing, a line of naked women and children in a queue and finally their executed bodies. Two particularly harrowing photographs show German police standing among heaps of naked corpses of women strewn on

Photographing the Holocaust

either side of the ravine. In Figure 21 one of them is aiming his gun at those believed to be still alive.[50]

Not enough is known about the motives of those who took photographs of these atrocities. Many reasons have been suggested: racial and cultural supremacy, the effect of anti-Semitic propaganda, a defence mechanism against witnessing horror, willing participation, curiosity, fascination or a 'mass psycho-pathological behaviour' – this being the reason the Nazis gave themselves, in the book *Polish Acts of Atrocity*, for the crimes supposedly committed by the Poles against the Germans in 1939. It is likely that individuals took photographs for a combination of these reasons.[51]

Even though Nazi officials were concerned that such a deluge of atrocity photographs could get into enemy hands, and apparently discouraged the activity, it seems impossible to believe, because of the sheer amount of extant pictures, that soldiers were castigated for taking photographs at every execution. As masters of propaganda, it is possible that the Nazis might have considered that a documentary record of the extermination of the Jews – which was a matter of policy – was evidence of that policy being accomplished. Apparently the Nazis had planned to memorialize the destruction of European Jewry through lavish displays of artefacts and photographs. A museum was apparently planned to portray the life of the Jews of Eastern Europe in Prague as a 'triumphant memorial to their annihilation'. These photographs might have formed a part of this macabre remembrance.[52]

By late 1941 the increasing demand for cameras and photographic materials was beginning to take its toll on supplies. According to a 'secret' report, sent from Switzerland in September by a J. B. Wager to the Ministry of Information in Britain, both cameras and materials were in short supply in Germany, and the quality of those that were being produced were reported to be inferior. This, according to the author of the detailed report, was due to the severe bombing raids on Germany by the allies. Wager also referred to a survey of the illustrated Nazi magazine *Signal* in the second month of the Russian campaign which established that many PK photographers had, he said, 'suddenly disappeared'. He commented that although PK photographers were usually well protected by their units, and used telephoto lenses for their action shots, it was possible that many had already been killed by the Russians.[53] It has been estimated that they suffered the same casualty rate as other front-line troops: 30 per cent.[54]

In mid-1943 severe restrictions were placed on the production of official photographs, but by that time thousands more had been taken throughout the occupied territories, including in the concentration camps and the ghettos of Poland.

FOUR
Cameras in the Ghettos

The Ghetto Tourist

By the end of 1940 the two largest Jewish ghettos had been established in occupied Poland and hundreds more were to follow. On 1 May 1940 the ghetto at Łódź (called Litzmannstadt by the Germans), housing some 160,000 people, was declared 'closed'. In November that year the Warsaw ghetto was inaugurated, housing over 400,000 people in 995 acres enclosed by a 3-metre-high wall. On 15 December, *Ilustrowany Kurjer Polski* (*IKP*) carried a full-page photo-feature on the Warsaw ghetto, with an emphasis on order (see Figure 22). It shows a smiling street vendor, a group of male Jews 'going to work' and the Jewish police in control.

Under the authority of the Nazis, each ghetto had its own Jewish administration, known as the Judenrat, which was responsible for the enforcement of German orders, establishing a police force and generally dealing with all education, work and housing matters. Chaim Mordechaj Rumkowski and Adam Czerniaków were appointed chairmen in Łódź and Warsaw respectively. Czerniaków was among a number of Warsaw ghetto inhabitants to keep a diary, until his suicide in 1942. In the Introduction to Czerniaków's diary, published in 1979, Józef Kermish wrote that the diary confirms the fact that the Judenrat 'represented mainly the well-to-do, was closer to the upper classes, and more frequently backed these classes during the selection for the camps where the Jews were sent for forced labour and extermination'.[1] But for the majority of inhabitants, extreme poverty, disease and starvation were rife. Polish underground courier Jan Karski wrote about his clandestine visit to the Warsaw ghetto in 1942. 'To pass that wall was to enter into a new world utterly unlike anything that had ever been imagined. The entire population of the ghetto,' he wrote, 'seemed to be living in the street.'[2] This desperate poverty supplied the Nazi propaganda machine with the required images of impoverished Jews and these were widely used in exhibitions, in films and in the press. On 15 February a full-page article in *IKP*, headlined 'Death walks alongside them', juxtaposed photographs of

Text visible within the newspaper clipping image:

WARSZAWSKIE GHETTO

Na, — owoce obamażone — palce oblizo-wać.

Żydowska kolumna porządku idzie do pracy.

Warszawa jako miasto, które posiada na kontynencie europejskim największą bo-daj ilość mieszkańców żydowskich, od dawna starała się załatwić ten trudny problem. Żydzi rozsiani po całym mieście posiadali największe swoje skupienie w dzielnicy zaczynającej się za tzw. Żelazną Bramą, za Ogrodem Saskim.

Podczas urzędowania.   Na granicy ghetta.   fot. Blazewski

a ciągnącej się dosyć daleko w głąb miasta.
    Obecnie przeprowadziły władze niemieckie przesiedlenie wszystkich żydów z całego mia-sta do jednej dzielnicy. Oczywiście, że tak olbrzymia przeprowadzka nie poszła łatwo: widziało się rodziny przenoszące swój dobytek na wozach, ale też na wózkach ręcznych, a nawet niekiedy na plecach. Tak czy owak doszło do stworzenia ghetta, przypomi-nającego swoim odosobnieniem od reszty mia-sta stosunki, jakie panowały w mieście w wie-ku XVIII. Żydzi w murach swojej dzielnicy żyją własnym życiem, zarząd dzielnicy spoczywa w rękach rady żydowskiej, która utrzymuje również straż porządkową, składającą się z ty-siąca ludzi. Jednym z najważniejszych zadań będzie oczywiście podniesienie higienicznego stanu tej dzielnicy, który jeszcze pozostawia wiele do życzenia. Według dotychczasowych obliczeń zamieszkuje dzielnicę żydowską prze-szło 400.000 osób, stanowi więc ona spore osobne miasto. Ghetto warszawskie jest pierw-szym załatwieniem zagadnienia żydowskiego w ramach zamkniętego obszaru, jakiego doko-nano od czasu obecnej wojny na terenie Ge-neralnego Gubernatorstwa.

22 · A page from *Ilustrowany Kurjer Polski*, 15 December 1940, 'Warsaw Ghetto'. (Author's collection)

insects with scrawny, dirty-looking Orthodox Jews.[3] Nazi camera crews and photographers were frequently sent into the ghettos to record aspects of life there. The anti-Semitic film *Der ewige Jude* (The Eternal Jew), was also compiled mainly from newsreel footage taken of the squalid conditions in Warsaw, Łódź and other ghettos in Poland.[4] At other times the Germans wanted material for alternative propaganda purporting to show the relatively luxurious life of the ghetto rich, forcing Jews to pose for such scenes in restaurants.

Films and photographs of ghettos were not only taken by official camera teams

23· A page from a private leather-bound photo album entitled: '*Das Warschauer Ghetto: Ein Kulturdokument für Adolf Hitler*' ('The Warsaw Ghetto: A Cultural Document for Adolf Hitler') which belonged to a German Luftwaffe soldier. (Yad Vashem Film and Photo Archives)

but also by inquisitive soldiers. The overcrowded streets and the poverty were an endless source of fascination and curiosity to members of the Wehrmacht. To enter the ghetto was to catch a glimpse of a foreign and exotic environment; a world apart. They did not see the ghettos as products of the Nazi regime, but as the natural habitat of the Jews. In early 1941 Czerniaków made reference in his diary to Wehrmacht 'tourists' who were taken on guided tours around the ghetto.[5] So popular did excursions into the ghettos become that Ulrich Keller, in his 1984 Introduction to *The Warsaw Ghetto in Photographs*, wrote that, to members of the Wehrmacht, the Warsaw ghetto was 'simply a kind of Baedeker sight' with picturesque scenes to be photographed.[6] Dr Hans-Joachim Gerke, who had graduated from Leipzig University with a PhD in journalism, served in the Luftwaffe transport unit. He was a keen amateur photographer who was prompted to visit the ghetto by what he called 'the journalist's curiosity, which', he said, 'overcame even the fear of disease'. Like many of his colleagues, it gave him 'a chance to see the unique world of the Eastern European Jewry, a world which he had not had the opportunity to see before'.[7]

As photographs of social occasions, picture-postcard views and hangings were pasted on to the pages of German photo albums, so were photographs from the ghettos. They were kept as private mementos, or to pass on to friends or colleagues. One unidentified Luftwaffe soldier dedicated his forty-page leather-bound album to Adolf Hitler with the inscription: '*Das Warschauer Ghetto: Ein Kulturdokument für Adolf Hitler*' ('The Warsaw Ghetto: A Cultural Document for Adolf Hitler'). The perspective of most of these photographs suggests that they were taken from the window of a vehicle, which is partially visible in the bottom left-hand corner. Some individuals in the streets are looking at the camera, some have stopped to pose, even occasionally smiling. In Figure 23, in the bottom left-hand photograph, a Judenrat policeman stands to attention saluting the passing car.

In the summer of 1941, radio operator Willy Georg was stationed in Warsaw. As a former professional photographer, Georg made portraits of his colleagues to earn a little extra cash. One day he was asked by his commanding officer to go and take photographs of the ghetto with his Leica camera. 'There are some curious goings-on behind that wall,' the officer said. 'I am issuing you with a pass to enter the enclosed area through one of the gates. Take your Leica, and food for the day, bring back some photographs of what you find.' By the end of the day he had taken four rolls of film and had loaded the fifth when he was spotted by a German police detachment who confiscated his camera. He said nothing about the four films in his pocket, thus managing to save them. He developed the films in a photo-laboratory in Warsaw and sent them for safe-keeping to his wife in Münster.[8] Georg's status as a professional photographer is apparent in these photographs. His pictures published in the book *In the Warsaw Ghetto: Summer 1941* are well composed and well lit. More important – and what is extraordinary about these photographs – is his apparent affinity with his subjects: he photographs them close-up, as though with their approval. Many of those he photographed were prepared to pose for the camera and some even respond with a dignified smile. Figure 24 shows a group of boys and men gathered together in the street. Their broad smiles and relaxed jovial poses reflect a rapport with the photographer. Another image shows a smiling mother tenderly pulling a shawl from the face of the baby she is holding in her arms so that Georg could take a photograph. An elderly bearded Jew is photographed sitting in a doorway, looking comfortably into the camera lens. As implausible as it may seem, this and other of Willy Georg's photographs could be mistaken for those taken of Jewish communities by Roman Vishniac.

On 19 September 1941, amateur photographer Sergeant Heinrich Jöst treated himself to a photo-excursion round the Warsaw ghetto for his forty-third birthday. 'I was given the day off,' he said, 'and decided to see what went on inside those walls. Because I was in uniform I went in without difficulty. I walked the streets and although it was against regulations I photographed what I saw.'[9] Jöst

24 · 'People on
the street in the
Warsaw ghetto',
by Willy Georg,
June–August 1941.
(Rafael Scharf,
courtesy of USHMM
photo archives)

took 140 photographs in the ghetto with his Rolleiflex camera. Compared with those of Willy Georg they are amateurish and distant from their subjects; there is none of the empathy. His pictures are voyeuristic, showing beggars, emaciated children, the sick and the dying. Jöst is fascinated with the contrast between the destitute and the well-to-do inhabitants he photographs in the street. One image shows a woman whom he described in an interview for *Stern* magazine forty years later as 'well-groomed'. He reflected that at the time he had questioned his right to photograph her. 'Strangely enough,' he said, 'I didn't think that about the poorly dressed people.'[10]

Although Jöst said that he had no difficulty photographing in the ghetto, Joe J. Heydecker, a photo laboratory technician with PK (Propaganda Kompanien) 689, indicated there was a certain amount of risk involved. He made a few visits to the Warsaw ghetto in February 1941 'driven on', he said, 'by the inescapable whip of horrified fascination.'[11] He later wrote about what he photographed. 'Every now and then I stopped to take a photograph: street scenes, wretched children, a remarkable head, a poverty-stricken face'.[12] On 1 March 1941 Heydecker made his last excursion to the ghetto with three colleagues. Heydecker's wife, who worked for the Warsaw government of occupation, managed to secure her husband and his colleagues official ghetto passes by 'doing business particularly

25 · 'A photograph by Heinrich Jöst. An undertaker pulls a cart laden with corpses into the Jewish cemetery on Okopowa Street for burial in a mass grave. Jöst's caption reads: "The arms of the dead hanging over the side of the body cart moved by themselves. It was an eerie sight. In the background is the entrance to the Jewish cemetery", 19 September 1941.' (Günther Schwarberg, courtesy of USHMM photo archives)

with Leica cameras'. They arrived at the ghetto boundary openly carrying their cameras. The German guard said nothing.[13] However, in the laboratory where he worked, a colleague who had taken photographs of corpses in the ghetto cemetery and distributed 9cm x 12cm photographic enlargements of them among the unit was taken to task by a superior about this activity. The negatives and prints were confiscated on the basis that 'Germany might suffer if such pictures got into enemy hands and were used as atrocity stories'.[14]

As conditions in the ghettos grew worse, the number of visits by soldier-tourists and camera crews increased. A number of the ghetto diaries refer to these visits. In his diary Czerniaków noted in May 1941: 'The movie camera crews are with us again.' The same month Czerniaków submitted photographs of starving children in communal shelters in a report to the Gestapo, informing them that in the first half of May 1941 more than 1,700 people died of starvation. By the end of May the death toll had reached 3,821; the mortality rate was much the same in the Łódź ghetto.[15] By the summer the death rate had increased to between

5,000 and 6,000 per day. The cemetery in Okopowa Street, which by then was overflowing with corpses, had become one of the main ghetto attractions for both German visitors and soldier-photographers. On his birthday trip to the ghetto Heinrich Jöst photographed the skeletal corpses waiting to be buried (see Figure 25), as did PK photographer Albert Cusian, who commented: 'I photographed everything in sight. The subject matter was so interesting. I took pictures in the morgue and at the Jewish cemetery. Bodies of Jews who had died during the night were laid out on the pavements for collection in the morning. I'd wait until the collectors came and then take pictures of them.'[16]

Czerniaków and most of the other ghetto diarists refer to frequent visitors to the cemetery. On 20 May 1941 Jewish historian Emmanuel Ringelblum, who was later to save the ghetto archive, wrote: 'Various groups of excursionists – military men, private visitors – keep visiting the graveyard. Most of them show no sympathy at all for the Jews. On the contrary, some of them maintain that the mortality among the Jews is too low. Others take all kinds of photographs. The shed where dozens of corpses lie during the day awaiting burial at night is particularly popular.'[17] On the previous day Jewish historian, educationalist and writer Chaim Aron Kaplan had noted in his diary: 'A few days ago the Nazis came to the cemetery and ordered the Jews to make a circle and do a Hasidic dance around a basket full of naked corpses. This too they recorded on film.'[18]

Another diarist, Michael Zylberberg, a high-school teacher of Jewish history and literature, made similar observations. He wrote: 'It was not only the funeral processions that made the cemetery so strangely lively, but the constant presence of hundreds of German soldiers. They gleefully photographed the dead and the accompanying relatives, and even went so far as taking snapshots of the corpses as they were laid out in the mortuary. The Nazis were particularly active in this respect on Sundays, when they would visit the cemetery with their girlfriends. This, rather than a cinema, was a place of amusement for them. The bereaved regarded them with scorn and loathing, but in the circumstances silence was the only protest.'[19]

On 1 May 1942 Czerniaków wrote that 'the German propaganda people' were filming in the prison, the refugee shelter at Tłomackie Street and were going to film the activities of the 'Council and life in the Quarter'. On 5 May he wrote: 'They are filming both extreme poverty and the luxury (coffee houses). The positive achievements', he wrote, 'are of no interest to them.'[20] A number of ghetto diarists recorded a particular intensification in the regularity of film crew visits. On 8 May, teenager Mary Berg, an inhabitant of the ghetto, wrote in her diary about the 'commotion' the Nazi film crews were causing during their shoot in the community building, where 'powerful spotlights were set up at different parts of the building and long wires and electric cables lay on the ground'. Berg described how the crews seized 'the best dressed passers by' and ordered them to sit around a table in 'one of the most elegant apartments' and 'eat, drink and talk'.[21]

On 19 May Kaplan recorded a similar film shoot in his diary. 'At ten in the morning,' he wrote, 'three trucks full of Nazis, laughing, friendly, with complete photographic equipment, stopped near Schultz's famous restaurant.' He described how 'every beautiful virgin' and 'every well-dressed woman' were detained and ordered to move around 'gaily' and 'sound animated'. They filmed in the restaurant showing 'abundance' and 'good fortune in the ghetto'. 'Why did the Nazis do this?' asked Kaplan. He answered his own question: to show as 'propaganda abroad'.[22]

On 12 May Czerniaków was asked by the German authorities to supply '20 Orthodox Jews with earlocks and 20 upper-class women', for a film shoot in the ritual baths which would include a demonstration of a circumcision.[23] Kaplan also noted this event in his diary. He wrote that the Germans had 'captured' a 'few dozen young and beautiful women' and some 'strong, powerful, virile men' and taken them to the same bath-house. They were ordered to strip naked and get into the bath together and were forced to perform, 'lewd and obscene acts imitating the sexual behaviour of animals … While one Nazi cracked his whip over the heads of the captives, his partner set himself up in a corner with a camera.'[24] This footage was apparently included in an anti-Semitic propaganda film, *Asia in Central Europe*, to prove the decadent habits of the ghetto Jews.[25]

The renowned musician Władysław Szpilman who escaped from the ghetto, barely with his life, described the same scenes, in the cafés and the bath-house, in the account he published after the war, adding that it was only 'much, much later' that he discovered their purpose: 'The Germans were making these films before they liquidated the ghetto, to give the lie to any disconcerting rumours if news of the action should reach the outside world. They would show how well off the Jews of Warsaw were – and how immoral and despicable they were too, hence the scenes of Jewish men and women sharing the baths, immodestly stripped naked in front of each other.'[26]

This hideous voyeurism was not unique to Warsaw. Lurid photographs and films were also made in the Łódź ghetto. An entry of *The Chronicle of the Łódź Ghetto 1941–1944* on 6 May 1942 referred to the fact that photographs of circumcisions were being made in the ghetto: 'In the last few days considerable filming has been done in the ghetto (by the Germans), as it was last year as well. They filmed outside in the streets and inside in workshops, institutions, and hospitals. Among other things, a circumcision ceremony was filmed in Hospital No. 1.'[27]

As film crews and individuals made excursions to and from the ghettos, the Nazis' chief accountant in the Łódź ghetto, Austrian-born Walter Genewein, was busy making his own photographs. As a keen amateur photographer, Genewein, who described the ghetto as 'a kind of small Jewish town', made colour transparencies with a Movex 12 camera which had been confiscated from a Jew. He photographed Jews in the streets, in ghetto factories and workshops and made self-portraits in his office. Genewein was more concerned with the quality of his film than with those he photographed. On more than one occasion in correspondence with Agfa he complained about the 'reddish-brown' hue which he said spoiled his photographs.[28]

In January 1942 he was given the task by the German administration of making plans for a museum 'to portray the life of the Jews of Eastern Europe' and their customs. The museum never materialized. The idea had been submitted to the Reichspropagandaamt, which concluded that the 'Jewish Question' was being dealt with 'in a series of exhibitions' and that 'life in the ghetto' was intended to separate Jews from the rest of the community, not make them appear interesting to outsiders.[29] In 1944, instead of a museum, an exhibition was mounted which showed ghetto factory products for potential customers in the Reich.[30]

By the time this exhibition took place the ghetto population had been severely reduced. The deportations had begun in May 1942, when more than 10,000 Jews were sent to the Chełmno death camp and murdered. By the end of August 1944 the entire ghetto had been liquidated. In Warsaw, the deportations began in July 1942. Czerniaków, who as chairman of the Judenrat was responsible for organizing people for deportation, wrote in his diary on 23 July: 'The orders are that there must be nine thousand by four o' clock … There is nothing left for me but to die.' Rather than authorize the expulsion order, he killed himself by taking cynanide. By 12 September, 265,000 had been deported from the Warsaw ghetto to Treblinka death camp and murdered.[31] Kaplan was among them. His diary abruptly ends on 4 August 1942 with the words: 'If my life ends – what will become of my diary.'

Despite the fact that by the spring of 1943 hundreds of thousands of Jews had been murdered in death camps, the Nazis were still obsessively publishing their propaganda material made in the ghettos. In March the Polish-language weekly illustrated paper *7 Dni* reported the opening of an anti-typhoid exhibition in Warsaw which included a film about 'a hospital, mortuary and a typhoid cemetery' and the 'sloppy flats' of the Jewish ghetto.[32] In October, *IKP* gave a double-page spread to an exhibition in Kraków called 'The World Plague of Jews', which put the blame for the war squarely on world Jewry.[33]

Six months earlier the Warsaw ghetto had been liquidated, but not without a fight. On 19 April 1943 German troops entered the ghetto to begin the final round of deportations. They met with unexpected resistance. The Warsaw Ghetto Uprising continued for twenty days before it was quashed under the command of SS Brigadeführer (Major-General) Jürgen Stroop. Of those who

survived the Warsaw Ghetto Uprising, 7,000 were deported to Treblinka death camp and 42,000 to the SS concentration camps in the Lublin area: Majdanek, Poniatowo and Trawniki.[34]

As a commemoration of the liquidation of the ghetto, a report was commissioned from Stroop by SS-General Friedrich Wilhelm Krüger, head of the SS police in the General Government in Kraków. The *Stroop Report* was essentially a photo album bound in black leather with a title page, 'The Jewish Quarter of Warsaw is no more!' It was divided into three parts: a summary of SS operations, daily communiqués and approximately fifty-four photographs taken of the uprising with handwritten captions in gothic script. One of the photographs, which shows a young boy with his hands up standing among those arrested, surrounded by German troops, was captioned, 'Pulled from the bunkers by force.' This photograph (Figure 26) would become an icon of the destruction of European Jewry and one of the most widely used images of the Holocaust. The use of this picture will be discussed in Chapter 9.[35]

26 · A page from the *Stroop Report*. The original German caption on this page reads: 'Pulled from the bunkers by force.' (Main Commission for the Prosecution of the Crimes against the Polish Nation, courtesy of USHMM photo archives)

The Ghetto Photographers

As German photographers and film crews were busy making bizarre and lurid images of the ghettos, Jewish photographers were also taking pictures. Officially, all photographers in the ghetto were commandeered to work for the Judenrat to photograph the apparent efficiency of ghetto institutions and its workforce and to please the German authorities. However, some of these photographers also took clandestine photographs as evidence of the abominable conditions, in the hope that the world would later learn about ghetto life. For this reason also, secret archives were established to collate documents, diaries, artwork and photographs. In the Warsaw ghetto in 1940 the organization Oneg Shabbat ('The Joy of the Sabbath') was established by Emmanuel Ringelblum. Its purpose was to preserve any documentation relating to the ghetto, including official papers, private letters, drawings, private journals, pre-war books and the Jewish underground press. A large part of Ringelblum's archive survived, including seventy-six photographs, among them portraits and images of ghetto life.[36]

In November 1940, an archive, based in the Jewish administration offices, was established in the Łódź ghetto. Ghetto postal worker Nachman Zonabend was one of a group of people who decided 'to document for posterity ... all that was happening around them'.[37] Apart from collecting official correspondence, statistical data, printed and visual material, a ghetto *Chronicle* was compiled by a number of people which recorded daily life.[38] In the Kovno ghetto George Kadish secretly took around 1,000 photographs over a period of three years and buried them in the ghetto. In 1945 he was able to retrieve them.[39] Apart from Kadish's photographs, and the archives of the Łódź and Warsaw ghettos, few collections from other ghettos survived.

About 500 photographs of the Warsaw ghetto, thought to have been taken in 1940, show a variety of aid establishments, which include soup kitchens, orphanages, hospitals, dental surgeries, offices, food distribution depots and workshops and are now preserved in four photo albums at Yad Vashem. The copyright stamp on the photographs is that of Foto-Forbert (the fashionable portrait studio, mentioned in Chapter 2), which had been established in central Warsaw before the First World War by film producer and photographer Leon Forbert. A colleague of Forbert, Henryk Bojm, also worked in the studio. Popular with actors and the Jewish establishment, it also regularly produced press photographs, occasionally credited to Foto-Bojm-Forbert, for pre-war Jewish newspapers and journals in Warsaw. After the death of Leon Forbert in 1938, the studio was run by Bojm and Forbert's two sons, Adolf and Władysław, until in September 1939 the two brothers left Warsaw for the eastern front.[40]

Foto-Forbert continued to function during the war under Bojm. The ghetto photographs, the only known surviving photographs of Foto-Forbert during this period, were thought to have been commissioned as evidence of the dire living conditions by the American Joint Distribution Committee, or 'Joint', as

Kinderheim für orthodoxe Kinder
Twarda 21

Vor der Mahlzeit

Copyright by
„FOTO - FORBERT"
Warsaw   Poland
11 Wierzbowa Str.

it was known, to endorse the need for funds to provide relief aid to the ghetto inhabitants.[41] The German captions on the photographs indicate that they were probably sanctioned by the Judenrat. They maintain the distinctive style of Foto-Forbert's pre-war large-format photographs published in the Warsaw Jewish press. Just as in their photographs of official Jewish functions, so in those of the ghetto soup kitchens, hospitals, nurseries or shelters for the homeless, groups of people are carefully placed in dignified poses looking towards the camera. They are reminiscent of the sympathetic eye of August Sander and other social documentarists of the 1930s. In Figure 27, taken in a ghetto children's home, the two rows of children are seated in front of meticulously placed bowls and spoons. The image has a symmetry which conveys a message of order, uniformity and discipline, in contrast to the disorder and desperation portrayed in most images taken by Nazis in the ghettos. The aesthetic formal qualities of this and the other Foto-Forbert photographs means that they are often overlooked

27 · A page from an album of photographs captioned, 'Children's home for orthodox children, before meal time', taken by Foto-Forbert. (Yad Vashem Film and Photo Archives)

Cameras in the Ghettos   **85**

as examples of ghetto life, presumably because they do not fit the stereotyped image of the ghetto. In the Yad Vashem photo archive the collection is defined as 'Judenrat' photographs.[42]

During the war Foto-Forbert operated from its pre-war location, close to the ghetto boundary and near to the German office of ghetto administration. It continued to be popular with ghetto artists and actors, and high-ranking Nazi officials were among its customers.[43] Foto-Forbert was, however, the exception rather than the rule. As poverty increased, the ghetto population had little need for photo studios and gradually they were forced to close. In the Łódź ghetto professional photographer Lajb Maliniak's studio, Foto Kasprowy, survived until 1941, although by then the majority of his photographs were made for the Judenrat.[44]

By the end of 1941, by order of Rumkowski and the Judenrat authorities, all personal and private photography in the Łódź ghetto was forbidden. After his studio closed, Maliniak joined photographers Henryk Rozencwajg-Ross and Mordechaj Mendel Grosman as official Judenrat photographers at the Ghetto Statistics Department.[45] On 8 December 1941 Rumkowski wrote to Grosman: 'I inform you herewith that you are not allowed to work in your profession for private purposes and that you have to liquidate your business immediately. Your photographic work is confined only to the activity in the department in which you are employed. You are therefore strictly prohibited to do any photographic work.'[46]

Rozencwajg-Ross and Grosman had both been photographers before the war. Rozencwajg-Ross was a photojournalist and Grosman an artist. According to Nachman Zonabend, a close friend of Grosman, their photographic styles and ways of working were very different. Rozencwajg-Ross, in his capacity as a news and sports photographer for Polish newspapers, was comfortable with organizing and photographing groups of people. Grosman, on the other hand, essentially an artist and self-taught photographer who had made a meagre living from photography before the war, was shy and unobtrusive and preferred to take photographs of people when they weren't aware of his camera.[47]

Working as an official photographer for the Judenrat in the ghetto involved taking portraits of officials, covering social functions and meetings and making photographs of every ghetto inhabitant for their identity cards. According to Rozencwajg-Ross, photographs were ordered of those who had died on the streets and on whom no documents were found. The prints had to be marked 'unidentified'. In addition, the German ghetto authorities demanded photographs of particular buildings or neighbourhoods which were to be destroyed.[48]

They also photographed workers in factories and workshops and their products, to demonstrate their efficiency to the German authorities and to encourage orders from German companies. It was apparently the belief of some ghetto officials, not least the chairmen, that a productive and efficient factory regime

would make the ghetto indispensable to the German war effort and therefore ensure its survival and save the inhabitants from deportation and death. Officials or employees of factories sometimes gave gifts of photo albums to the Judenrat chairmen, portraying their efficiency, both as a way of heaping praise on them and showing gratitude for 'saving' the ghetto. In the Kielce ghetto on 1 January 1942 an album was presented to Judenrat chairman Hermann Levi by his employees.[49] Similarly, a photo album was made by the manager of the Schultz factory in the Warsaw ghetto, which in mid-1942 employed 4,500 workers.[50]

The Judenrat chairman most renowned for his determination to please the German authorities was Rumkowski, a powerful and influential figure whose belief in the exploitation of the ghetto population as a means of their survival was fundamental to his doctrine. There are nine extant photo albums at Yad Vashem thought to have been commissioned by factory directors, administrators or foremen as gifts to Rumkowski, probably in the hope of securing extra food rations, or simply to curry favour. They were made in the Ghetto Statistics Department by photographers and artists including Grosman and Rozencwajg-Ross, and designers, bookbinders and graphic artists, including Mieczysław Borkowski, Moshe Grienwald and Pinkus Szwarc, and darkroom worker Hans Rubiček.[51] The albums, which represent the workers of the ghetto factories and workshops as efficient, productive and content, combine the German administration's demand

28 · A page from a 'Judenrat' album which shows a large portrait of Chaim Mordechaj Rumkowski (left-hand side) surrounded by workers and factory directors. The text reads: 'A celebration of work' (original in colour). (Yad Vashem Film and Photo Archives)

29 · A page from a 'Judenrat' album dedicated to child labour, entitled: *'Das Erziehungswerk in Litzmannstadt-Getto'*, ('Educating for Work in the Łódź Ghetto'). The page is captioned '245 Young people VI. 1943' (original in colour). (Yad Vashem Film and Photo Archives)

for detail with innovative design. Charts, graphs, accounts and statistics of factory production levels are combined with photographs, photomontage, colour graphics and handwritten text, mostly in German but occasionally in Hebrew or Yiddish. They are fine examples of photomontage, clearly influenced by Russian constructivism. In one album a page which shows a photograph of a group of workers reads in German and Yiddish: 'Everyone in the Ghetto Must Work.' The same album contains a large portrait of Rumkowski surrounded by smiling workers and factory directors with the text: 'A celebration of work' (see Figure 28). A ninety-page album dedicated to child labour, entitled 'Das Erziehungswerk in Litzmannstadt-Getto' ('Educating for Work in the Łódź Ghetto'), juxtaposes statistics of the number of children working in the textile, leather and tailoring factories with photographs of them at work. One page shows a photograph of girls making hats; in the foreground is a drawing of two fashionable summer hats (see Figure 29). A seventy-nine-page album documents the process of production at the 'boots department'. On one page is an elderly woman sorting a pile of old leather products; in the foreground is a drawing of a new shoe and handbag (see Figure 30).The exquisitely fashioned products stand in stark contrast to the lives of those who made them.

This album does not mention that most of the goods being recycled had been taken from Jews deported from Łódź and other ghettos to Chełmno or Auschwitz-Birkenau. Whether or not those in the Łódź ghetto knew this is hard to

Vom Abfall zum fertigen Schaft

30 · A page from a 'Judenrat' album. The text reads, 'From Waste to the Final Boot' (original in colour). (Yad Vashem Film and Photo Archives)

say. Lucjan Dobroszycki, editor of *The Chronicle of the Łódź Ghetto 1941–1944*, makes the point that 'the chroniclers were not in the habit of asking too many questions'. In May 1942, as the deportations to Chełmno began, the *Chronicle* reported how the people of the ghetto were 'tremendously puzzled' by the large shipment of clothes and 'other things' arriving daily by trucks. An entry in the *Chronicle* for 6 September 1943 noted, 'More old shoes have come into the ghetto', and that 'twelve freight cars' of them had been unloaded and were waiting to be sorted. The chronicler did not speculate on where they might have come from.[52] In 1944 a railway carriage at Auschwitz-Birkenau loaded with clothes belonging to 'Jews murdered on the previous day' was marked to be sent to Textilverwaltung Litzmannstadt (the German Textile Administration) in Łódź.[53]

Many ghetto inhabitants were incensed by the propaganda in the Judenrat albums, including the artists and photographers who made them. An extant group photograph of Grosman, his sister Fajga Frajtag, Grienwald and Szwarc shows them looking mockingly at a page of one of these albums which features Rumkowski's portrait.[54] As a reaction to the Judenrat albums and in opposition to Rumkowski's regime, Arie ben-Menachem (then known as Artur Printz), a factory worker and founder member of the Zionist youth movement in the ghetto, Jewish Youth Front (FMZ), secretly made his own photo album, which he said was 'honest and truthful', as opposed to those of the Judenrat which he considered to be 'flattering to the Germans'.[55]

Arie ben-Menachem's remarkable eighteen-page album used some of the same photographs, all of which had been taken, officially or unofficially, by

31 · A page from Arie ben-Menachem's photo album with the text: '45,000 evacuated from the ghetto vanished into thin air.' (Copyright Arie ben-Menachem)

Grosman, to satirize the Judenrat propaganda, and like all good satire it made a strong political point of its own. Ben-Menachem used constructivist design and photomontage, not unlike the official albums, but subverted the meaning of the images with an ironic text (in Polish) in order to denounce what he saw as the betrayal of the ghetto Jews. One montage of a photograph of workers removing sanitary waste from the ghetto, which was used in the official albums to show the efficient workforce, is captioned, 'Shit movers: Galley Slaves of our Time'. Two pages highlight the deportations. A photograph of a group of people carrying their belongings has the caption, 'They came. They left … '. On the next page with a photograph of a woman and a child carrying bundles of belongings is a large question mark with the text: '45,000 evacuated from the ghetto vanished into thin air' (Figure 31). Ben-Menachem and his family sometimes feature in the photographs. A page with the text 'Beware the "Sonder" [special department of the social security] are looking for you' features a photograph, in the bottom right-hand corner, of ben-Menachem being searched by a ghetto policeman (Figure 32). With reference to the obsessional charts and diagrams in the official albums, another page shows a chart displaying the increasing death rate of the ghetto, with a small photograph inserted in the top right-hand corner of a group, including ben-Menachem, at a grave side. The text reads: 'Peace and quiet in the Ghetto.' Another page has a montage of ten photographs of the faces of murdered ghetto inhabitants, captioned simply, '5.IX–12.IX.1942'.

Although photographing the dead in the ghetto was strictly prohibited, these

Photographing the Holocaust

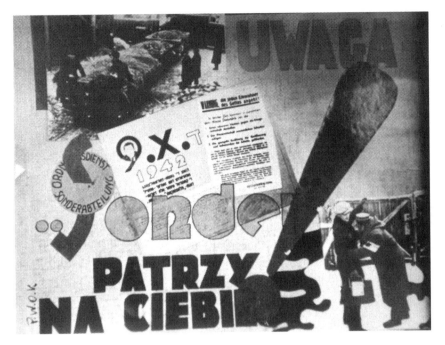

32 · A page from Arie ben-Menachem's photo album with the text: 'Beware the "Sonder" are looking for you.' (Copyright Arie ben-Menachem)

photographs were taken on instructions from Rumkowski. During a curfew in September 1942, members of the Wehrmacht were rounding up ghetto inhabitants for deportation to Chełmno. Aware of what was happening, some of the young, the old and the sick attempted to hide in their homes. Those who were found were shot dead on the spot. Due to the large numbers of dead, the hot weather and the possibility of disease, Rumkowski received permission from the German authorities to bury the corpses. He called on Grosman to photograph each dead person with a number written on a card which could be attached to the grave, so that families could identify their relatives. Grosman asked that ben-Menachem be allowed to write the numbers, effectively saving his life.[56]

Despite Rumkowski's orders, both Grosman and Rozencwajg-Ross continued to photograph secretly in the ghetto. Aware that the appalling conditions might not be believed, they compiled the evidence hoping that it would survive. Rozencwajg-Ross took many clandestine photographs of those who had died from hunger and in 1942 photographed the deportations to Chełmno and a hanging at Bazarny Square.[57] When he presented some of his pictures as evidence at the trial of Nazi official Adolf Eichmann in Israel in 1961, he described how on one occasion he had disguised himself as a cleaner to gain access to Radegast railway station where deportations to Auschwitz were taking place. He asked a friend to lock him in a storeroom for several hours so that he could take photographs through a hole in the storeroom wall of the brutal treatment of the deportees by the Germans.[58]

Cameras in the Ghettos

33 · Mordechaj Mendel Grosman, foreground right, photographing the deportation of Jews from the Łódź ghetto. (Wiener Library, London)

Grosman also secretly photographed deportations, the sick and the starving. Before the war, he had owned two Leica cameras. In the ghetto he used one for his official work and the other for his clandestine photographs. He was helped by engraver Menachem Printz, ben-Menachem's father, who made Grosman a primitive zoom lens to make it easier to take secret photographs. In the Ghetto Statistics Department, Grosman was able to order extra film for his clandestine work by simply saying that some of the films taken for his official work hadn't come out properly. No one asked questions. To print the photographs, despite his overcrowded living conditions, Grosman made a darkroom in a corner of his one-room ghetto flat at 55 Młynarska Street, which he shared with seven other people. It was here that ben-Menachem would spend evenings with Grosman, selecting photographs for his album which Grosman would then print.[59]

In the ghetto, Grosman often worked with his camera hidden under his coat. With holes in his coat pockets he was able to operate the camera without being seen. Sometimes he would carry his camera in a bag and quickly take the camera out to make his photographs. Figure 33 shows Grosman with a bag in one hand and a camera in the other, photographing a deportation. It is possible that Rozencwajg-Ross took this photograph, as the Judenrat policeman in the foreground is not reacting, indicating that the photographer may have been recognized as working for the Judenrat. There are a number of surviving photographs of both Grosman and Rozencwajg-Ross taking photographs in the ghetto. One features the two of them in the darkroom with Rubiček and Borkowski. Apparently it was not unusual for Grosman to ask friends to photograph him with his camera in different locations around the ghetto. Ben-Menachem was asked on a number of occasions simply to 'press the shutter' for Grosman when he wanted to include himself in a photograph.[60] Seemingly, Grosman considered a record of himself, the photographer at work, an important contribution to the underground ghetto archive. Zonabend also recognized the importance that photographs could have later. From time to time he took Grosman's photographs to hide in his home. He was eventually to save 417 of them.[61]

By July 1944, the workforce of the Łódź ghetto had finally outlived its usefulness. With the Red Army only 75 miles from Warsaw, the final deportations were about to begin.[62] From July to September, nearly all of the remaining 68,000 people were deported to Auschwitz-Birkenau,[63] including chairman of the Judenrat Chaim Rumkowski, who is presumed to have perished in the gas-chambers along with his 'subjects'.

With the threat of deportation looming, Rozencwajg-Ross hid his negatives in barrels which he then buried. Grosman continued to take photographs until he too faced deportation. With the help of his sister Fajga Frajtag and ben-Menachem he placed around 10,000 negatives in crates and buried them in the wall of his home. Grosman was deported to Germany and died there, aged 32.[64] On 28 August ben-Menachem arrived with his parents at Birkenau. His mother was immediately sent to the gas-chamber while he and his father remained at this camp before being transferred to others. He had arrived at Birkenau with a small bundle of possessions including his photo album. They were taken from him and he assumed the album would be destroyed. After the final deportation Zonabend was one of around 800 workers ordered by the German authorities to remain in the Łódź ghetto to clean up. He was able to hide documents, paintings, sketches and Grosman's photographs, which he had personally collected, in various locations and ultimately to save this unique archive.

After liberation Rozencwajg-Ross returned to the ghetto to retrieve his negatives. The majority were saved. Fajga Frajtag also returned to the ghetto to recover Grosman's negatives. It was decided to send them to Israel for safe-keeping. She gave them to a British soldier to deliver to ben-Menachem, who had survived the camps and had made his way to Kibbutz Nitzanim in Israel. He kept them in an ammunitions box under his bed until 1948 when, during the first Arab–Israeli war, Egyptian forces occupied the kibbutz and the negatives disappeared. In 1948 there was an indication that these photographs had survived. The Cairo daily newspaper *Al-Ahram* published a photograph, purportedly showing people in Tel Aviv queueing for bread. In fact, according to ben-Menachem and Zonabend, it was one of Grosman's photographs of a bread queue in the Łódź ghetto. Attempts to trace Grosman's photographs in Egypt have so far failed.[65]

While Grosman's photographs were lost, ben-Menachem's album survived. In 1946, a friend showed him a copy of the book *Zagłada Żydostwa Polskiego, Album Zdjęć* ('The Extermination of Polish Jews, an Album of Photographs'), published in Łódź the same year, which reproduced six pages of his album, credited to PWOK (Pomoc Więźniom Obozów Koncentracyjnych – Help for the Prisoners of Concentration Camps), a war-time organization based in Kraków and linked to the Polish underground. (The initials PWOK are clearly visible in Figures 31 and 32.) There is evidence to show that the album was indeed sent by the resistance movement from Auschwitz-Birkenau concentration camp to the underground in Kraków. On 20 November 1944 a letter, written in code by a member of the camp resistance to a colleague in Kraków, lists documents being secretly sent from the camp. It included what was referred to as an album from the Łódź ghetto.[66]

In the 1960s ben-Menachem met a Polish journalist in Israel and asked him to try and track down the album in Poland. In 1967, a few days before the Six-Day War, he received a package from Poland in the post which contained a set of black and white photographic prints; copies of each page of his album. No information was enclosed. During that war diplomatic relations between Eastern Europe and Israel were severed and ben-Menachem was unable to correspond with the journalist. Since then he has been unable to trace either the journalist or the album.[67]

As I listened to ben-Menachem's story in his home in Ramat Sharon, Israel, I wondered why, despite his contact with archives as an authority on documents of the Łódź ghetto, his album is little known and does not feature in any of the major Holocaust exhibitions. On the very rare occasions when pages from his album are used, he is not acknowledged as the author. Nor is his story widely known. It was only as I filed through pictures at the Ghetto Fighters' House photo archive in western Galilee, that my curiosity about these intriguing photo-montages, which I had not come across before, led the archivist, who knew very little about them himself, to suggest I might meet the author who lived near Tel Aviv. His album, and the photographs of Grosman and Rozencwajg-Ross, are not only vital evidence of the ghetto but a truly uplifting testament to the strength of the human spirit in the most terrible adversity.

Whose Reality?

The various photographers of the ghettos, Heinrich Jöst, Joe J. Heydecker, Dr Hans-Joachim Gerke, Willy Georg, Walter Genewein, members of the PK camera teams, the Judenrat, Mendel Grosman, Henryk Rozencwajg-Ross, George Kadish and other unidentified photographers, each had a different story to tell. Many of the photographs taken by the Jewish photographers resurfaced after the war ended, but few people were interested in them. Those photographers who had risked their lives to document the infernal life around them found an unsympathetic audience in the West, and even in Israel. Rozencwajg-Ross survived the war, stayed in Łódź and opened a photography shop. Some years later he moved to Israel and tried to find a publisher for his photographs, without success.[68]

In the past two decades, some of the photographs taken by German photographers have come to be publicly known. Men who, for most of their lives, had kept their ghetto photographs hidden away, in their later years decided to make them public. In 1981 Joe J. Heydecker, then living in Brazil, decided to publish some of his Warsaw ghetto photographs in *Where is Thy Brother Abel? Documentary Photographs of the Warsaw Ghetto*. He wrote: 'I find it hard to explain why nearly forty years have passed before I was able to publish these pictures. I believe I simply had not the strength enough to write the text, although I tried several times. I still feel unable to do so. Now I do what I can to set down what is seared into my memory, weak as it may be, because time is running out.'[69] In November 1982 Heinrich Jöst, the soldier who had taken photographs in the ghetto on his forty-third birthday, then an ailing man in his eighties, called an editor at *Stern* magazine in order to hand over his Warsaw ghetto negatives. Günther Schwarberg, a reporter from *Stern*, went to interview him and facilitated the publication of some of the images.[70] Jöst claimed he had never shown his photographs to friends, family or comrades. Contrary to his claim, in recent years, a few of his photographs have reached the Yad Vashem archive, from different sources. Some had been apparently found among the possessions of two dead German soldiers at the end of the war.[71]

Dr Gerke kept his photographs at his home in a desk drawer until, in 1994, after conversations with a Polish historian, he donated 500 of them to the National Museum in Warsaw. Pondering on the reason he had taken the photographs in the first place, he said: 'That is all I could do as a simple soldier of a foreign army.'[72] Some time in the 1960s, Willy Georg had offered his photographs to members of the Jewish community in Münster, but they had shown no interest in them and turned them down. It wasn't until 1991 that Georg was given the opportunity to make them public. It was then the Polish-Jewish writer Rafael F. Scharf heard of an elderly man in Münster who had photographs of the Warsaw ghetto. Scharf went to visit the eighty-year-old Georg, who readily gave him his photographs and negatives without payment because, he said, he wanted his photographs to be in 'good hands' so they might survive him.[73] Georg had said that when he saw his photographs anew and recalled those times he was 'shocked to the core'. Scharf, however, refrained from asking him how he felt about taking photographs in the ghetto. He decided there was no point. 'All he would have said', wrote Scharf, 'is what he thinks of it now, or, rather, what he thinks would be appropriate to say to me now.'[74]

In 1987, a collection of 600 of Walter Genewein's colour slides were discovered by chance in a Viennese second-hand bookshop. In 1998 Polish film-maker Darusz Jabłoński made a film based on the photographs. Arnold Mostowicz, a former Łódź ghetto doctor who appears in the film, said of the photographs: 'I was shocked to see those pictures – some of the first colour slides in the history of photography, taken by ghetto official Walter Genewein. The slides pictured the ghetto in Łódź but it was not the ghetto from my memory even though they showed the same people, the same buildings, the same streets. Where is the truth to be found? Is it in my memory or in the pictures taken by Walter Genewein? Where is the truth? In the archives? In old documents? In the cemetery? How to grasp the sense of this colourful vision contained in Genewein's slides.'[75]

These comments by Mostowicz define the problem of using photographs as records of reality and truth. 'I cannot even place myself in that reality,' he said. In an article about Jabłoński's film, journalist Nick Fraser wrote that for Mostowicz the photographs were 'worse than memory' because while Genewein had 'contrived to record the appearance of Łódź', he had been 'constructing a lie'.[76] In fact, he had constructed his own truth. Photographs do not represent a single reality. They exclude, include, distort and misrepresent. Walter Benjamin quoted Bertolt Brecht as saying that representing reality 'is complicated by the fact that less than ever does the mere reflexion of reality reveal anything about reality. A photograph of the Krupp works or AEG tells us next to nothing about these institutions.'[77] What, then, should a photograph of a ghetto show? A studio photograph taken in the Łódź ghetto of a young fashionably-dressed couple is printed as a Jewish New Year card (see Figure 34). The style of their portrait is the same as any other European studio portrait photograph at this time. Both are staring boldly and comfortably into the camera lens. Their image is framed by the words 'Litzmannstadt Getto'. It was presumably meant as a memento to send to family or friends as evidence of their being together. Are such photographs taken in the Łódź ghetto of Jewish family gatherings any more true representations of the ghetto than Genewein's vision, or that of the soldier-photographers? Genewein could not have recorded these realities, just as the ghetto Jews could not have recorded his. Besides, neither he nor other German photographers would have taken these photographs, because the subject-matter would have been of no interest to them. The people in them did not fit their perceived view of the Eastern European Jew. Apart from the fact in some

לשנה טובה תיכתבו

19   40

LITZMANNSTADT GETTO

34 · 'A portrait of a Jewish couple in the Łódź ghetto printed as a Rosh Hashana (Jewish New Year) greetings card.' (Jerzy Tomaszewski, courtesy of USHMM photo archives)

of these photographs they are wearing their required armband, there is little to distinguish them, or the couple, from other Europeans in the 1940s.

The secret photographs of Rozencwajg-Ross and Grosman, of deportations, hangings, poverty and suffering, do not necessarily differ from photographs of the same subjects taken by German soldiers or by Genewein. We cannot necessarily 'read' the motivation of the photographer or the meaning of the photographs simply by looking at them. Willy Georg was a German soldier who photographed the Warsaw ghetto in uniform, yet his images are touching and humanistic. We cannot know what his motivation was. Was he really sympathetic to the people he photographed, or was he as a professional photographer simply able to establish the rapport needed to encourage his subjects to co-operate?

What do photographs of the ghetto factories tell us? Grosman made photographs in the factories because it was his job; Genewein made photographs in the same factories to show the administration's 'achievements'; the Judenrat used photographs of factory production for similar ends; ben-Menachem used them to put across an opposite message. Indeed, the use of the same or similar photographs in the Judenrat albums and ben-Menachem's own album indicates how dependent on context photographic meaning can be.

When Nick Fraser commented that Genewein had constructed a lie, he was probably drawing on his own idea of ghetto life. My perception of ghetto life was challenged when I read the diary of Mary Berg. As a ghetto inhabitant she suffered hardships, though as the daughter of an American citizen she was eventually allowed to leave for the USA. With friends in the ghetto she formed a theatre troupe and her diary contains accounts of their celebrated performances in ghetto halls and cafés. In July 1942, prior to her departure from the ghetto, she went with friends to Foto-Forbert for a souvenir photograph.[78] This had not been my perception of the ghetto. Where is the reality?

The tragedy of these photographs lies not in what they show but in what we now know about the fate of the people in them. Arnold Mostowicz said: 'Those whose existence was recorded died shortly afterwards. They were betrayed by these photographs. And I feel that this expresses a paradox about art – that it can be made to harm as much as it can heal or console.'[79] He was expressing an essential paradox about photography: isolated from their context, photographs can be regarded as works of art, as beautiful, comforting or uplifting; not as the fragments of the cruel history they sometimes are.

FIVE

Cameras in the Camps

The Lili Jacob Album

In December 1964, trials of German guards who had served at Auschwitz concentration camp took place in Frankfurt. Lili Zelmanovic, a thirty-eight-year-old resident of Miami, Florida, gave evidence. She showed the court a photo album which, according to Bernd Naumann's account of the trial, she said she had found 'in a night table at Mauthausen'. The dedication apparently on the first page read: 'As a remembrance of your dear, unforgettable Heinz.' She said of the album: 'When I opened it I recognised the picture of the rabbi of my home town who officiated at my parents' funerals. When I leafed through it I recognised my family and myself. Since then I have come to feel that it is the only possession left to me'.[1]

Lili Zelmanovic was referring to a set of photographs said to have been taken of the arrival of Hungarian transports at the ramp at Auschwitz II-Birkenau. She and her entire family were on the transport. Originally from Bilky, a small Slovak town annexed by Hungary in 1939, they had been sent to the ghetto at Beregovo from where they were deported to Auschwitz on 24 May 1944. Judge Hofmeyer read out the captions to the photographs in the album: 'Resettlement of Jews from Hungary; Arrival of a Transport; Sorting Out; Arriving Men; Arriving Women; After the Sorting Out of Still Able-bodied Men; Still Able-bodied Women; Not Able-bodied Men; Not Able-bodied Women and Children; After Delousing; Assignment to Labour Camp; Personal effects.' Closing the album, Judge Hofmeyer commented, presumably referring to the inscription, 'peculiar mementos they gave each other'.[2] Figures 35 and 36 show two pages from the album.

Eight years earlier, on 22 November 1956, two former Auschwitz prisoners of Czech nationality had arrived at the Auschwitz State Museum with sixty-four of the same photographs. The museum confirmed them as authentic. The two men, Ota Kraus and Erich Kulka, explained that they were prints taken from a set of 203 photographs they had found in the State Museum in Prague, where

Aussortierung

35 · A page from
the Lili Jacob album.
The watchtower
and arched gateway
of Birkenau can
be seen in the
background of both
photographs. The
text reads: 'Sorting.'
(Yad Vashem Film
and Photo Archives)

apparently, in 1947 or 1948, a woman, whose identity was not known, sold the museum copies for 10,000 Czech crowns.[3] The woman was then called Lili Jacob (her name later changed to Zelmanovic, then Meier). She had wanted to sell the photographs in order to finance her emigration to the USA.

In 1949, thirty-seven of these photographs were reproduced for the first time in *The Tragedy of Slovak Jewry* published in Bratislava. In 1958 Kraus and Kulka published some of the same photographs in the third edition of their book, *The Death Factory* (Die Todesfabrik). Kulka, also a witness at the Frankfurt trials, had presented some of these photographs as evidence prior to Lili Zelmanovic. He handed them to the court and said, 'It is the only complete photographic document of the last stage of the crime the Nazis called the "Final solution of the Jewish problem".'[4]

Accounts of how the photo album was originally found vary. In 1958 Kulka and Kraus wrote that it had been discovered 'in a town in northern Czechoslovakia,

Frauen bei der Ankunft

in a house which once served as an SS photographer's home'.[5] In 1980 the *New York Times* incorrectly reported that Lili Jacob had found the album at Auschwitz, 'on the day Auschwitz was liberated by Allied troops in December 1944'. (Auschwitz was of course liberated by the Soviet army in January 1945).[6] It is now more widely accepted that Lili Jacob found the photo album at Dora-Nordhausen concentration camp where she had been transported from Birkenau.[7]

The photographs in the album, now commonly referred to as the Lili Jacob album, are of great importance as the only surviving photographs known to have been taken of the sorting of the arrivals at the ramp at Birkenau, the biggest and most ruthlessly efficient extermination operation in human history. Photographs from the album had been presented as evidence in the Adolf Eichmann trial in 1961 but they attracted little publicity. Mrs Esther Goldstein, of Hungarian origin, then living in Israel, was able to identify herself and her family in copies of the photographs.[8]

36·A page from the Lili Jacob album. The text reads: 'Women at the arrival.' (Yad Vashem Film and Photo Archives)

Lili Zelmanovic kept the photo album until 1980, when she was finally persuaded to hand it over to Yad Vashem Martyrs' and Heroes' Remembrance Authority in Israel. The *New York Times* reported Lili Meier, as she had now become, as saying: 'I felt this was all I had left. I never thought of parting with it. But I'm feeling relieved that I'm doing the right thing ... I want to close the past.'[9] As Lili Meier quietly closed the door on her own past, another door was opening. The photographs in the album were to become central to the visual representation of the Holocaust. Apart from their value as evidence, they would be imbued with an emotional intensity and reproduced in books, films and museums world-wide. But who took the photographs, and for what purpose, is still not established.

The Camp Photographers

Photography was integral to the operation of some of the concentration camps. Whether taken for prisoners' identity papers, or as evidence of the most abhorrent medical experiments, photographs appear to have played an important role. For the official production of photographs, specialist departments were established, known as the Erkennungsdienst, or camp identification service. Although not every camp had this facility, Sachsenhausen and Buchenwald in Germany, Auschwitz and Stutthoff in Poland and Mauthausen in Austria are all known to have had Erkennungsdienst departments. At Mauthausen, François Boix, former news photographer and Spanish prisoner of war, who worked in the Erkennungsdienst, said of the department's work that, 'pictures of everything happening in the camp could be taken and sent to the High Command in Berlin'.[10]

The most comprehensive collection of Erkennungsdienst photographs to survive the war were taken at Auschwitz II-Birkenau. At other camps they were either removed or destroyed as the liberating armies drew closer. At Buchenwald, the Erkennungsdienst department was demolished by an allied air raid in 1944 and many pictures were destroyed.[11]

There were no official photographs taken at the extermination camps at Bełżec, Chełmno, Treblinka and Sobibór in occupied Poland. Unlike the concentration camps, which were slave labour camps for those opposed to the Nazi regime, where thousands died of maltreatment, starvation, disease or execution, these camps were built specifically to exterminate Jews. As almost everybody on the transports was gassed within hours of arrival, there was no need for official identity photographs or any other photographic representation. However, there is one extant exception: the last commandant of Treblinka, SS Untersturmführer (Lieutenant) Kurt Franz, made his own personal photo album of the camp entitled, incredibly, 'The Best Years of My Life'. Franz's photo album includes photographs of a holiday in Italy, his dog, animals at Treblinka camp zoo and the cranes used to exhume bodies for burning during the closure of the camp in 1943.[12]

At Auschwitz the Erkennungsdienst was established at some time in late December 1940 or early January 1941. It came under the direct control of the camp's political department (Politische Abteilung) headed by SS Obersturm-führer (Lieutenant) Maximilian Grabner. In January 1941 SS Hauptscharführer (Sergeant) Bernhardt Walter arrived at Auschwitz to run the Erkennungsdienst and manage the camp cinema on the orders of camp commandant SS-Obersturm-bannführer (Lieutenant-Colonel) Rudolf Höss. Walter had joined the National Socialist Party in 1933 and in 1935 had become a member of the SS 'Totenkopf' division, said to have been one of the 'most brutal German divisions' to serve in the Second World War and whose members served as camp guards at Dachau, Sachsenhausen or Buchenwald.[13] Walter had previously run the Erkennungsdienst at Sachsenhausen, the camp where Höss had held the position of 'Adjutant to the Commandant' from 1938. Höss had been promoted and transferred to Auschwitz on 1 May 1940.[14]

In the summer of 1941 SS Unterscharführer (Corporal) Ernst Hofmann, a former school teacher, became Walter's assistant and, at Walter's request, photographer Franz Maltz, a communist and German political prisoner, was transferred from the Erkennungsdienst in Sachsenhausen to take up the position as department Kapo or foreman. However, in 1943, Maltz was executed in the camp for 'inappropriate behaviour'. He allegedly told a group of SS men about a dream he had had in which he saw Germany surrounded by barbed wire and Hitler and Himmler as prisoners.[15]

After the execution of Maltz, Polish political prisoner Tadeusz Bródka was appointed Kapo. Bródka was on the first transport of 728 Polish prisoners from Tarnów which arrived at Auschwitz on 14 June 1940, as was graphic artist Tadeusz Myszkowski, who worked in the Erkennungsdienst from late 1943.[16] On 31 August 1940, the second Tarnów transport to arrive at Auschwitz included a Polish political prisoner, twenty-two-year-old Wilhelm Brasse, who worked as a labourer in the camp before becoming one of the main Erkennungsdienst photographers in early 1941. Before the war began Brasse had been a profes-sional photographer in a studio in Katowice called Foto-Korekt. He also spoke German, a requirement for working in the Erkennungsdienst, as speaking Polish was not allowed.[17]

The Erkennungsdienst was an efficiently-run department where at any one time there were around a dozen prisoners, some with professional skills as photographers, darkroom workers, retouchers, painters, graphic artists or writers. The department, established on the ground floor of block 26 at Auschwitz, consisted of two darkrooms, a third room for loading cassettes, an office and a large room where prisoners' identity photographs were taken. This room was specially equipped with a large-format camera and a revolving adjustable chair with a crescent-shaped head support. Three poses were taken of each prisoner: full front portrait, a three-quarter profile, and profile. Around forty or fifty negatives were made each day. In the early days of the camp, film was easily available and ordered by Walter from either Agfa or from a firm called 'Opta' in Bydgoszcz. The photographic prints which were made from these negatives were filed on a 8cm x 8cm index card with the prisoner's name, number, date and place of birth and the place the prisoner was transferred from. The index system was divided into three groups: the living, the dead, and those who had been transferred elsewhere.[18]

During 1940–41 this highly efficient system for photographing newly arrived prisoners, who at this time were mainly Poles, was the main work of the Erkennungsdienst. Later, as more nationalities and racial groups came to the camp, only those considered to be in the political prisoners' category were registered, given prison numbers and photographed. This excluded the thousands of Soviet POWs and later Gypsies and Jews, who were not photographed unless on special orders from the political department. Making identity photographs continued until 7 July 1943 when, due to the lack of photographic materials, severe restrictions were imposed on camp photography on order from the Reichssicherheitshauptampt (RSHA – the Reich Security Head Office) in Berlin. Except for German prisoners who continued to be photographed until the end, the camp number, generally tattooed on the left forearm, replaced the identity photographs.[19] Identity photographs were also made of civilian workers in the camp, SS men and high-ranking officials. SS men were also known to use the Erkennungsdienst facilities to develop personal photographs or to order the prisoners to make them. Although this activity was forbidden, it was widespread. On 2 February 1943 Rudolf Höss issued a notice which explicitly prohibited unofficial photography. Order no. 4/43 stated: 'I want to point out once more that taking photographs in the camp is forbidden. I shall punish with the utmost severity those who do not observe this order.'[20] Despite the warning, Bronisław Jureczek, a Polish political prisoner who from 1943 worked in the Erkennungsdienst darkroom, claimed that SS men frequently visited the darkroom and that, 'with regularity', they printed secret photographs or occasionally had them made by prisoners. According to Jureczek, on occasions even Höss's son Klaus visited the Erkennungsdienst to learn about photography under the instructions of prisoners.[21]

Walter, who was known in the camp for his love of gambling and alcohol, saw an opportunity to make photographs for commercial gain. When he saw a photograph of a vase of flowers which Brasse had taken in the Erkennungsdienst office, he apparently liked it so much that he ordered several thousand prints to be made into postcards which were then sold from kiosks outside the camp. Some time later, on Walter's orders, Brasse was accompanied by Hofmann to take a photograph of the view of the town of Auschwitz (Oświęcim in Polish) from outside the camp. It was the only time in almost four years that Brasse had left the camp. The photograph entitled, 'The view of the bridge into the town' was coloured by Myszkowski and sold as a postcard.[22]

The photographs ordered by Walter were not always scenic. Captured partisans, dead and alive, were also photographed, as were camp inmates who had committed suicide 'on the wire' (camp terminology for those who could no longer endure the misery and threw themselves at the high-voltage electrified fence) or who were shot for trying to escape. Others committed suicide by hanging themselves from their bunks. These situations were photographed mainly by Walter and Hofmann.[23] In his reminiscences about the camp, SS man Pery Broad, an employee of the political department, said that after the death of a prisoner had been reported by the block senior at roll-call, 'the officers of the Erkennungsdienst hurried to the place and photographed the body from all angles'.[24] Photographing suicides and executions was not a rare occurrence. Brasse recalled how Walter enthusiastically showed a number of films he had personally made with his 16mm Agfa Monik film camera to the Erkennungsdienst workers. It showed 'scenes of the liquidation' of Soviet POWs. In one of the films, according to Brasse, there were several thousand Soviet prisoners in the execution yard at block 11, clothed and later naked, probably before their execution. Another film included scenes of thousands of Soviet prisoners being murdered with axes. In a testimony given to Auschwitz-Birkenau State Museum in 1984, Brasse recalled the horrifying film. 'Despite that a few decades have passed since this,' he said, 'I have never forgotten, and probably will not forget the scenes in this film.' Walter, according to Brasse, sent the original to the RSHA in Berlin and later received a copy-print in return.[25] Following the German invasion of the Soviet Union in June 1941, Soviet POWs, whose status was not respected, were brought west in their thousands. As far as SS Reichsführer Heinrich Himmler was concerned, the 12,000 Soviet POWs who arrived at Auschwitz during the winter of 1941 and 1942 were a 'gift from heaven'.[26] The shortage of labour, which threatened the elaborate construction plans to build another camp at Brzezinka (Birkenau), 3 kilometres from Auschwitz main camp, was resolved.[27] The Soviet POWs were put to work in appalling conditions. Within months the majority, too weak to work, were shot and buried in mass graves. After six months only 150 were still alive.[28] On 3 September 1941 around 600 Soviet POWs and 250 sick Poles were the first groups to be used for Zyklon B experiments which were carried out in the basement of block 11.[29]

On 16 September, 900 more Soviet POWs 'inaugurated' a new experimental gas-chamber in what was formerly the morgue of the Auschwitz crematorium.[30] According to SS man Pery Broad, Russians were considered 'just as unimportant as the Jews'.[31]

At Mauthausen and Majdanek, the latter set up as a camp for POWs in October 1941, the treatment of Soviet POWs was equally brutal. François Boix, Erkennungsdienst worker at Mauthausen, in a testimony made during the Nuremberg trials in 1946, said the Soviet POWs were massacred 'by every means imaginable'. In 1941, within three months of the arrival of 7,000 Soviet POWs at Mauthausen, only thirty were still alive. Boix claimed that these thirty survivors were photographed by the Erkennungsdienst, 'as a document'. Boix recalled other photographs being taken of the Soviets by the head of the Erkennungsdienst, SS Oberscharführer (Lance Sergeant) Paul Ricken. On one occasion, in block 20, which housed 1,800 half-starved Russian internees, Boix was called to a photo-shoot to 'handle the lights'. Describing the scene he said: 'Large kettles of spoiled food were emptied on the snow and left there until it began to freeze; then the Russians were ordered to get at it. The Russians were so hungry, they would fight for this food.'[32]

According to Boix, propaganda photographs were also made to show how well the Russian prisoners were treated. In 1943 a transport of Soviet officers arrived at the camp. Some were given 'new prisoners' clothing' and put to light work in the quarry, where Ricken photographed them with his Leica. He took about forty-eight pictures. Boix developed the photographs and made five 13cm x 18cm copies of each which, along with the negatives, were sent to Berlin. After the photo-shoot, all the Soviet prisoners were 'sent to the gas-chamber'.[33]

At Auschwitz, none of the photographs or films of Soviet POWs is known to have survived, although a photographic documentation of the construction of Auschwitz II-Birkenau did. Towards the end of 1941, a second smaller photographic laboratory, known as the Bauleitung, was established specifically to deal with the photographic documentation of the construction work. The department came under the direct control of Karl Bischoff, chief of the Zentralbauleitung (Central Construction Office) and was run by SS Corporal Uscha Dietrich Kamann. The idea of a separate photography workshop had been proposed to Kamann by Polish political prisoner Ludwik Lawin, whose job it was to make photo albums to record the progress of the construction work. Kamann, who wished to avoid being sent to the front, thought it an excellent idea and obtained authorization,[34] but according to Wilhelm Brasse, Kamann was not a professional photographer and his skills were minimal. In the early days of the Bauleitung he would frequently visit the Erkennungsdienst to ask for advice.[35]

The majority of Bauleitung photographs were taken in 1943 when the building work in Birkenau was at its peak. All aspects of the work were photographed, including drainage, barracks, gas-chambers and crematoria. The camp authorities were so proud of the construction work that an exhibition of these photographs, enlarged to 13cm x 18cm, were displayed on a collective noticeboard in the hallway of the Bauleitung.[36]

Pery Broad thought this public display was not altogether a good idea. He later wrote: 'The building section of *Auschwitz* concentration camp was so proud of their achievements that they placed a series of pictures of the crematoria in the hall of their main building for everybody to see. They had overlooked the fact that civilians, coming and going there, would be less impressed – with the technological achievements of the building section; on seeing the enlarged photos of fifteen ovens, neatly arranged side by side, they would, instead, be rather apt to ponder on the somewhat strange contrivances of the Third Reich.' For this reason the exhibition was short-lived. According to Broad, Grabner was quick to quell 'the bizarre publicity', and the photographs were removed.[37] However, Lawin, who recognized the significance of these photographs and what he called their 'documentary value', persuaded Tadeusz Kubiak, a prisoner and photographer in the Bauleitung, to make extra prints so that he could give them to Stanisław Dubiel, a fellow prisoner and gardener at Höss's family house in the camp, in case he didn't survive. Dubiel welded them into a pipe in Höss's greenhouse. After the war when the pipe was sawn in half, the packaging was there but the photographs were missing. They were never found.[38]

The construction photographs were pasted into photo albums which Lawin said were made to pay homage to distinguished SS men.[39] One surviving eighty-eight-page photo album, known as the Bauleitung Album, contains 398 photographs and is now kept at Yad Vashem archive.[40] Although the photographs in the album are generally thought to have been taken by Kamann, it is possible that some were also taken by Walter. In a statement given to Auschwitz-Birkenau State Museum, ex-prisoner Władysław Plaskura names Walter as one of the Bauleitung workers. Jureczek claimed that Walter had made photographs of the 'individual stages of the building of the crematoria' and in a few of the photographs a parked motorbike is visible. Walter was a motorbike enthusiast and he was well known for riding it around the camp.[41]

In keeping with the industrial nature of the camp, at Auschwitz photo albums were produced as a part of an efficient production line, personalized not by members of the armed forces but by prisoners, albeit under orders. As a graphic artist it was Myszkowski's main task to decorate and bind the albums and to write captions to the photographs. The albums not only included photographs taken in the camp; on one occasion Hofmann commissioned Myszkowski to make a 'beautifully illustrated' album of German fairytales.[42] Other SS men ordered Myszkowski to make caricature drawings of SS officers and rural scenes, sometimes for the camp museum which officially opened in 1941.[43]

From 1942, with the arrival of the SS doctors, the work of the Erkennungs-dienst photographers became increasingly macabre. Eduard Wirths, chief camp physician, and Johanne Paul Kremer, Professor of Anatomy from the University of Münster, were sent to Auschwitz in 1942. In May 1943 Hauptsturmführer (Captain) Josef Mengele arrived. The prisoner-photographers were frequently ordered to photograph the medical experiments performed on prisoners. Dr Kremer noted some of these occasions in his diary in the same casual tone that he described his travels abroad, the weather or his abundant meals in the camp. On 6 September 1942 he gave a full description of an 'excellent Sunday dinner'. On 16 October 1942 he wrote: 'Had a photo taken of a syndactylous Jew in camp (father and uncle had the same affliction).' On 4 November he noted a trip to Prague and the photographs he had taken around the city. Back in Auschwitz a few days later he wrote: 'Fresh material (liver, spleen and pancreas) from a Jewish prisoner of 18, extremely atrophic, who had been photographed before.'[44] It was said that Kremer would often have prisoners photographed if they had unusual physical features, or before their murder – an injection of phenol – in order to extend the collection of fresh organs.[45]

On many occasions Brasse was ordered to make photographs of Dr Men-gele's and Dr Wirths's pseudoscientific experiments. For Dr Mengele he photo-graphed Hasidic and traditional-looking Jews whose dress or physical features were regarded as 'interesting'. Triplets, twins, Jewish and Gypsy children were also photographed as were people regarded as 'strange', 'diseased', 'deformed', 'disfigured', 'disabled' or on the verge of dying.[46] This morbid curiosity for documenting sickness and disease among prisoners was also extended to include the SS. On one occasion Dr Wirths ordered Bródka and Brasse to make photo-graphs of SS men, sick with malaria, during a feverish 'fit'. The photographs, which apparently showed their terrible distorted faces and trembling bodies, were processed and printed in the Erkennungsdienst and sent to Berlin.[47]

Prisoners who had what were regarded as 'interesting' tattoos were also lined up for the camera. Brasse recalled being ordered to photograph a prisoner who had 'a beautiful tattoo' on his chest of Adam and Eve, in two colours, red and blue. He later saw the tattoo 'stretched on a special canvas'. According to Jureczek, these photographs of tattoos were placed in a special photo album which Walter kept in his office under lock and key.[48] 'This is what they found entertaining,' said Brasse, who photographed many tattoos, 'photographs of this sort. Why anyone wanted to look at this kind of thing I haven't a clue. But this is what they thought was fun, looking at photographs like this.'[49]

Brasse was frequently ordered by Dr Wirths to take black and white or colour photographs of women prisoners in block 10 during pseudoscientific medical experiments supervised by Dr Maximilian Samuel. Dr Samuel was a German-Jewish professor and gynaecologist from Cologne who, although he collaborated with the Nazis' medical experiments, was suddenly put to death at Auschwitz for reasons that remain unclear.[50] 'They would bring the women into the room', said Brasse, 'and strip them naked.' Dr Samuel would inject them with a kind of anaesthetic, unless they were Jewish in which case experiments would be performed without. 'Gynaecological equipment and other special equipment was inserted into them … They had special forceps and the womb was taken out and I took photographs of the wombs. It was horrendous. They claimed that the work was about examining cancers of the womb but they could have been doing anything'.[51] Brasse would develop and print the black and white photographs and either Dr Wirths or Dr Samuel would collect them. The colour negatives were sent to a specialist laboratory in Berlin. Dr Wirths also ordered Brasse to make 'colour photographs of eyes' at the women's camp at Birkenau to be used in pseudoscientific research. On one occasion, Brasse and Bródka told Dr Wirths that these films 'hadn't come out properly'. They were ordered to return to Birkenau to retake them. This ruse enabled Brasse and Bródka to smuggle medicines to Birkenau in a tripod case.[52]

Occasionally young healthy women were photographed. They were stripped naked and brought in front of the camera and photographed from the front, profile and from the back. Brasse said: 'I made photographs of young women for Dr Mengele. I was fully aware that they were going to die. They didn't know … To photograph these women and to know that they were going to die was so highly distressing. They were so full of life and so beautiful … ' In my interview with him in August 2000, in his home town of Żywiec, he broke off at this point, unable to say more about these events that had taken place fifty-five years earlier.

In the spring of 1944 Dr Emil Kaschub, an advanced medical student, carried out experiments on the limbs of healthy 'young and middle-aged' male prisoners in a room in block 28. He would infect their limbs with various substances which caused sores, abscesses and other painful symptoms. Every few days Kaschub would photograph their limbs in various states of decay with a Leica camera and take the film to be processed and printed by prisoners in the Erkennungsdienst.[53] Hofmann, who personally oversaw the making of these photographs, stressed to the prisoners that they were 'top secret and extremely important'. All prints, Hofmann told them, whether good or bad, must be given to him and nothing taken from the workshop.[54]

Despite these horrific tasks, prisoners were known to make 'secret' photographs for their own personal use, possibly as a way of bringing an element of humanity into their inhumane existence.[55] When I asked Brasse if he had ever secretly taken a photograph in the camp he paused and then said: 'Only once. It was just a photograph of a woman who looked extremely pretty.' This simple demure act in such a barbaric environment was important to Brasse. At great risk he smuggled the picture out of the camp to his mother. After the war ended he found the woman he had photographed and gave her the print. She looked at it and then destroyed it, saying that she didn't look good enough.[56]

Even though all the photographs carried out in the Erkennungsdienst were considered top secret, and Grabner frequently warned prisoners that if any should leave the workshop they would be shot, its workers smuggled material to the outside world via the camp resistance movement.[57] Alfred Woycicki, who had been arrested on 18 February 1942 as a result of his participation in the resistance movement in Kraków, was known for his continued resistance work in the camp. As a fluent German speaker, he was in charge of written matters in the office and photographic archive, and regularly passed on discarded prints or documents to the camp resistance. Brasse also participated in making forged documents and photographs for prisoners attempting to escape.[58] Myszkowski also later admitted to belonging to what he referred to as a 'secret organization'.[59]

From January 1944, Auschwitz became the main centre for the extermination of the Jews. The four temporary death camps in occupied Poland, where an approximate total of 1.5 million Jews had been murdered, had been closed down. In the first four months of 1944, 6,000 people a day were arriving at Auschwitz II-Birkenau. Due to a severe labour shortage in the Reich, prisoners were sorted into those who were fit for work and those who were not. Those considered unfit were dispatched to the gas-chambers. By late April, in order to process the transports more quickly, a new railway siding was completed which enabled the transports to come through the famous watchtower archway into the camp itself. On 29 April one of the first transports of 1,800 Hungarian Jews arrived on this new rail spur. By July the number of Hungarian Jews alone had increased to around 437,000.[60] According to Pery Broad, 'the weeks of the Hungarian action constituted the craziest climax'.[61] Throughout May and June the number of people murdered exceeded the official incarceration capacity of 132,000 corpses per month; 'The frenetic gassing and burning continued through July.'[62] The crematoria were unable to cope with such large quantities and pyres were lit to dispose of the corpses. During the summer of 1944, transports of Jews arrived from France, Holland, Greece, Bohemia, Moravia, Belgium, Germany and Austria. In August–September, 67,000 came from the Łódź ghetto.[63]

It was on the platform alongside the new rail spur, known as the 'ramp', and at different vantage points around the area, that the majority of photographs in the Lili Jacob album were taken. Some photographs, taken from a high vantage point, suggest that the photographer was standing on top of the train trying to capture the enormity of the operation and the dense crowds. In some of these high-angle photographs the watchtower can be clearly seen in the background (see Figure 35). Others are taken from a slightly lower vantage point, maybe from the train itself, while some were taken among the crowds. A few were taken after the women and children had been segregated from the men. In the latter pages of the album are photographs of men and women who have been selected for work in their camp uniforms. The elevated angle of some of these photographs, which show an overview of the camp with prisoners in the foreground and the camp in the background, indicate these were not clandestinely taken. Of the last eight pages, seven have photographs which show the enormous piles of belongings being sorted at the warehouses, known to prisoners as 'Kanada', because Canada was seen as the land of plenty. Prisoners worked in more than thirty such warehouses, sorting goods and clothes of all kinds to send back to the Reich or for recycling in the Polish ghettos.[64] The last page of the album has two photographs: the exterior of one of the crematorium buildings and the interior, showing the ovens.

It was well known among the Erkennungsdienst prisoners that those who worked in the political department received these transports at the ramp and attended the 'mass actions' – the gassing of the deportees.[65] According to Dr Kremer, men competed to taken part in 'such actions' as they were given additional rations, '$^1/_5$ litre of vodka, 5 cigarettes, 100 grammes of sausage and bread'.[66] Jureczek, Brasse and Woycicki all claimed that both Walter and Hofmann frequently went to the ramp. Walter was often seen by prisoners riding his motorbike to Birkenau for the arrival of the bigger transports and sometimes he took his camera. When Walter returned from these 'actions', Woycicki observed that he was often tired, dirty and dusty, his voice was hoarse and he was frequently drunk. He would wash and then sometimes sit with Hofmann in the office for long periods talking and laughing. At other times he would close himself in the photographic darkroom, where he would process his films and make prints which he then took away.[67] Occasionally Walter would give Brasse the film to process – generally one 36-frame film – then either Hofmann or Walter would choose those to be printed. According to Brasse, 'at least three photo albums' were made up of photographs taken at the ramp. One of them included photographs taken by Hofmann of people entering the gas-chamber. Brasse recalled developing and printing one of these photographs for Hofmann: 'It was a photograph taken of one woman at the moment she was entering the gas-chamber, just to see her face, just to see her reaction – the photograph showed a bit of her torso and her face, her face was terrible, frightened and with a horrible expression.' Some of these albums, Brasse claimed, were sent to Berlin.[68]

37 · A photograph taken by the Sonderkommando at Birkenau. In the bottom left-hand corner are naked women running. (Państwowe Muzeum Auschwitz-Birkenau w Oświęcimiu)

One morning in the spring of 1944 a Hauptscharführer (Sergeant) photographer, allegedly from the RSHA in Berlin, arrived by car to take photographs of the mass actions in Birkenau. He was, he claimed, under direct orders to make a series of photographs for the Reichsführer himself. He started by photographing at Birkenau, where they had just gassed a recently-arrived transport. According to Woycicki, he photographed the most horrendous scenes there, including 'SS guards standing on a heap of dead corpses laughing'. He also took photographs at the women's camp and the hospital blocks before taking the film to be processed by the prisoners in the Erkennungsdienst. Woycicki, who saw the photographs, was surprised by their content. 'The greatest enemy of the SS', he said, 'couldn't have chosen more discrediting material.' The photographer took his film and left the camp. It was discovered the next day that the RSHA knew nothing about this photo-reporter.[69] But Woycicki was able to secretly make 'one print of each photograph' before he left, which were then 'smuggled out of the camp'. They have since disappeared.[70]

In the autumn of 1944 more secret photographs were smuggled from the camp,

38 · Photograph taken from a window by the Sonderkommando at Birkenau. The Sonderkommando is burning bodies. (Państwowe Muzeum Auschwitz-Birkenau w Oświęcimiu)

taken by members of the Sonderkommando, a special unit of prisoners responsible for burning the bodies of those who had been gassed (see Figures 37 and 38). How the prisoners acquired the camera is not known but Kraus and Kulka claimed that cameras were sometimes smuggled by prisoners from the 'Kanada' warehouses.[71] From a window a few photographs were taken of the burning pyres and women being sent to the gas-chamber. They were smuggled to Kraków, around

50 kilometres from the camp, via the Polish Socialist Party in Brzeszcze, a small town near Oświęcim. The note which accompanied the photographs was dated 4 September 1944 and signed 'Stakło', a pseudonym for Polish prisoner Stanisław Kłodziński, a leading member of the camp resistance. It said:

> Urgent. Send two metal rolls of film for 6x9 camera as fast as possible. Have possibility of taking photos. Sending you snaps from Birkenau – gas poisoning action. These photos show one of the stakes at which bodies were burned, when the crematoria could not manage to burn all the bodies. The bodies in the foreground are waiting to be thrown into the fire. Another picture shows one of the places in the forest, where people are undressing before 'showering' – as they were told – and then go to the gas-chambers. *Send film roll as fast as you can!* Send the enclosed photos to *Tell* – we think you should send the enlargements further on.[72]

Tell was the pseudonym of Teresa Łasocka-Estreicher, a member of the underground movement in Kraków. These photographs are frequently credited to Dawid Szmulewski, a member of the camp resistance movement, although it seems doubtful that he personally took them. Some years later former Sonderkommando Alter Fajnzylberg, a Jew from France, gave his own account of how the photographs were taken:

> [S]omewhere about midway through 1944, we decided to take pictures secretly to record our work: that is, [to record the] crimes committed by the Germans in the Auschwitz gas-chambers. In order to do that, it was necessary to get a good camera and film. I do not remember precisely all the details, but we actually managed to get such a camera … Having decided to take such pictures, I was unable to operate entirely alone. From the very beginning, several prisoners from our Sonderkommando were in on my secret: Szlomo Dragon, his brother Josek Dragon, and Alex, a Greek Jew whose surname I do not remember.
>
> On the day on which the pictures were taken – I do not remember the day or the month exactly – we allocated tasks. Some of us were to guard the person taking the pictures. In other words, we were to keep a careful watch for the approach of anyone who did not know the secret, and above all for any SS men moving about in the area. At last the moment came. We all gathered at the western entrance leading from the outside to the gas-chamber of Crematorium V: we could not see any SS men in the watchtower overlooking the door from above the barbed wire, nor near the place where the pictures were to be taken. Alex, the Greek Jew, quickly took out his camera, pointed it towards a heap of burning bodies, and pressed the shutter. This is why the photograph shows prisoners from the Sonderkommando working at the heap. One of the SS was

standing beside them, but his back was turned towards the crematorium building. Another picture was taken from the other side of the building, where women and men were undressing among the trees. They were from a transport that was to be murdered in the gas-chamber of Crematorium V.

Describing this event, I want to emphasize once again that when these pictures were taken, all the prisoners I mentioned were present. In other words, even though the Greek Jew, Alex, was the person who actually pressed the shutter, one can say that the pictures were taken by all of us. Today, I cannot remember what the camera looked like, because I had never taken pictures before and I did not hold the camera, but I think it looked like a German Leica.[73]

On 7 October 1944 several hundred members of the Sonderkommando were murdered. They were no longer needed for their duties. On 31 October 1944 the gas-chambers ceased to operate. Around 1.1 million Jews had been murdered at Auschwitz-Birkenau, along with approximately 150,000 Poles, 23,000 Gypsies, 15,000 Soviet POWs and 25,000 people from other nations.[74] By 25 November the demolition of crematorium II had begun and throughout December the remaining crematoria were dismantled. By December most of the Erkennungs-dienst prisoners had been evacuated to other camps in the west – Gross-Rosen, Mauthausen and Sachsenhausen – and Bernhardt Walter was busy packing the photographic evidence. Brasse said: 'During mid-December 1944 everything in the Erkennungsdienst took place slowly and calmly and photographs were being packed up into suitcases and crates. These were photographs from the ramp, the film that Walter made of the Soviet POWs, and all the photographs ordered by Dr Mengele and Dr Wirths.'[75]

During mid-January 1945, after the last evacuation transport had left Ausch-witz II-Birkenau and as the Soviet army grew nearer, 'the panic started'.[76] Only Walter, Jureczek, Brasse and seven Jews were left in the Erkennungsdienst. By that time most photographs had been sent elsewhere, except the prisoners' identity photographs which were still kept in the department. Walter ordered the men to burn all the photographs and negatives. Jureczek recalled the situation:

At almost the last moment we were ordered to burn all the negatives and pho-tographs which were in the Erkennungsdienst. First, we put wet photographic paper and also photographs and then a large number of photographs and nega-tives into the tile stove in such large numbers as to block the exhaust outlet. This ensured that when we set fire to the materials in the stove only the photographs and negatives near the stove door would be consumed, and that the fire would later die out due to the lack of air. After the war I learned that our assumption had been right, and that a high percentage of the photographs and negatives had survived and found their way into the right hands ... Moreover, under the pretext of haste, I had deliberately scattered a number of photographs and negatives in the rooms of the lab. I knew that with the hurried evacuation of the camp, no one would have time to gather them all and that something would survive.[77]

On 15 January Walter left Auschwitz to join an SS police division in Berlin.[78] When the camp was liberated on 27 January 1945, all those who had recorded the Nazis' crimes had moved on. It was the turn of the Soviet and Polish liberating army photographers to record the results. Although photographs taken during the existence of the camp were used as evidence in war crimes trials, who took them and why was considered of little importance. The photographers of the Erkennungsdienst were forgotten.

The Auschwitz Archive

In April 1946 a group of around eighteen former Auschwitz prisoners returned to the camp with the aim of setting up a museum of martyrology in memory of all those who had suffered and died there. Other former prisoners later joined them. In June 1947 an exhibition marked the formal opening of the museum and the seventh anniversary of the arrival at the camp of the first transport of Polish political prisoners; 50,000 people attended. A month later the museum was officially sanctioned by the Polish government. For the next ten years a community of former prisoners, which was referred to by one of them as 'one big family', lived and worked in the camp to preserve buildings and documents. From the outset, visitors, mainly from Eastern Europe and the USSR, came to pay tribute and the ex-prisoners gave guided tours.[79] As the former prisoners were living evidence of the history of the camp, there was little need at the time for a research-based institution in the museum; that would not happen until the mid-1950s. Consequently no research was carried out and details about how or where documents and photographs were found were not always recorded. Although former Erkennungsdienst worker Tadeusz Myszkowski worked at the museum at this time, he did not think it necessary to record his experiences as a prisoner at the camp.

The 40,000 identity photographs saved by the ingenuity of Brasse and Jureczek were the only photographs found when the camp was liberated. Over a period of twenty years, other photographs taken at the camp gradually surfaced.[80] On 25 September 1946 Ludwik Lawin returned to Auschwitz to retrieve the fifty-three photographs from the Bauleitung department which he had secretly buried in the camp grounds in a corked bottle in the winter of 1944. The photographs were still where he had buried them – fourteen steps from the third Bauleitung barracks – and in good condition.[81] In 1944 Lawin had given another set of the same photographs to a colleague to bury elsewhere, but the colleague did not survive the war, and where they were hidden is still unknown.[82]

In the late 1940s, thirty-eight photographs of Dr Kaschub's experiments on prisoners' limbs were used as evidence at the Auschwitz trials in Kraków. In his evidence to the court, Woycicki confirmed they were authentic. It is thought that they were sent to the underground in Kraków after the liberation, though no specific information exists. After the trials they were kept in the Main Commission for Research into German Crimes in Warsaw until the mid-1950s when they were returned to the Auschwitz archive.[83] In 1955 a microfilm of each page of the Arie ben-Menachem album was sent to the Auschwitz archive from the Main Commission. However, in recent years the commission – now Instytut Pamięci Narodowej (IPN) – has claimed the album is no longer in its collection.

In 1958, a suitcase containing around 2,500 family photographs, thought to have been brought to the camp by deportees, was returned to the archive by an office worker at the museum. It is not recorded who that person was. It is thought that the photographs were found on the liberation of the camp and sometime later taken away by a camp museum worker, although there are no details.[84]

In June 1959 Brasse returned to Auschwitz to give a statement about his experiences in the camp. He identified the photographs from the Lili Jacob album which Kulka and Kraus had brought to the archive as the work of Hofmann and Walter. Some, he said, were from a film delivered personally by Höss to the Erkennungsdienst.[85] In 1961 Jureczek returned to Auschwitz to give his testimony. He also identified the same photographs as authentic. Although he could not be certain whether he had seen these particular photographs at the Erkennungsdienst, he was certain that 'these, or thematically similar photographs were both made or owned by Walter'.[86] When I met Brasse and showed him a copy of the album, he instantly recognized some of the photographs as those which, he said, he had made prints of in the Erkennungsdienst darkroom. He stated categorically that the gothic handwritten captions in the album were by Myszkowski. He also was certain that not all the Jews in the photographs were from Hungary but came from other countries as well.

On 17 October 1960 Władysław Pytlik, a leading member of the resistance movement in Brzeszcze during the war, gave a testimony to the Auschwitz State Museum about his wartime activities. Pytlik brought with him three photographs. They were the photographs taken secretly by the Sonderkommando in 1944. In 1947 one of the same images had been displayed in the first exhibition at Auschwitz. Two of them were later published in 1959 and 1960 in *1939–1945 We Have Not Forgotten*.[87] As a member of the resistance, Pytlik recalled receiving the photographs sixteen years before. He said: 'In 1944 we received a piece of mail from the camp including a photographic film. It included photographs made near one of the crematoria at Oświęcim. The film had been passed on to Kraków and a number of prints made from it.'[88] Pytlik was prepared to give the museum copies of the three photographs, but not his own original prints. Why Pytlik chose to wait for sixteen years before donating them to the museum is not known; nor is there any evidence that the copies made in Kraków in 1944 were received in the allied countries.

In 1985, following the death of Pytlik, his wife donated her late husband's set of photographs to the Auschwitz-Birkenau State Museum Archive. They revealed that the three donated by Pytlik in 1960 had been severely cropped. This was the first time the museum had seen the 'originals'. In the 'original' two images of the Sonderkommando burning bodies the window from where they were taken is visible (see Figure 38), whereas in the cropped photographs it is not. In the 'original' image of the women running to the gas-chambers (see Figure 37), the women cover only a corner of the frame, whereas in the cropped version their image has been blown up to cover the entire frame and their faces retouched (as in the 'original', their faces are not distinguishable). Those published in *1939–1945 We Have Not Forgotten* in 1959 and 1960 are noticeably retouched, as the pencil lines to accentuate the outlines of the women's figures can be clearly seen. Apparently, after the war underground worker Teresa Łasocka-Estreicher had asked Polish photographer Stanisław Mucha to make prints of these photographs.[89] It is assumed that it was he who cropped them, presumably because he considered the images of the burning bodies and running women to be more important than the surroundings.

In August 1964, the fifty-three-year-old Bernhardt Walter was called as a witness to the court in Frankfurt where, three months later, Lili Zelmanovic would give evidence with her album. During the pre-trial investigations Walter was asked if he had ever been at the ramp when the transports arrived. He answered 'No'. Neither had he seen, he said, any prisoners being killed. His job was 'merely to photograph prisoners from the identification section, to register them, and possibly to identify those who might have been shot while trying to escape or who had committed suicide'. In response to Walter's comment a former SS Blockführer Baretzky, who had been earlier identified at the ramp in the album photographs (shown to the court by Erich Kulka) jumped to his feet in the courtroom and called Walter a liar. 'I still remember the motorcycle he used to ride around on,' he shouted to the court.[90]

In May 1947 Walter had been arrested in Poland. In a statement made to a Kraków court in September of that year he claimed that he had only once visited a crematorium at Auschwitz which he said was to cremate his son who had died of typhus.[91] On 8 April 1948 he was convicted and received a three-year prison sentence. The leniency of the sentence indicates that no serious charges were proven against him; the mere fact that he was a member of the SS would have been enough to guarantee this minimum sentence.[92] In a letter to Auschwitz-Birkenau

State Museum in 1963, Myszkowski wrote that he had declined to testify against Walter in the trials in Kraków because, in his experience, Walter was lenient towards the prisoners. Myszkowski did recognize, however, that Walter 'must have earned his SS Hauptscharführer status somehow', and suggested that other prisoners be consulted. Myszkowski claimed that the Erkennungsdienst was a place where 'every "muselman" found nourishment' and described how, from time to time, Walter sent him or other prisoners to his home in the camp to help his wife work in the garden. 'This help', claimed Myszkowski, 'consisted of my lying the whole day under a redcurrant bush eating as much as I could. When I was there at lunchtime,' he wrote, 'Walter's wife set the table and gave me lunch.'[93]

Whether or not Walter took the photographs at the ramp has never been firmly established. There has been much speculation in recent years as to their origin and purpose. In 1979 Martin Gilbert, in his book *Final Journey*, wrote that the photographs were taken by both Hofmann and Walter for an official record of the 'Resettlement of Hungarian Jews' which was to be published as Nazi propaganda, although it was never released.[94] According to Serge Klarsfeld's analysis of the album, in 1959 Walter had sworn that he took the photographs with Hofmann, but he denied it at the Frankfurt trials. Klarsfeld claims the photographs were most likely to have been taken by Hofmann. He bases his theory on the fact that former prisoner Ota Kraus had met Hofmann during his time as a prisoner at Auschwitz and found him to be 'understanding'. According to Klarsfeld, Kraus believed that Hofmann was the kind of man willing to 'express the truth through these pictures'.[95] Just what truth Hofmann was supposed to be expressing was not explained.

After the war those Erkennungsdienst workers who survived returned to civil life. Bernhardt Walter, after serving his sentence, became a movie projectionist in Bavaria. Hofmann disappeared shortly after the war and was never found. According to Brasse, he never returned home to his family in Germany. Bródka moved to Sweden and Myszkowski stayed at Auschwitz and was appointed head of Auschwitz-Birkenau State Museum until, in 1950, he emigrated to Israel. Woycicki returned to work in the theatre in Kraków and Jureczek found employment in the steel works in Bytom, a few miles from Oświęcim. The former professional photographer Wilhelm Brasse returned to his home town of Żywiec, a few miles from the camp, and would never take another photograph.[96]

The Last Execution at Auschwitz

On 16 April 1947 the last execution took place at Auschwitz-Birkenau. Rudolf Höss, the former Commandant of the camp, was condemned to death in a Warsaw court, taken back to the scene of his crimes and hanged on specially erected gallows in the former camp grounds.

39 · The hanging of Rudolf Höss at Auschwitz 16 April 1947 taken from the attic of block 2 by former Auschwitz prisoner Henryk Porębski. Two men taking photographs can be seen in the bottom right-hand corner. The hooded man behind the gallows also appears to be taking photographs. (Państwowe Muzeum Auschwitz-Birkenau w Oświęcimiu)

Höss had been arrested by the British Military Police near Flensburg in March 1946. He was interrogated and handed over to the allied authorities at the International Military Tribunal at Nuremberg. In May he was handed over to the Polish War Crimes Commission and taken to Warsaw to await trial. In his prison cell, between October 1946 and April 1947, Höss wrote a statement that became known as his 'autobiography', in which he stated that over one million people had been gassed at Birkenau. It was the first official admission that Auschwitz-Birkenau had not only been a labour camp but also an extermination camp.[97]

In Poland, the period of his trial was highly charged. Höss symbolized not only the barbarous regime at Auschwitz-Birkenau but the suffering of the nation as a whole. Even so, the execution was not intended to be public and the date was changed a number of times. The day before the eventual hanging large crowds flocked to the former camp, but were turned away by the militia.[98]

One photographer who recorded the execution was Stanisław Dąbrowiecki

from the agency Film Polski. Immediately after the execution Dąbrowiecki's camera and film were seized by officials from the Ministry of Public Security who told him that the film was being requisitioned. On 21 April Film Polski made a request to the Minister of Justice, Henryk Świątkowski, that its film be returned. The agency believed that it had sensational photographs that would fetch a substantial amount of money abroad. On 6 June Film Polski was informed that Świątkowski had turned down its request and that the film was to be put 'in the Ministerial archive forever' at the Main Commission for Research into German Crimes in Poland.[99]

In the early 1980s, journalist Andrzej Gass, who was writing a drama-documentary about Höss's trial for Polish television, set about trying to find the pictures. Initially the Main Commission refused to acknowledge that it had the film. However, his determination, together with a change of staff at the commission and the political and social turmoil of the period, led to the commission conceding that it was in its archive. Inside a safe, designated for prohibited material, was an envelope containing eleven photographic prints, taken from Dąbrowiecki's film but, to the surprise of Gass and the staff, no negatives. It was concluded that they had probably been stolen and sold to the west. If so,

41 · Rudolf Höss
hanged at Auschwitz,
16 April 1947.
Photographer
Stanisław
Dąbrowiecki.
(Państwowe Muzeum
Auschwitz-Birkenau
w Oświęcimiu)

they have never surfaced. In 1995 Gass included three of the pictures in an article headlined 'Photographs which have never been published'. There was no reaction either from official quarters or the public.[100]

It transpired that these were not the only photographs taken of Höss's execution. In 1958, following a reorganization of the Auschwitz-Birkenau State Museum, seven photographs of the hanging were found on the premises. One of them (Figure 41) was taken by Dąbrowiecki. It was from his confiscated film; how it came to be at the museum no one knows. The others were probably taken by former Auschwitz prisoners living or working at the museum at the time. In 1979 a former prisoner from Bielsko-Biała sent a photograph of the hanging to the museum and in 1980 former prisoner Ludwik Lech sent four more photographs. Both stated that they did not know who the authors were. One of the pictures (Figure 40) shows a group of people gathered around the gallows. The camp can be clearly seen in the background. In 1998 seven more photographs were sent to the museum by former prisoner Wilibald Pająk. He claimed that Henryk Porębski, also a former prisoner, had taken the photographs from the attic of block number 2. In one of them (Figure 39) are two people in the right-hand side of the frame taking photographs. Behind the gallows, a second hooded executioner also seems to be holding a camera to his eye.

Until now none of the photographs of Höss's execution kept at Auschwitz-Birkenau State Museum has ever been published. They have been considered classified material, as those in the Main Commission were intended to be. Auschwitz museum was given copies of Dąbrowiecki's photographs by the Main Commission but archivists do not consider they have the authority to show them to anyone. The Auschwitz Head of Archives, Dr Piotr Setkiewicz, does not know why those kept at the museum are considered classified as no explanation has ever been recorded. There is, however, a genuine fear that Holocaust deniers would attempt to use the photographs to support their contention that Höss's prison statement had been beaten out of him. Additionally, Dr Setkiewicz believes that to use them for commercial or sensational purposes would be morally wrong. He also doubts whether the photographs have any 'historical or informative value'.[101]

Andrzej Gass suggests that the decision to classify the images of Hoss's execution in 1947 was not necessarily a political one. Following widespread revulsion at gruesome scenes filmed at the Lublin hangings in 1944 and particularly at the public hanging of Arthur Greiser, Nazi governor of Warthegau, in Poznan in 1946, it was decided that there should be no more public executions. Höss's case was an exception – but the authorities did limit the attendance and suppress publication of the pictures. In fact, according to Gass, Polish editors had already agreed, under the instruction of Świątkowski, that images of executions should no longer be published. These were the oppressive early years of communist rule, when, says Gass, many things were shrouded in secrecy. It is possible that the order to keep the Höss photographs secret, which has little if any relevance today, has remained unchallenged simply due to bureaucratic inertia in Warsaw.

The photographs of Höss's execution are unquestionably symbolic, not least for the Polish nation. They show the last death at Auschwitz and the last public execution on Polish soil. Whatever the reasons for the secrecy, there is some irony in the fact that while the Commandant of Auschwitz seems to have been granted a reprieve from the public display of the indignity of his final moments, the cruel fates of his victims are commonly displayed in museums around the world.

SIX
Liberations

The Western Camps: Seeing is Believing

During April 1945 the story of the concentration camps of Western Europe, liberated by British and American troops, began to unfold. Newspapers, magazines and cinemas were flooded with images of tangled naked skeletal bodies, corpses stacked in mass graves, starved emaciated faces, the dead and the dying in unimaginable conditions. So numerous were newsreel films shown in cinemas in Britain that at the end of April the *Daily Mirror* reported that the British Ministry of Information had granted 'an extra allowance of film stock' to newsreel companies so that they could include in their films 'full scenes of conditions in concentration camps'.[1]

British and American photographers and film-makers who had the task of photographing these scenes later described their traumatic experiences. American photojournalist Margaret Bourke-White wrote: 'Using a camera was almost a relief. It interposed a slight barrier between myself and the horror in front of me.' When people asked her how she could bear to photograph such scenes, she said: 'I have to work with a veil over my mind. In photographing the murder camps, the protective veil was so tightly drawn that I hardly knew what I had taken until I saw prints of my own photographs. It was as though I was seeing these horrors for the first time.'[2] British photojournalist George Rodgers was so appalled by the way he found himself photographing the dead that he promised never again to photograph a war. Author Jorge Lewinski wrote about Rodgers: 'He started to shoot, subconsciously arranging groups and bodies on the ground into artistic compositions in his viewfinder. He suddenly realised that he was treating this pitiful human flotsam as if it were some gigantic still-life.'[3]

Bert Hardy, a British Army Film and Photographic Unit (AFPU) photographer who took photographs at Belsen, said that, although he did not like taking photographs of corpses, 'I controlled my feelings of rage for long enough to take some'. He later made a point of carrying around a contact print of what he said was 'one of the most horrifying of my photographs' to show Germans who didn't believe that 'such things had really happened'.[4]

The Jackboot Code: Thousands see Horror Camp crimes—in pictures

On 18 April another AFPU photographer, Sergeant A. N. Midgley, described Belsen in a letter: 'Today I visited a German concentration camp at BELSEN near Celle. I saw some of the most horrible sights imaginable. No words can describe the havoc of this place ... I am now convinced that the Nazis are not human beings, but vermin that must be exterminated.' He described the 'hundreds of bodies lying about' which, he said, 'were piled in many cases 5 and 6 high. Amongst them sat women peeling potatoes and cooking scraps of food. They were quite unconcerned and when I lifted my camera to photograph them, even smiled.' Midgley finished his letter: 'I have read about such camps as this, but never realised what it was really like. It must be seen to be believed.'[5]

On 1 May 1945, 'Seeing is Believing', an exhibition of atrocity photographs organized by the *Daily Express*, opened at the newspaper's reading rooms in Regent Street, London (see Figure 42). The *Daily Express* reported that on the first day visitors had filed through the exhibition in 'shocked silence'.[6] A Mass-Observation survey carried out at the exhibition to gauge public reaction reported that although some of those interviewed said they had known about the camps, either they had not visualized anything so bad or had considered previous reports and pictures exaggerated. The report concluded that everyone who was interviewed felt 'the deepest horror and revulsion at the pictures'. Several people had found it difficult to look at them. 'I couldn't bear to look at them all,' said one person. 'It made me feel sick.' Some interviewed were certain the pictures couldn't lie. 'I believe it's true. I can see with my own eyes. Pictures don't lie.'[7]

Others had their doubts and even now referred to the atrocity campaign of the First World War and the government White Paper on German Atrocities published in 1939. A welfare worker commented: 'After the atrocity stories we invented in the last war, people could always defend themselves against such horrors by saying, "I expect it's much exaggerated" or, "Of course it's only propaganda".'[8] C. J. Charters, a British army film projectionist who witnessed the horror of Belsen, sympathized with the British public's cautious attitude. In a letter to his wife in May, he wrote that had he not seen the camp for himself

42 · The *Daily Express* exhibition 'Seeing is Believing' at Regent Street, London, May 1945. (Copyright Express Syndication)

he too might have thought the photographs propaganda. He wrote: 'I realise that I should possibly have been the first to cry out "Propaganda! – selected pictures", if I had seen the pictures in England but, like St Thomas, the proof has been put before my eyes.'[9] An article in *The Times* stated it was the public's duty to see the pictures and was critical of those who felt the images were faked. 'The camera, it is true, can, on occasions, lie and photographs can be "faked" but the very size and scale of these German enormities carry their own guarantee of authenticity.'[10]

The shocking discoveries at the camps surpassed even what the British government had in mind for a series of anti-German propaganda exhibitions and films which were being considered as early as 1943. In April of that year, a confidential report written by the British Film Producers' Association stated that 'upon cessation of hostilities' there would be a 'vast demand' for 'films of all kinds'.[11] By February 1944 the Ministry of Information and the American Office of War Information (OWI) had been approached by the pictorial division of the Psychological Warfare Branch (PWB) of the Supreme Headquarters Allied Expeditionary Force (SHAEF) to make a series of photographic exhibitions for information centres in liberated countries which would serve British and American interests and 'tell Europe the *true history of the last five years*' (their italics).[12] In December the Ministry of Information were considering the production of a series of films called 'Evidence' which would pin the blame for atrocities on Germany as a whole rather than on the Nazi Party. According to a memorandum, it proposed to use material captured from the Germans juxtaposed with 'a few beatings, tortures and rapes which have taken place in Germany, Czechoslovakia and Poland'.[13] By February 1945, these films were being prepared by Sidney Bernstein, head of the film division at the British Ministry of Information.[14] In a ministry memorandum an official, who did not mention Bernstein (who was Jewish) by name, expressed concern about the large number of Jews in the film business. In his opinion this could be used as proof, by 'reactionary forces', of the 'nazi proposition' and might, he said, 'reflect dangerously on our position'. Bernstein rebuffed him and the matter was apparently dropped.[15]

On 22 April Bernstein visited Belsen. From then on the ministry's previous film projects were put to one side. No one had foreseen the horrific scenes in the concentration camps. The following day he began making plans for an Anglo-American production for SHAEF about Nazi concentration camps, intended for showing 'around the world' – including in Germany. Bernstein said the film should 'take the form of a prosecuting counsel stating his case', and ordered photographers and film-makers to capture as much detail as possible in the camps. He wanted photographs of those responsible and pictures of anything which identified German industry's involvement in the construction of crematoria and gas-chambers.[16] But the production of the film was fraught with problems. The London film laboratories were unable to cope with the amount of film to be processed and there was even a search for an editing machine. By June no director, producer or writer had been appointed. The Americans suggested that Billy Wilder complete the film in Munich, but in late June film director Alfred Hitchcock arrived in London as a 'treatment adviser'.[17] However, by September the film was still not complete. Meanwhile, footage taken in the camps was released to newsreel companies in Britain and the USA. Their content was so shocking that one distributor, Movietone, took the view that the public might not believe they were true and proposed not to use them. However, the Ministry of Information decided that 'the horror impact of the pictures' would kill any question in the minds of the public as to their authenticity.[18] On 26 April the first one-reel film, *Nazi Atrocities*, was shown at the Embassy Theater in New York. A few days later the *New York Times* reported that the 'notorious Nazi "death" camps' newsreels … were generally received by audiences in silence or with muttered expressions of outrage'. The report said that the films made at Nordhausen, Buchenwald, Ohrdruf and Hadamar, are 'probably the most frightful pictures of death and woe ever exhibited in American newsreels'. The Radio City Music Hall in New York was the only 'first-run' theatre that did not show them. Managing director Guy S. Eyssell was reported as saying that he did not want to take a chance on 'shocking and sickening any squeamish persons in the audience'.[19]

In Britain, film censor C. Matthews also questioned whether public cinemas were a proper place to show them. 'Much of the material', he said, 'is too dreadful for exhibition in a place of entertainment.'[20] The newsreels were shown in cinemas with films which some considered to be inappropriate. A Mass-Observation survey of the public's reaction to the newsreels noted that 'many found it distasteful to see a Donald Duck film immediately after the horror film'.[21] One person interviewed at a newsreel cinema in London felt 'thoroughly ashamed' of the way in which the film was shown. The interviewee said: 'though the film is terrible, it's very short – too short to be properly convincing and of course you know quite well that the worst shots have been cut out. And then it's followed up by a Walt Disney, and that sort of removes any impression it made, people are laughing again within a minute. And it's all mixed up with a propaganda film about Noble London and how wonderful Londoners were in the Blitz, and that makes you feel the whole show really only is propaganda.'[22]

The Media Circus

As more camps were liberated, more and more horrific photographs and films were produced. American and British freelance photographers were commissioned by Western European and American magazines, and newspapers and news agencies sent their own photographers. Although AFPU photographers had recorded scenes at Bergen-Belsen, it was the American Army Signal Corps photographers who made the majority of photographs at Buchenwald, Nordhausen, Wobbelin, Dachau and Mauthausen. In the USA in 1945 the Signal Corps photographic laboratory made over one million prints.[23]

From the time they joined the war in 1941, the Americans had become known for their skill and efficiency at producing high-quality pictures. The influence of the Hollywood film industry was paramount, and film directors and 'motion picture actors' became involved, including the film actor Louis Hayward and film directors John Ford, Frank Capra and John Huston.[24]

Signal Corps photographers attended specialist training courses set up by leading players in the media industries. By late December 1941 the Signal Corps Photographic Center (SCPC) had purchased the old Paramount studio on Long Island and by January 1943 employed 1,258 staff and had branches in Detroit and Hollywood.[25] Help in training photographers was offered by leading newspapers, magazines, education establishments, Hollywood film companies, picture and news agencies. In Paris the American army opened a school where cameramen, returning from the front, went to have 'experts' critique their work.[26]

The American 'liberal humanist' documentary tradition influenced the way the Americans photographed not only the war but also the camps. This documentary tradition had developed from 1935 when the historical division of the Resettlement Administration, later to become the Farm Security Administration (FSA), had employed photographers to document the story of the Depression in the USA and the plight of the rural poor. During the seven years of its existence, FSA photographs had appeared in all major magazines, exhibitions and museums and had had a major influence on documentary style, not only in the USA but also in Europe.[27] In 1939 the popularity of the FSA was reflected in the publication of *Let Us Now Praise Famous Men* by journalist James Agee and FSA photographer Walker Evans, which documented the plight of the rural poor in the southern states.[28] When the FSA project folded in 1942, the historical division became the photographic section of the Office of War Information (OWI) and some of the photographers transferred their skills to the armed forces. Photographer Russell Lee headed the photography division of the air force and a colleague, Arthur Rothstein, was in a group of elite photographers in the army.[29] In the opinion of one commentator, the professional documentarists' influence gave war photographs an 'artistic integrity'.[30] But this integrity also produced disconcerting results. Margaret Bourke-White and US army accredited photographer Lee Miller, who had previously worked on *Vogue* magazine, took photographs of piles of skeletal corpses and emaciated survivors at Buchenwald and Dachau with a technical merit and an aesthetic quality which appear incongruous. The large-format quality with flashlight added a drama that seems superfluous and not only filmic but painterly. Bourke-White's renowned photograph taken in April 1945 of a group of male prisoners standing at the barbed-wire fence at Buchenwald has the *chiaroscuro* and expressiveness of a Dutch old master.

British AFPU photographers had neither the equivalent documentary tradition to influence their work, nor the technical support. When AFPU photographer Sergeant William Lawrie arrived in Bergen-Belsen he said that they were given no instructions on what to photograph; they just 'did what they saw at the time'. There was an apparent difficulty in finding people with 'the requisite combination of skills', and those chosen to join the ranks of army photographers were 'rapidly' trained at the AFPU's school at Pinewood film studios. In the opinion of cameraman Captain E. H. Walker, the problem was that 'they wanted soldiers to be trained as cameramen rather than cameramen to be in combat'.[31] The Ministry of Information photographic division issued a set of guidelines to all new photographer recruits called 'Sergeant Photographer: This is Your New Job'. The five-page guide was as bland as its title. It advised soldier-photographers to take note of *Life*, *Illustrated* and *Picture Post*, but cautioned that 'some feature stories may take weeks or even months to work out'. The technical advice amounted to little more than simple photographic effects, which could add, for example, 'the extra touch of drama' when 'shooting against the sun'. It concluded: 'When you go to work in the battle areas there is little that can be said now to help you'.[32]

The efficiency of the American media machine far outshone that of the British. Although in 1942 an article in *Illustrated* attempted to reassure the public that the AFPU distribution system was a 'model of efficiency', pictures published in the British press after 1941 were frequently taken by American cameramen.[33] This was not entirely surprising as each US Signal Corps company included twenty stills photographers, thirty film cameramen, twenty darkroom technicians, two film recorders and three maintenance men.[34] The American system for distributing photographs was sophisticated and fast. By 1944 the Army Pictorial Service (APS) had its own laboratories in Paris and London and eighteen smaller labs around Britain employing hundreds of staff. In 1945, as the 163rd Signal Corps approached Germany, a 'jeep–airplane courier system' was in place, which meant that films could be taken by plane to the nearest lab and processing could be done within minutes. From there the film could be radioed or flown direct to Paris or London or the USA on APS's regular air courier service. Either way photographs could be in American or British newspapers within twenty-four hours.[35] In a scathing attack on the lack of British front-line pictures, a *Picture Post* editorial in 1944 thanked the Americans for their help and praised their 'brilliant cameramen'.[36]

The Americans also had the upper hand in publicity. In the camps liberated by the Americans, photo opportunities and camp tours were of paramount importance. Tours were organized for dignitaries, officials, Congressmen, Members of Parliament, British and American officers and soldiers, editors, journalists and photographers to see for themselves. As author Robert H. Abzug points out, surviving prisoners were more than willing to show the visitors around the camps. He writes: 'Prisoner guides eagerly showed the highlights to arriving troops, dignitaries, and press persons: crematoria, mass graves, instruments of torture, gas chambers, and the endless personal stories of sacrifice and heroism that had given some meaning to existence for the prisoners themselves.' Buchenwald and Dachau became the focal points for official tours. At Buchenwald visitors filed past 'neatly stacked piles of bodies' and a table was set up to exhibit 'pickled' human remains used in medical experiments, shrunken human heads and tattooed human skin. At Dachau a train full of bodies apparently 'remained untouched for days while visitors inspected it'.[37] Photographs of the camp tours featured in major press reports, showing delegates peering at human remains in the crematoria, staring at piles of emaciated dead bodies, pointing at 'autopsy tables', 'inspecting' the bunk beds on which the inmates slept, or filing past truckloads of tangled emaciated bodies. These macabre excursions around the camps call to mind the visits made by German soldiers to the cemetery in the Warsaw ghetto, where they took photographs of piles of skeletal corpses. In 1945,

44 · 'Solemn-faced Washingtonians view the evidence of German brutality portrayed in the large photomural exhibit at the Library of Congress.' (Martin Luther King Memorial Library, courtesy USHMM photo archives)

American soldiers in the camps who owned 35mm cameras were encouraged to make their own photographs of piles of bodies, as evidence for those back home who may have been sceptical of official reports. In Figure 43 American soldiers can be seen with cameras making pictures of a row of dead inmates at Lager Nordhausen concentration camp. At Dachau, Lee Miller wrote that 'soldiers were encouraged to "sightsee" around the place, they were abetted to photograph it and tell the folks back home'.[38] But it proved difficult for some soldiers to show them at home. Many found that they were either dismissed as fabrications or seemed too shocking to show. As a result many remained silent about their experiences in the camps and kept their photographs hidden.[39]

At the end of April 1945 an American congressional delegation visited Buchenwald and Dachau. It included eighteen newspaper editors and publishers, among them Joseph Pulitzer, editor of the *St Louis Post-Dispatch*. Pulitzer had initially been sceptical about reports of the camps but on his return he said: 'Since my return to the United States, I have been asked by many people if the concentration camps were as bad as the newspapers have been saying. I can answer in one word: Worse.'[40]

On 30 June, 'Lest We Forget', an exhibition of camp photographs cosponsored by the *St Louis Post-Dispatch* and the *Washington Evening Star* was formally opened at the Library of Congress in Washington, DC. The exhibition was followed by a film show of 'war and indoctrination films' which were first shown at the Kiel Auditorium in St Louis. On the opening day of the exhibition, the *St Louis Post-Dispatch* reported that, despite it being Washington's hottest day of the year, the attendance had reached 5,229. Three weeks later the *Washington Evening Star* reported that the exhibition had 'broken all records' – 88,891 people had seen it – and that 'thousands of persons have been flocking to the motion pictures at various public schools throughout the city and in some instances the crowds have been so great an extra showing has been necessary'.[41]

The exhibition went to great lengths to dramatize the horrors of the camps. A photograph of an emaciated man, naked except for a garment he is holding over his genitals, was enlarged to more than double life-size. A line of smartly dressed visitors was photographed staring up at the picture, making an incongruous juxtaposition. Behind them the text on a large wall mural of prisoners reads: 'The living dead' (see Figure 44).

The reactions of people in the USA and Britain towards this glut of atrocity images varied. There were indications that some had grown weary of them and felt saturation point was being reached. Others seemed perplexed, and could not grasp the enormity of what they were seeing. In July 1945, Susan Sontag, as a young girl, saw photographs of Bergen-Belsen and Dachau in a bookstore in Santa Monica, and found it hard to make sense of them. She later wrote: 'Nothing I have seen – in photographs or in real life – ever cut me as sharply, deeply, instantaneously. Indeed, it seems plausible to me to divide my life into two parts, before I saw those photographs (I was twelve) and after, though it was several years before I understood fully what they were about.'[42]

Sontag later questioned if any good had been served by seeing photographs of suffering that she found hard to imagine.[43] One eyewitness to the camps, British MP Mavis Tate, also wondered what could be achieved by looking at atrocity photographs. 'They are infinitely less terrible than the reality we saw,' she said, 'because you can photograph results of suffering, but never suffering itself.'[44] Sontag has written that photographs of horror do not necessarily 'strengthen conscience and the ability to be compassionate. It can also corrupt them. Once one has seen such images, one has started down the road of seeing more – and more. Images transfix. Images anesthetize.' Sontag felt that after seeing these images, 'some limit had been reached'. Not only did she feel 'grieved' and 'wounded' but, she said, 'something went dead'.[45]

Sontag's observations are echoed in comments made by members of the public in Britain. In a Mass-Observation report, made to assess the response to atrocity films, one person who did not intend to see them said: 'I'm beginning to get fed up with all these pictures in the papers. I know it's very terrible and I was as horrified as anyone at the beginning … I do think they've overdone it … I mean you keep on looking at dead bodies heaped on top of each other – well, you just get used to it. Just as we've had to get used to the idea of death all through the War.' Another interviewee admitted to feeling disgusted at the photographs, 'not even with the Germans, but with the people themselves. They look so horrible and disgusting – their cracked faces, and their skinniness and sloppiness and horribleness.' The interviewee confessed at having the same kind of feelings when confronted with 'any kind of serious illness or deformity'.[46] Such views may have been encouraged by the dehumanizing way in which those liberated in the camps were often described in the press: 'pitiful specimens', 'the living dead', 'ape-like living skeletons', 'skeletons held together with rags', 'wrecks of humanity'.[47] Photographer David E. Scherman described how he and Lee Miller 'held flashbulbs for each other while photographing stripe-clad skeletons who had just been freed'. He added: 'A few of them simply died of exhaustion, or perhaps excitement, before we could get their pictures.'[48]

There was also confusion and misunderstanding over the nationality of the prisoners and the purpose of the camps. Seldom did anyone ask the prisoners for their own stories. They were sometimes generalized as 'European nationalities', as Italians, Poles or Russians and sometimes as Jews. In the USA the leaflet for the exhibition Lest We Forget claimed that as a result of Nazism, more than 7.5 million people had lost their lives 'in some 100 concentration camps for political prisoners set up in all parts of Germany and in invaded countries'. In an attempt to explain why these people had been sent to the camps in the first place, it suggested two main reasons '(1) to reduce and weaken populations of other European states, thereby giving the German people a future advantage in numbers and physical sturdiness; (2) to ruthlessly exterminate or intimidate anti-Fascist opposition in over-run and satellite countries'.[49]

In Britain, a book compiled by the Daily Mail, Lest We Forget, mentioned the death of 5 million Jews but went on to define the prisoners as political internees and Jews from Germany, Austria, Czechoslovakia and Poland. Common to all camps, it reported, were the 'butcher's hooks, the gas ovens, the gas-chambers, the torture cells, the whipping posts'.[50] Although it mentioned Auschwitz as being 'the worst camp of all', where it said 'at least' 4 million people 'were done to death in circumstances of peculiar horror', it did not explain what the 'peculiar horror' was, and kept its report firmly centred on western concentration camps.[51] The American leaflet Lest We Forget did not mention Auschwitz at all.

This confusing representation of the slaughter, its purposes and who exactly had suffered and died at the hands of the Nazis, was a consequence of how little was known at the time about the genocidal Nazi policies which had led to the Final Solution and the extermination of the Jews, and about the terror unleashed on the Slavic peoples of Eastern Europe. It was as if the sensationalism of the images was a barrier to understanding; for without this knowledge, the numbers of the dead simply didn't make sense. Nobody asked why these millions of people had been killed. This lack of understanding was to have far-reaching effects on how the public understood Nazism and the Holocaust for a long time to come. The fact that the majority of those liberated at Belsen were Jewish went unreported in Britain and the USA. And Margaret Bourke-White, according to her biographer, 'maintained her own secret' and did not mention Jews when she wrote about Buchenwald.[52] The secret referred to was, presumably, that Bourke-White's father Joseph White was of Polish-Jewish origin.

While the British and American public were looking at atrocity images in cinemas and exhibitions at home, in Germany Western allied forces made it their duty to confront the German population with the consequences of Nazism. German civilians were either forced to look at displays of photographs and films taken in the camps, or were taken to the camps themselves. By the end of April a report in the *Daily Mirror*, headlined 'Holding the Mirror up to the Huns', said that British forces were fly-posting copies of the newspaper in order that Germans see 'The Pit of Belsen'.[53] A Ministry of Information memorandum stated that 'all German civilians will be required to view the atrocity film' and that ration cards should be stamped 'with an indication that this film will be viewed'. Whether or not this policy was carried out is unclear.[54] Entire German communities were forced to watch newsreel films of *Belsen – The Atrocities*, and before and after the screenings British army cameramen took photographs of the audiences in an attempt to 'gauge the intensity of their remorse'. The German population of Burgsteinfurt, referred to by the British military as the 'Village of Hate', were forced to watch footage of atrocities at Belsen and Buchenwald. Apparently, 'those who laughed at the exit were subjected to a second showing'.[55]

The *Daily Mirror* further proposed that German POWs in Britain should also be made to see atrocity films and photographs. An article headlined 'Show Horror Films to Huns Here' said that 'public demand is growing hourly' for the five-minute Movietone film *Horror in Our Time* to be shown to the 196,000 'double ration' German POWs in Britain.[56] The Ministry of Information had its doubts, not only about showing atrocity films to German POWs, but about how they were being received in Germany. In a memorandum, Davidson Taylor from the Psychological Warfare Division in SHAEF wrote to Sidney Bernstein:

We discovered that both Nazis and anti-Nazi prisoners of war disassociate themselves almost unanimously from any responsibility for the atrocities depicted. Furthermore, they say that many of the pictures remind them of photographs of the German victims of allied air raids, which they have seen constantly in the German press ... They say yes it is true that many innocent people must have suffered in the concentration camps. But ... many Germans have also suffered at

the hands of the Nazis. It seems that the great danger in making any atrocity document for German consumption is not that the Germans will believe the atrocities
were faked, but that they will steadfastly refuse to recognise that they have any
responsibility for them. This is the thing I most fear in the atrocity film.[57]

Throughout April and May 1945 there was a growing sense that some kind
of revenge against the Germans was being sought by the public. In mid-April a
Mass-Observation survey conducted on the response to atrocity films and photographs concluded that 'the majority of people are definitely strongly antagonistic
towards the German nation as a whole'. One male interviewee thought that the
German race were 'not fit to live', and a female commented that 'we ought to
turn their gas-bombs on them and exterminate them'.[58]

A large number of newspaper reports in Britain and the USA included photographs of German civilians either being made to look at scenes in the camps,
digging graves or burying the victims. In the *Illustrated London News*, some of
the photographs in a five-page picture-led report showed the citizens of Weimar
looking at 'a truckload of tortured and murdered prisoners'.[59] On 19 April the
Daily Express published a front-page photograph of Germans who were 'Forced
to Bury Their Murdered Victims' at Nordhausen. *PM* also carried a photograph
of Germans burying the dead at the same camp. At the end of May a Reuters
report said: 'Horror photographs of the Dachau and other concentration camps
have been posted up all over Germany. Underneath the photographs is the
question "Who is Guilty?"'[60]

Whether or not the German population as a whole was responsible for the
atrocities was the subject of heated debate in Britain and the USA. Writer and
journalist James Agee, who chose not to see the atrocity films in the USA, wrote
in the *Nation*: 'I have not felt it necessary to see the films themselves ... I cannot
get my thoughts in order, yet, to write what I think needs writing, about such
propaganda and the general reaction to it. But I want to go on record against
it.' In his view, 'the passion for vengeance is a terrifyingly strong one', which,
Agee thought, was being confused with a passion for justice.[61] The Western world
wasn't ready to deal with arguments about the consequences of revenge. An
article by the philosopher Bertrand Russell in *Picture Post*, headlined 'WHOSE
GUILT' underneath a half-page photograph of German civilians being made
to dig graves, gave what the introduction to the article said was 'an unusual
answer' (see Figure 45). Like Agee, Russell questioned the validity of blaming the
entire German race for the atrocities. He argued that 'undoubtedly' the British
government had known about the atrocities perpetrated by the Nazis 'from the
very beginning' but continued with its policy of appeasement. If, he argued, the
nation is content in the collective blame of the German people then, he wrote,

German Civilians are Compelled to Dig Graves in their Own Town Square for the Victims of Their Concentration Camps
They disclaim all knowledge. They say it was "nothing to do with them" what happened at Wobbelin, the S.S. concentration camp a few miles from their
town. But now the British and Americans have come, and they are forced to realise what has been going on. They must dig graves for the victims.

WHOSE GUILT? The Problem of Cruelty

One of the worst Nazi concentration camps is uncovered by British and American troops at Wobbelin, north-west of Berlin. Allied soldiers feed the starving, treat the sick, then compel citizens of the nearby town to exhume the dead and give them honoured burial in the town square. These pictures raise again the questions "Who was responsible for such organised horror! How can it be prevented in the future?" In this article Bertrand Russell gives an unusual answer.

Atrocity Victims are Exhumed for an Honoured Re-burial
Huge pits had been dug as the Allies approached. The victims were crammed in. Now
the Germans must exhume the bodies, and give them decent burial.

A German Keeps the Tally
When they were alive he preferred to know nothing
Now they are dead he must know all about them.

10

45 · 'A page from a *Picture Post* article by Bertrand Russell, published 16 June 1945, showing German civilians digging graves for victims of the concentration camp at Wobbelin.' (Getty Images/Hulton Archive) 'we are not understanding what has happened'.[62] Russell had a point. Press reports tended to concentrate on the discovery of the western camps, rather than on reporting the reasons why the British and American governments had been reluctant to publish information about them throughout the war. Apart from a generalized idea of Germany as an 'evil' nation, the reasons that lay behind the images of atrocities were unclear.

This general lack of understanding of what Nazism had meant in occupied Eastern Europe was partially the result of the vague, conflicting information disseminated throughout the war, particularly concerning the Jews. On 19 April 1945, the second anniversary of the Warsaw Ghetto Uprising, an exhibition called 'Heroes and Martyrs of the Ghetto' opened at the Vanderbilt Museum, New York, under the auspices of the Jewish Labor Committee. It was organized by A. R. Lerner, who had edited bulletins about the plight of the Jews under Nazi occupation for the Polish News Agency in New York during the war.[63] Although this exhibition opened before 'Lest We Forget', it did not capture the public's imagination, nor receive the kind of publicity that the exhibitions of atrocity photographs did. To understand this exhibition required more knowledge about what had happened in occupied Europe than the general public at this point possessed. The stories of the ghettos and camps of Eastern Europe was, as yet, largely untold.

This point had been highlighted in August 1944 by a three-page article about the liberation of Warsaw in *Picture Post*. The report focused on the suffering of the Poles and congratulated the people of the city for their 'astonishing vitality' during the war: 'Even the inmates of the ghetto – half a million Jews were now huddled together behind its walls – seemed to settle down to some sort of "normal" life.' Although the article mentioned what it called the 'Battle of the Ghetto', the heroic fight of the Jews and the massacres, nowhere did it mention the deportation of the defeated inhabitants to the extermination camps, nor even the camps themselves. The article gives the impression that after the war the Poles and Jews simply returned to a 'normal' life. This impression was not helped by the two main photographs of Warsaw, one showing a picturesque skyline of church spires and the other of children playing in an old cobbled street. In truth, Warsaw was by then almost entirely flattened.[64]

The most consistent message in all the shock-horror reporting was the allied victory and the superiority of Western democracy. Photographs that could convey that story were keenly sought-after. A Ministry of Information memorandum stated: 'The war office material contains some very good shots of children in the Belsen camp and our soldiers looking after them and entertaining them. The children are very attractive and I thought that an inclusion of these items into some newsreels would help the propaganda angle.'[65] The *Illustrated London News* reported the British heroism angle in a story on the liberation of

Belsen. The report said: 'And, over all, flies the Union Jack, "the symbol of the completion of the great task of liberation". That is Belsen to-day; what it was yesterday is being shown to the German people by means of films.' The article went on to report 'the dawn of a new era' in Prague and the first Czechoslovak government's cabinet meeting in the 'liberated city'. It somehow failed to mention that Prague had been liberated by the Red Army.[66]

In fact, as the Western democracies were absorbed in publicizing the horrors unearthed by their own liberations, discoveries made by the Russians were ignored. By the time the Western allied forces had begun to liberate the camps in Germany, the Soviet army had already liberated Majdanek and Auschwitz-Birkenau in Poland, and three Nazi war crimes trials had been concluded in the Soviet Union and Poland. To the majority of the British and American public, these events were unknown. Although a large amount of information had reached the West about the extermination camps during the war, their liberation was hardly reported in the Western press. With the end of the Second World War in sight as the Russian front moved west, and with the Cold War about to begin, the attitude of the Western powers towards the Russians was beginning to shift from regarding them as heroic allies to a communist threat.[67] The Soviets were the wrong kind of heroes and their liberations were largely seen as the making of their own propaganda. As a result, the British and American public were left with the impression that the western concentration camps represented the entirety of Nazi atrocities.

The Camps in Eastern Europe: Ignorance and Disbelief

On 14–17 July 1943, in the Soviet city of Krasnodar, north-east of the Black Sea, a military tribunal gathered to hear the case of war crimes and atrocities committed on Krasnodar territory by Nazis and their collaborators.[68] In August *Soviet War News Weekly* ran a report on the trial, including four photographs of corpses under the headline 'THIS IS WHAT THE NAZIS DID IN KRASNODAR'. It reported that 'eight traitors' had been hanged and three imprisoned for their crimes.[69] Later the same year, from 15 to 18 December 1943, a military tribunal took place in Kharkov. Those accused were publicly hanged in Kharkov City Square on 19 December 1943.[70]

It was seven months later, in July 1944, that the Kharkov trials were reported in *Life* magazine. *Life*'s two-page picture-led report announced that a Russian military tribunal had tried, convicted and condemned to death three Germans and 'a Russian traitor'. All the published photographs, including four of the public hanging, had been reportedly taken from a 'full-length movie' made of the trial by Soviet cameramen.[71]

In May 1945 the film of the Kharkov trials, called *Atrocities* (and also *We*

Accuse), was screened at the Little Carnegie Hall in New York but was then withheld from general release. Although at the time the cinemas were full of images from camps liberated by the Western allies, the Production Code Administration, known as the Hays Office, 'a voluntary system of self-regulation administered by the Motion Picture Producers and Distributors of America', decided that the film be rejected on the basis that it used the word 'damn' and included images of atrocities and 'the prolonged hanging of war criminals'.[72] Although the film was shown at the Tatler Theatre in London in July 1944, the British Foreign Office regarded the Kharkov trials and the Soviet judicial system generally with scepticism.[73] It felt that it was no coincidence that the trials – well publicized in the Soviet Union – had followed closely on preliminary meetings in London of representatives of United Nations governments to discuss the punishment of war criminals.[74] The decisive action taken against the accused in the Soviet Union drew a resigned response from Foreign Office official Roger Allen, who saw no possibility of an international tribunal for war criminals. He wrote: 'The gulf which separates our ideas of justice from the Russians' is too wide to be bridged – and perhaps, if the truth be known, some of our other allies would be found on the Russian side of it.' He did admit, however, that if there were to be trials of war criminals, the Russian way 'may well be the best way of doing it but it is not the British way'.[75]

On 23 July 1944, after capturing the Polish city of Lublin, the Red Army, accompanied by Soviet and Polish photographers and film-makers, entered Majdanek camp, 3 kilometres outside the city. Adolf Forbert was among them. In 1943, Forbert, then in Tashkent, had joined the photography and film section of the newly formed First Division of the Tadeusz Kościuszko regiment of the Polish army, called Czołówka Filmowa Wojska Polskiego. It was with this group that he and his brother Władysław returned to Poland.[76]

These army film-makers and photographers were ill equipped. In contrast to the media circus that flocked to the concentration camps liberated by the Western allies, at Majdanek there were no journalists or photographers from Western press agencies or illustrated magazines. There were no crowds of soldiers with their own 35mm cameras, none of the slick and efficient production facilities available to the American forces. The war in the east had taken its toll on all forms of production, and film and photographic materials were in short supply, as were the means to publish them. The photographers and film-makers assigned the task of recording the liberation of the camps in Eastern Europe had to make do with the meagre means at their disposal. Adolf Forbert later wrote about his frustration at not having any film stock to record what he called the 'wonderful and unforgettable sight' of the colourful spectacle of columns of Polish, Russian and partisan soldiers and horsemen as they approached Majdanek.[77]

Aleksander Ford, a well-known Polish-Jewish film-maker born in Łódź and head of Czołówka Filmowa Wojska Polskiego, had the task of directing film and photographic operations at Majdanek. After joining the Communist Party in 1939, Ford had left Poland for the Soviet Union to make instructional and documentary films for the Red Army. With no film production facilities in Lublin, the first job of the film crew was to find a suitable base from which to work. They took over the most notorious residence in the city, the already abandoned former villa of SS Gruppenführer (Lieutenant-General) Odilo Globocnik, who had been responsible for Operation Reinhard, the code-name for the administration of the extermination camps. Within a few weeks, with the help of local people, he and his team – which, as well as Forbert, included well-known Soviet film-maker Roman Karmen and Czołówka Filmowa Wojska Polskiego members Jerzy Bossak, Stanisław Wohl and technicians Stanisław Jakubowski and Bogdan Siwek – transformed the villa into what Forbert called a 'film factory'. Some equipment was made available by the Soviet Union, but everything else had to be made or found. Siwek travelled 150 kilometres in search of suitable wood to make developing tanks with army food rations as his only currency. When the wood was brought to Lublin, two local carpenters were employed making the tanks with a lathe that had been found in a warehouse left by the Germans. The cellar of the villa was converted into a room for developing film and the bathroom into a sound studio. An American Akeley sound camera was used for recording the testimonies of former prisoners and 'hangmen'. As a part of the operation to lay cables through the villa, a section of the yard had to be dug up, which revealed 'beautiful sandstone slabs'; they turned out to be gravestones from a nearby Jewish cemetery.[78] Despite the conditions, the film, *Majdanek, Cemetery of Europe*, was completed in 1944 – the first film to be made about a concentration camp. By November a museum had been established at Majdanek – the first on the site of a former concentration camp.[79]

By December 1944, commanders of the Majdanek camp had been tried in Lublin and hanged.[80] For the Soviet people, wrote Russian-born British journalist Alexander Werth, the discovery of Majdanek 'was devastating ... Everybody had heard of Babyi Yar [sic] and thousands of other German atrocities; but this was something even more staggering. It brought into sharper focus than anything else had done the real nature, scope and consequences of the Nazi regime in action.'[81] Unlike the British and American public, the Soviets had little need of large displays of atrocity photographs and sensationalist headlines to convince them of the authenticity of Majdanek. They had endured a three-year war with Germany and atrocities committed by the Nazis were widely known about. But according to Werth, the effect of Majdanek on the Soviet Union was enormous and thousands of Russian soldiers were made to visit the camp.[82] Meanwhile, in Britain, reports about Majdanek were received with caution. In August 1944 the eminent Russian journalist Konstantin Simonov wrote in the *Polish Jewish Observer* that for three years the newspaper had published many terrible accounts from 'underground sources' of German atrocities in the Majdanek camp but 'so incredible' were they 'that few people were able to believe them'.[83]

Throughout August and September, Konstantin Simonov's lengthy, factual reports about Majdanek were published in the Russian English-language press but were ignored in the West.[84] In contrast to the emotive style of Western journalism, his reports were dry and detailed, but they did show that the Soviets had understood Nazi policies far more clearly than the press in the USA or Britain. Simonov made extensive reference to 'the wholesale extermination of the Jewish population', including specific reports on the deportation of many thousands of Jews from the Warsaw and Lublin ghettos.[85]

On 16 September 1944, a report on Majdanek was transmitted to the British Foreign Office by the Soviet news agency Tass.[86] A Foreign Office memorandum noted that, on 27 September, Mr E. P. Smith asked in a question in Parliament whether 'His Majesty's Government have received official information concerning the massacre by the Germans, by means of poison gas, of thousands of Jewish men, women, and children at Lublin; whether the names are known of any of the persons guilty of this atrocity; and whether he can make a statement'. Foreign Secretary Anthony Eden replied, 'a full report prepared by a Polish–Soviet Extraordinary Commission had been recently published and that those chiefly responsible were named and would be answerable to UN for their crimes'. However, a note attached to this memorandum stated that it would be 'unlikely' that this commission's finding would be submitted to the UN War Crimes Committees as 'neither the Polish National Committee nor the Soviet government are represented'.[87]

In the West the liberation of Majdanek went almost unreported, as did the deaths of hundreds of thousands of people there. A set of photographs of the camp, the majority taken by Red Army photographers V. Temin and M. Mikhailov, were released in Britain and the USA by the New York-based Soviet agency Sovfoto. *Life* and the *Illustrated London News* published some of them. In the same week as the *Life* article was published, a group of Western foreign correspondents made an official visit to Majdanek, including Alexander Werth. As a BBC commentator in the Soviet Union since 1941, he filed a 'detailed report' but the BBC refused to broadcast it on the basis that 'they thought it was a Russian propaganda stunt'.[88] The tone of the full-page article in *Life* was equally cautious, even though it published images which showed ashes in the crematoria, a mass grave and piles of shoes. Under the headline 'LUBLIN FUNERAL', all the key words were in inverted commas: 'murder vans', 'ovens', 'Cyclone' gas and 'extermination camps'; the death in Majdanek of Leon Blum, the pre-war Prime Minister of France, was reported as 'a circumstantial Russian story'.[89]

The *Illustrated London News* did not share *Life*'s scepticism. A picture-led double-page story headlined 'CAMP OF ANNIHILATION' reported: 'It is not the custom of "The Illustrated London News" to publish photographs of atrocities, but in view of the fact that the enormity of the crimes perpetrated by the Germans is so wicked that our readers, to whom such behaviour is unbelievable, may think the reports of such crimes exaggerated or due to propaganda, we consider it necessary to present them, by means of the accompanying photographs, with an irrefutable proof of the organized murder of between 600,000 and 1,000,000 helpless persons at Majdanek Camp, near Lublin.' Who the 'helpless persons' were was not explained, though in *Life* all the victims were reported as Jews (see Figures 46 and 47).

In comparison to the emotive images of human suffering which would be used to represent the camps liberated by the Western allies, those which were released to represent Majdanek showed the industrial scale of the camp – Zyklon B cylinders, the interior of 'gas cells', the interior of barracks 'showing remnants of rope used to hang victims' and the exterior of the 'torture chamber', piles of shoes and boots, ashes of human remains in the crematoria and a pile of identity cards – the kind of detailed photographic evidence that police photographers might take in the course of a criminal investigation.[90] *Time* and *Life* correspondent Richard Lauterbach, one of the few foreign correspondents to have visited Majdanek, wrote that he was largely unaffected by seeing the gas-chambers, the open graves, the fertilizer made from human ashes and the crematoria. 'Too machinelike', he reported. 'The full emotional shock', he wrote, came when he saw a warehouse full of people's shoes – 800,000 pairs of them. 'There's something about an old shoe, as personal as a snapshot or a letter.'[91]

Barbie Zelizer, in her authoritative study of the liberations of the camps, *Remembering to Forget*, interprets this lack of images of human suffering at Majdanek as a 'relative absence of vivid documentation' which provided, she writes, 'less evidence' than was required to dispel disbelief. She argues that the way in which Majdanek was represented was merely 'a dress rehearsal for the western press's entry into the camps, where scenes of massive decay and death could be photographed more easily'. It was only with the images of western camps, Zelizer argues, that 'the scope and magnitude' of Nazi atrocities would be realized.[92]

Zelizer's point implies that photographs of human suffering were more explicit than those taken at Majdanek. Certainly, the Western coverage of the camps in Germany prompted a more emotive response from the public than did photos taken at Majdanek, but this was largely to do with the enormous amount of press coverage given to them. More significantly, Russian reports about Majdanek were considered, by the West, to be propaganda. Zelizer states that it was the lack of photographs of 'dead bodies and other gruesome scenes' which helped facilitate the disbelief about Majdanek, but even if photographs of this type had been published there is nothing to suggest that they would not have been dismissed as propaganda.[93] After all, during the war there had been no shortage of images of Nazi atrocities committed in the Soviet Union which, rather than inspiring outrage among the Western allies, had simply fostered distrust.

When the Nazis left Majdanek there were around 1,500 prisoners left in the camp. Most were disabled Soviet POWs and Polish peasants from the Lublin district.[94] A few poor-quality photographs show survivors dressed in rags, many supported by crutches, standing behind the barbed-wire fence. There is no evidence that these photographs were released to the West by the Soviet Union. It is worth considering whether Britain or the USA would have released photographs of the western liberated camps with quite the enthusiasm they did, if the camps had been full of their own nationals. After all, it had been policy in both countries throughout the war not to release photographs of their dead. In the USA they were withheld, 'for reasons of privacy and out of respect for families ... if faces were shown, or if death or injury was too graphically portrayed'.[95] This respect given to dead Americans seemed not to apply to the people in the camps.

Neither Alexander Werth's report from Majdanek nor Simonov's coverage mentioned the prisoners. It's possible that by the time journalists arrived they had been removed. Following the liberation, apparently Polish prisoners who were able to immediately left the camp and Russian POWs were 'taken to the camps in their homeland'. One source suggests that crippled Russian POWs were shot by the Red Army. By late August part of the camp had been taken over by the NKVD, Stalin's secret police, and was used to intern members of the Polish Home Army (AK, Armia Krajowa, the nationalist war-time underground movement) and the Peasant Battalions, who, despite their heroism, were regarded as enemies of the new political system in Poland. From Majdanek many were transported to the gulag in the Soviet Union.[96]

Some of the film-makers and photographers who had taken pictures at Majdanek went on to record the horrendous scenes at Auschwitz-Birkenau. On 28 January 1945, the day after the camp was liberated by the Red Army, Adolf Forbert was one of the first Polish soldiers to arrive — as he later said, in a 'worn out Willys Knight jeep that had served me well'. He described his first impression of Auschwitz as being as 'macabre' as Majdanek, but on a 'larger

46/47 · (pages 144–5) A double-page picture story from the *Illustrated London News*, 14 October 1944. (Illustrated London News Picture Library)

THE MOST TERRIBLE EXAMPLE OF ORGANISED MASS MURDER BY THE GERMANS AT

barbed wire, it was never intended to provide permanent accommodation for the inmates, and the barracks were cleared just as fast as the prisoners could be killed off. Some, it is true, died of hunger and disease, but the favourite method of extermination was by poison gas. In the ferro-concrete cells provided for the purpose, the victims were packed so tightly that they died on their feet as the gas was pumped in. Fifteen minutes after the introduction of the gas, the executioners entered the cells and removed the dead. In the centre of the camp stands a huge stone building—

LUBLIN'S "CAMP OF ANNIHILATION"; THE BARRACKS' INTERIOR, SHOWING REMNANTS OF ROPES USED TO HANG VICTIMS.

THE EXTERIOR OF THE TORTURE CHAMBER AT THE MAJDANEK "ANNIHILATION CAMP," SITUATED SOME TWO TO THREE MILES OUTSIDE LUBLIN.

THE GAS CELLS INTO WHICH THE PRISONERS WERE PACKED SO TIGHTLY THAT THEY DIED ON THEIR FEET AS THE POISON GAS WAS PUMPED IN.

A FEW OF THE CYLINDERS CONTAINING POISON GAS THIS WAS THE NAZIS' FAVOURITE

THE FURNACES IN WHICH THE GERMANS CREMATED THE BODIES OF THE MEN AND WOMEN THEY HAD DELIBERATELY ASPHYXIATED BY POISON GAS.

IT is not the custom of "The Illustrated London News" to publish photographs of atrocities, but in view of the fact that the enormity of the crimes perpetrated by the Germans is so wicked that our readers, to whom such behaviour is unbelievable, may think the reports of such crimes exaggerated or due to propaganda, we consider it necessary to present them, by means of the accompanying photographs, with an irrefutable proof of the organised murder of between 600,000 and 1,000,000 helpless persons at Majdanek Camp, near Lublin. And even these pictures are carefully selected from a number, some of which are too horrible to reproduce. The Majdanek camp was called by the Germans themselves "the camp of annihilation"; built over an area of 20 square kilometres and surrounded by

THE OPENING IN THE ROOF OF THE GAS CHAMBER THROUGH WHICH "CYCLONE" CRYSTALS WERE POURED.

CRUELTY IN THE HISTORY OF CIVILISATION.
THE MAJDANEK "CAMP OF ANNIHILATION."

the world's biggest crematorium. In this crematorium are five large ovens, where five furnaces were never allowed to go out. Day and night, pillars of black smoke belched from the chimneys, as the bodies of the prisoners were dragged from the gas chambers and burnt. Even in this most horrible of all work the Germans were methodical: a layer of bodies, then a layer of logs, another layer of bodies, another layer of logs; and so on. One thousand four hundred corpses were so disposed of every twenty-four hours, and the ashes from the furnaces were carefully collected and sent to Germany as [*Continued below.*]

AN ENORMOUS QUANTITY OF LOCKS FROM THE PRISONERS' LUGGAGE WAS FOUND IN THE CAMP: FOREIGN CORRESPONDENTS VIEWING THESE LOCKS.

SOME OF THE PASSPORTS AND IDENTITY CARDS BELONGING TO THE VICTIMS OF NAZI BRUTALITY AT MAJDANEK CAMP.

USED FOR THE WHOLESALE SLAUGHTER OF PRISONERS. METHOD OF EXTERMINATION.

THOUSANDS OF PAIRS OF BOOTS AND SHOES, ONCE BELONGING TO FREE MEN AND WOMEN, HERE COLLECTED FROM THE VICTIMS FOR CONSIGNMENT TO GERMANY.

CANS OF "CYCLONE" CRYSTALS: SUCH CANS WERE FOUND BY THE SCORE IN THE MAJDANEK CAMP.

[*Continued.*]
fertiliser for Nazi kitchen gardens. This story as it stands is almost incredible in its bestiality, but German cruelty went further still at Majdanek. Prisoners who were too ill to walk into the camp—there to strip and neatly hang their clothes on pegs specially provided for the purpose before going to their death—were dragged alive to the furnaces and thrust in alongside the dead. And the man chiefly responsible for these mass murders? Herr Mussfeld was his name, the camp commandant. And yet no one man can be held responsible for these mass murders, not even Himmler; the whole German nation is involved, for it has chosen its leaders and presumably admires them. This camp, as it stands to-day, is a grim reminder of that streak of utter inhumanity which is found in every German.

THE CRYSTALS OF THE POISONOUS CHEMICAL KNOWN AS "CYCLONE." THE GERMANS USED THE WORD CYCLONE—"ZYKLON"—AS THE TRADE NAME FOR THIS GAS.

scale'. 'Long rows of lifeless barracks', he wrote, 'from piles of snow protruding limbs of the dead, and all around the silence of a cemetery'. Forbert stayed to film everything he could, but with only 300 metres of film, a camera 'of the Bell and Howell type' manufactured by the Russians, and one Leica, the possibilities were limited. He described his frustration at having so little film and no lighting equipment or tripod, which meant he was unable to film or take photographs inside the barracks. He wrote, 'everywhere dead bodies, but I am helpless, I cannot film, I don't have artificial lights'.[97]

He was taken by former prisoners to the women's hospital in Birkenau where, apart from the doctors and nurses, there were around 500 sick women. Forbert stayed at the camp for two days and one night. Nurses provided him and his colleagues with 'fold-out beds, even with clean bed linen'. He sat late into the night listening to the camp stories of Jadwiga Dąbrowska, Anna Chomicz and other prisoners, sharing food and vodka found in the former SS warehouses. On the second day he walked through Birkenau, which he called the 'gigantic factory of torment and death', and spoke with prisoners. Although Forbert had more than an adequate experience of photographing war, including the horrendous scenes at Majdanek, he nevertheless still found it difficult to photograph at Birkenau. 'Between the barracks under the snow', he wrote, 'laid the large and smaller piles of corpses, completely frozen people. A few here, a few dozen there, then another pile. Terror.' With an attitude to photographing the dead similar to that expressed by Margaret Bourke-White when photographing at Buchenwald, he said that it was only the distance that the camera put between him and the subject which made him able to confront what he saw. 'Only through the viewfinder', he wrote, 'could I calmly watch these macabre scenes. It must be part of my professional qualities.' Forbert travelled through Birkenau and Auschwitz filming general views, 'the watchtower and barbed wire in the sunset', panoramas, the destroyed crematoria, faces of sick or weak prisoners, a group of five able prisoners preparing to leave the camp and a Zyklon B canister which a prisoner offered to hold for him and pose for the photograph.[98] It is posed photographs such as this that, as Teresa Świebocka and Renata Bogusławska-Świebocka point out in their essay on photographs of the Auschwitz liberation, sometimes look surreal. During the transitional period, after the Nazis had left but while the prisoners were still in the camp, prisoners were photographed in such a way that before liberation would not have made sense. They cite the example of a group of children who are seen to be walking through a narrow channel of barbed wire which formerly would have been electrified. It is, the authors wrote, 'a potent cinematographic image' but unreal.[99] Nevertheless, it is an image that is commonly used to represent Auschwitz today.

Forbert found a warehouse with piles of camp uniforms and took twenty complete sets which he thought might be useful for future films. Having left the camp he gave his films to a 'laboratory' for development and never saw them again. They disappeared. Nor did he keep what he referred to as his 'private collection'. As a soldier in the Polish army, his duties were not yet finished. He travelled on to Kraków and later Dresden and Berlin.[100] Władysław Forbert went on to film the Nazi war trials in Nuremberg in 1946. After the war had ended the Forbert brothers became two of the most eminent film-makers in Poland, and Adolf Forbert became a teacher at the celebrated film school in Łódź.

The fate of Forbert's film and photographs of Auschwitz is not known. It is possible they were lost, or filed away in a Soviet state archive, or remain anonymous. He is not acknowledged by Auschwitz-Birkenau State Museum as being among the liberation photographers and film-makers. The film *Chronicle of the Liberation of Auschwitz*, made in 1945, is attributed to four Soviet army film-makers, N. Bykov, K. Katub-Zade, A. Pavlov and A. Vorontsev. The majority of now well-known stills photographs of the liberation – the mass graves, the sick in the hospital, the camp grounds, the piles of hair, suitcases, shoes and other belongings of former prisoners – are taken from this film.

Soon after liberation other photographers began to arrive to take photographs for the special investigative commissions established to collect evidence of Nazi crimes. Henryk Makarewicz and Stanisław Mucha took photographs for the Polish Red Cross team and the Soviet commission examining Nazi crimes in Auschwitz. In May, Stanisław Łuczko, of the Kraków Institute of Judicial Ex-pertise, also took photographs as evidence.[101] In April 1945 an illustrated article in *Przekrój*, which included photographs of the inscribed gates, human hair, the barracks, the barbed-wire fence and a Polish investigation committee at work, reported that the investigation into the crimes at Auschwitz had begun.[102] Four months after the liberation, on 29 May 1945, a British delegation headed by the Dean of Canterbury Cathedral, Dr Hewlett Johnson, known in the British media as the 'Red Dean' because of his communist sympathies, went to Auschwitz to inspect the camp. Polish photographer Stanisław Kolowca took photographs of the delegation's visit. By that time the press was full of images of the dead and the dying in the western camps, and no publicity appears to have been given to this visit. Even though regular reports had been received about Auschwitz-Birkenau throughout the war, there were hardly any reports in the British national press about its liberation, fewer even than about Majdanek, and no photographs were published in national newspapers.

Apart from the lack of publicity in the West, Zelizer states that there was an inconsistency in the way the Soviets reported the liberation of the camps in Eastern Europe generally. She argues that not only did they not publicize the liberation of Auschwitz until after the liberation of the western camps, but they did not issue press releases about the extermination camps at Bełżec, Sobibór and Treblinka.[103] But on 1 March there was a report in *Soviet War News Weekly* with five photographs, including two of emaciated survivors taken by Red Army photographer M. Redkin. The article, headlined 'More terrible than MAIDANEK!', stated that 'at least five million people were destroyed by the Germans at Oświęcim. Among them Soviet citizens, Poles, French Yugoslavs and Czechoslovaks.'[104] The lack of reporting of the extermination camps might have been due to the fact that by the time the Red Army reached their locations all evidence would have been removed. By the end of 1943 all three, including Chełmno, had been closed down. At Bełżec the Nazis had already landscaped and planted trees on the site of the camp and a farmhouse had been built which was given to a Ukrainian farmer who acted as 'caretaker' to deter locals from looting the site.[105]

The primary reason for the lack of press coverage about the liberation of Auschwitz seems to have been that by early 1945 the allied countries were more concerned about the war being won. It is doubtful whether anyone in the West would have been interested in more Soviet atrocity stories. During late January through to mid-February, the front-page lead stories in British national newspapers were solely concerned with the Soviets' heroic advance towards Berlin led by Soviet Marshals Koniev and Zukov. Although their advances through Silesia (where Oświęcim is situated) were reported in detail, there were only two brief mentions of the liberation of the camp. On 29 January, in the *Manchester Guardian*, the liberation warranted one sentence at the end of a short column on page 5 which outlined the success of the Russian advance.[106] On 3 February, the *Daily Express* gave Alaric Jacobs's report from Moscow on the liberation one column on page 4, headlined, 'Last Word in German Brutality'. It reported that there were 'several thousand survivors' and that during 1941, 1942 and 1943 'between five and eight trains full of people would enter the camp's own railway station daily … They came from Russia, Poland, France, Yugoslavia and Czechoslovakia'.[107] Neither of these reports mentioned the Jews.

In Poland itself few images were published of the liberation of either Majdanek or Auschwitz-Birkenau. At the end of the war there was a severe shortage of materials for making and publishing photographs. The publishing industry in Poland was virtually extinct. According to a survey of photographs in the Polish press between 1944 and 1946 conducted by Michał Gawałkiewicz, very few photographs were published during this period and those that were, were of such a low technical standard that it was difficult to identify people or objects. On 9 and 12 August the Communist Party newspaper *Rzeczypospolita* published photographs from the funeral services in Lublin and of the 'final days of Majdanek', but they were of such bad quality that they were heavily retouched and resembled drawings.[108] Despite the lack of resources, on 1 December 1944 an officially backed exhibition of 152 photographs opened in Lublin. Prominently placed was the work of the Czołówka Filmowa Wojska Polskiego. The Forbert brothers were awarded a joint first prize.[109]

It was to be decades before images of Auschwitz-Birkenau would become familiar in the West, and the tragedy which had taken place at the camps in Poland fully acknowledged. The films, *Chronicle of the Liberation of Auschwitz* and *Majdanek, Cemetery of Europe*, remained unseen in the West for the best part of fifty years. Although in the 1990s Auschwitz would become the universal symbol for the Holocaust, in 1945, for the majority of the British and American public, the true nature of the Final Solution, the concentration camps and extermination camps in Poland, the ghettos and the slaughter in the Soviet Union, were little known or understood. Even the images of the camps liberated by the Western allies would disappear and fade from public memory. Tony Kushner argues that the very nature of the atrocity photographs and films in 1945 assisted that process. Although the images had 'made an impression', the atrocity materials, he wrote, 'were such that many wished to put them out of mind as quickly as possible'.[110]

In the Soviet Union and Eastern Europe the story was different. The millions of war dead were remembered and honoured. Photographs of the camps liberated by the Red Army, and of Nazi atrocities in general served as a reminder of the horrors of fascism and were firmly fixed in the public consciousness. The changes in the way in which the extermination of 6 million Jews – the Holocaust – was remembered, were to be determined by changing world politics.

SEVEN

Constructing the Post-war Memory: 'Don't Mention the Jews'

The Disappearing Evidence

During the late 1940s, in Britain and the USA, official attitudes towards showing photographs and films of Nazi atrocities and the liberation of the concentration camps began to change. After the trials at Nuremberg ended in July 1949, the images which had been so powerfully placed in the public consciousness slowly faded from public view.[1] As the Western democracies began to see the strategic importance of West Germany as a buffer state against the Soviet Bloc, it was no longer politic to continue to remind the British and American public of the evils of Nazism. But just as the West chose to suppress Nazi atrocities in favour of the rebuilding programme for West Germany, so the Eastern Europeans, whose populations had suffered the greatest losses, chose to remember Nazi crimes. As each nation's interpretation of the events of the war changed, so did the use of pictures.

In mid-1945 Britain and the USA were collaborating on a number of books and exhibitions to reflect what a British Ministry of Information memorandum referred to as the 'true history' of the war. In the six volumes of *The War in Pictures* (in six languages), just four pages were given over to images from Belsen; the rest concentrated on the heroism of the allies.[2] In July and August, war exhibitions opened in Oslo, Copenhagen, Liège and Antwerp which showed photographs of the army, navy, and 'British and American Women at War'.[3] Although the exhibitions included some camp photographs, they were no longer central. Since the war had ended, rather than continue to demonize the German population, the allied governments were now keen to stress that West Germany was under their control, that the re-education of the population was underway and that Nazi war criminals would be punished. As early as May 1945, the *Daily Express* had sought to reassure the public that 'the task of de-Nazification and demilitarisation of the German mind and educating it along democratic lines has begun and is making progress'.[4] It was perhaps as a consequence that the graphic film about concentration camps on which Sidney Bernstein, head of the film division at the Ministry of Information, had been working since April, was by August in difficulties. On 4 August, a letter to Bernstein from Commander D. McLachlan of the political intelligence department of the Foreign Office stated that the 'policy at the moment in Germany is entirely in the direction of encouraging, stimulating and interesting the Germans out of their apathy, and there are people around the C-in-C who will say "No Atrocity film" '.[5] There is no evidence that the film was ever completed. The five roughly edited film reels – approximately 55 minutes of footage – along with the script, were deposited in the Imperial War Museum archive some time in the early 1950s along with other material from the Ministry of Information and War Office. According to the original film script, there had been a sixth reel containing Soviet film of the liberation of Majdanek and Auschwitz-Birkenau, but that reel was missing and has never been found. It was not until the early 1980s that an American film company, WGBH, assembled the original film footage and script and made a film entitled *Memory of the Camps*.[6]

As the Western allies' attitude towards Germany's past was changing, so a more cautious approach was being taken towards the collaborative war-time role of other Western European countries. In the summer of 1945 a Nazi War Crimes Exhibition sponsored by the UN War Crimes Commission (UNWCC) and the French government opened in Paris where, according to the *Daily Worker*, it 'caused a sensation'.[7] Brought to Britain 'at the expense' of the French government, it was opened in London on 6 December at the Prince's Galleries in Piccadilly by Lord Wright of Durley, chairman of the UNWCC, and the French Minister of Justice, Pierre Henri Teitgen. At the opening ceremony, Teitgen, a former member of the resistance, said that the exhibition was not propaganda but a 'series of war documents'.[8] He was even more keen to stress the speed at which 'trials of collaborators are functioning in France' and that out of 100,000 'dossiers', 60,000 had already been dealt with.[9]

Although the exhibition included 'horror pictures from concentration camps', and some camp film-footage, it was predominantly made up of a bizarre array of artefacts: 'torture instruments used by the Nazis', a 'blood-stained execution stake' and 'stretchers used for carrying corpses' in the concentration camps. The *Daily Worker* called it not only 'a horror exhibition, but an education in politics and contemporary history which no one can afford to miss'.[10]

While the exhibition was touring Europe, the Soviet authorities were compiling their own evidence on Nazi atrocities. A photo album made by the Provincial Commission on the History of the Great Patriotic War is entitled: 'Photo Album of atrocities and crimes committed by Nazi German aggressors in Drogobych province during the period 1941–44'. One page (see Figure 48)

48 · A page from a photo album compiled by the Provincial Commission on the History of the Great Patriotic War entitled, 'Photo Album of atrocities and crimes committed by Nazi German aggressors in Drogobych province during the period 1941–44'. The text on the page reads: 'Deputy Head of the Gestapo for Drogobych province (Deputy Head of the Gestapo's Political Department) Gertschultz'. (L'viv Regional State Archive, Ukraine)

is a montage of a portrait of a Nazi official surrounded by powerfully portrayed ghostly infernal figures reaching up to him, and, alongside, two people hanging. The official is described as the deputy head of the Gestapo political department in Drogobych province (in south-west Ukraine).

Images of atrocities were also presented at the International Military Tribunal in Nuremberg, established on 8 August 1945 by the UK, USA, USSR and France. The majority of documents and photographs presented to the court, however, came from British or American sources which, according to Robert Wolfe of the National Archives in Washington, DC, writing in 1974, were presented in a 'highly unsystematic' way and served 'the function of assembling documents for prosecution purposes rather than collecting source documents for any logical historical purpose'.[11]

Although Wolfe wrote that the documents presented to the tribunal by the USSR remained a 'considerable mystery' to him, they offered compelling visual evidence. Chief Counsellor L. N. Smirnov, assistant prosecutor for the Soviet Union, showed atrocity photographs and film-footage including a 'seven-reel' documentary film, *The Atrocities by the German Fascist Invaders in the USSR*, which, according to one observer, showed 'piles of corpses dwarfing those in Dachau and Buchenwald'.[12] Reports and photographs were also submitted about

Majdanek and Auschwitz-Birkenau, including stills from the film *Chronicle of the Liberation of Auschwitz*, although in the published transcript of the tribunal these were said to be 'Captured German Originals'.[13]

A photo album, certified by the Extraordinary State Commission, a board assigned to investigate Nazi atrocities, was also submitted as evidence. The twenty-nine-page album entitled 'The Germans in Lvov' deals with the crimes committed in and around the notorious Janovska camp referred to in the album as the 'Factory of Death'. It incorporates handwritten text and powerful graphics, and it displays a remarkable artistic flair, with black and white atrocity photographs taken by the Nazis or collaborators and images of murder sites taken by the commission. The photographs show public hangings in the city, the piles of exhumed corpses of those murdered at Janovska camp and their belongings and forensic teams at the sites of mass killings. In Figure 49 the image in the bottom left-hand side shows the Janovska camp orchestra. The text points out that the musicians were made to play the 'Tango of Death' during shootings at the camp and were later executed themselves. There is a carefully drawn musical stave across the top of the page. Although the camp had been predominantly for Jews from the eastern regions of Galicia, the album refers to those who were murdered as 'people', 'Soviet POWs' or 'local inhabitants', not specifically as Jews.[14]

The prosecuting counsel for the USA also presented photo albums to the tribunal; a report from SS Lieutenant General of Police Katzmann made in 1943 which documented the 'Solution of the Jewish question in Galicia'; and the *Stroop Report* (referred to in Chapter 4) which documented the suppression of the Warsaw Ghetto Uprising in 1943.[15] In addition the assistant counsel for the USA, US Navy Commander James Britt Donovan, presented a silent 90-second 'motion picture' entitled 'Original German 8-millimeter Film of Atrocities against Jews', which showed the physical abuse of men and naked and half-naked women in the streets. 'The pictures', he said, 'obviously were taken by an amateur photographer.' He also stated that it offered 'undeniable evidence, made by Germans themselves, of almost incredible brutality to Jewish people in the custody of the Nazis, including German military units'. It was not known exactly what events the film showed, or where it was made, but Counsellor Donovan believed that to be 'immaterial'.[16]

Apart from captured German film, the Americans presented two major films made specifically for the tribunal. The six-hour 'motion picture' *The Nazi Plan* included parts of *The Triumph of the Will*, Leni Riefenstahl's epic propaganda film about the Nazi Party, and other surviving Nazi footage. It was cut together by American directors and film-makers in an attempt to make a documentary history of the Third Reich.[17] It was, Robert Wolfe argues, a 'biased' film, in

49 · A page from a photo album entitled, 'The Germans in Lvov'. Text at the top reads: 'During the shootings at Janovska camp the Gestapo ordered an orchestra composed of prisoners from the best musicians in the Western Ukraine to play the TANGO OF DEATH.' Text in the middle reads: 'The musicians played to the last moment of their own lives and were then also shot.' (L'viv Regional State Archive, Ukraine)

which 'the villains were clear and the heroes were clear, that's the memory'. The atrocities were seen as the acts of 'monsters' and not of human beings.[18]

But the *pièce de resistance* screened at the tribunal was the hour-long American 'documentary motion picture' *Nazi Concentration Camps*. This used footage selected from more than thirteen hours of film shot by 'official Allied photographic teams in the course of their military duties' and was made under the direction of Commander Donovan and Commander E. Ray Kellogg, former director of photographic effects at Twentieth Century-Fox in Hollywood.[19] In their book, *The Film Till Now*, Paul Rotha and Richard Griffith state that the 'much heralded reportage film' was disappointing and its ' "English" narration was naive to the extent of embarrassment, attempting to infuse melodrama into visuals which were already dramatic in their authenticity'.[20] It presented an outline of the concentration camps at 'Leipsig, Pegnig, Ohrdruf, Hadamar, Breendonck, Hannover, Arnstadt, Nordhausen, Mauthausen, Buchenwald, Dachau and Belsen', but there was no reference to any of the death camps in Poland and only one reference to Jews, as 'German Jews'.[21] The failure to mention the Jews was not unique. Sidney Bernstein's film script had also mentioned the word Jew only once.[22] In context, these omissions were not necessarily incorrect, as Peter Novick points out, as Jews accounted for only about a fifth of those liberated by American troops. The images of the camps which have now come to symbolize the Jewish tragedy were then seen quite differently.[23]

The trials at Nuremberg did little to capture the British public imagination. In March 1946 a Mass-Observation survey concluded that the public were growing weary of hearing about them. Two out of every five people interviewed said they were taking no further interest in them. The main criticisms were that they were a 'waste of time', 'waste of money' and 'unnecessary from the start'. The vast majority of those interviewed felt that 'the defendants were obviously all guilty even before the trial opened'.[24] Nevertheless, as the end of the trials grew nearer, another 'War Crimes Exhibition' was organized in Britain in July 1946 by the War Crimes Investigation Unit. According to a War Office memorandum, the exhibition should be 'more than a display of mere horror photographs'; its primary purpose was 'to secure an indictment of the Nazi regime, in particular relation to war crimes and atrocities' and to 'illustrate the atrocity policy of the Third Reich as a deliberate State effort rather than the spontaneous action of a few'. The main exhibits included photographs from Neuengamme, Belsen and Ravensbrück concentration camps, the Łódź ghetto and 'well-known criminal types'. The remainder of the exhibition consisted of artefacts similar to those exhibited in the Nazi War Crimes Exhibition. All the captions, the memorandum added, should be in both English and German.[25]

It had become a matter of course that the democratic re-education process taking place in Germany was extended to German POWs in Britain. A number of exhibitions including 'The Housing Problems in Germany', 'The Exploitation of Europe Under Hitler', 'Men Against Hitler', 'British Press and Broadcast' were shown at Ettington Park near Stratford-upon-Avon and other POW camps. Another which aimed to highlight 'the differences between the English and the German characters' was among others considered suitable. The German POWs were encouraged to make their own exhibitions with photographs supplied by the Foreign Office. Camp officials made requests for pictures which included 'a debate in the House of Commons' (photography has always been forbidden in the House of Commons) to contrast with 'a stormy Reichstagsitzung', and 'a speaker in Hyde Park' to contrast with 'a stormy electoral assembly in Germany'. The 'Commandant' of Ettington Park said that he was concerned 'that they should feel that they are free to express their own ideas and preferences in these exhibitions without any propaganda "line" being imposed on them'.[26]

But a propaganda 'line' was being imposed on them. On 7 June 1946 an exhibition 'Germany Under Control', organized by the Control Commission for Germany, was opened with a ceremony at the Dominion Theatre, London, and was shown in Birmingham, Bristol, Leeds, Cardiff and Edinburgh. Its primary aims were to reassure the British public that not only were the Western administrations in control of Germany, but that the German people were being taught the lessons of democracy and that all Nazi elements were being got rid of, even though this was far from the case. As far as the Foreign Office was concerned, the exhibition 'must try to give the impression of firmness ... which', a memorandum said, 'will ultimately benefit the man in the street in Britain'.[27] An exhibition pamphlet called *Germany Our Way*, which told in 'simple language' the 'story of the British administration in Germany and the organisation of the Control Commission', was distributed free of charge. In addition, six 15-minute film programmes were shown daily, including *Military Government at Work*.[28] A meeting at the Foreign Office to discuss publicity for the opening of the exhibition had suggested that German POWs from Wilton Park camp, near Beaconsfield in Buckinghamshire, should be taken to the exhibition as a publicity stunt for the opening ceremony. 'It could make a story to the effect that we are reconverting them to our way of thinking,' a Foreign Office memorandum stated, adding that 'their recorded reactions to the exhibition would make useful data'.[29]

There were no Nazi atrocity photographs in this exhibition. As the message was about restructuring and re-education, to have reminded the public of Nazi atrocities in such a graphic way would have been inappropriate and, as far as the British government was concerned, would have given the wrong message. Rather than horrify the public with pictures, the intention now seemed to be to entertain them with inconsequential artefacts. A draft press release announced that 'British housewives will also see saucepans made from Wehrmacht helmets' and that 'a stone eagle from the Reichschancellory' would be on display. It was hoped that film stars Michael Redgrave, Jack Warner or Basil Radford, who had featured in the British film *The Captive Heart* (a story about British officers in a German POW camp), would be present at the opening ceremony; this, a Foreign Office official said, would provide an 'excellent attraction'.[30]

Not every visitor to the exhibition was convinced by the government's message. One member of the public remarked on the lack of reference to 'German exploits' in concentration camps. Another person was appalled by its propagandist tone and by one of its slogans: 'The Nazis are no longer active.' This person wrote in a letter: 'I have never been so horrified in all my life at the possible effects of propaganda as I was then ... but almost at the same time as I was reading this slogan reports were reaching London of the Nazi demonstrations in Hamburg ... and similar remarks appearing in the US Press that in the British zone the Nazis remained in office. The British alibi has apparently been that after so long it is only Nazis who have any administrative experience.' In response to this criticism and in anticipation of more, a letter from the Central Office of Information to the Foreign Office asked that the fact that the exhibition posters had been printed in Germany be 'left out in case of an outcry'.[31]

As well as aggravating some members of the British public, the British and American rebuilding programme in Germany was enraging the Soviet Union. During the Nuremberg trials, *Soviet Weekly* had published regular reports of the proceedings by distinguished Russian journalist Ilya Ehrenburg. As they drew to a close, the newspaper began a series of articles on what it saw as the contradictions between the conviction of leading Nazis at the trials, and the allies knowingly allowing other Nazis back into positions of power in Germany. On 25 October 1945, the front-page lead story headlined 'Nazi Conspiracy is Not Dead Yet' reported that Nazis were filtering back into German life and that '200,000 Gestapo agents are at work abroad'.[32] On 29 November, a further front-page story headlined 'The "Pity the Germans" Campaign' was critical both of the Vatican for not criticizing the Nazis, and of Britain and the USA for protecting the economic and military interests of Germany and the rebuilding programme. The article stated that according to a 'Washington correspondent' this was being done 'in order to use her as a barrier against the Soviet Union'.[33] They were of course correct.

When the trials ended, the Western allies embarked upon a strategy of ignoring all traces of Germany's Nazi past. The nature of the trials had allowed this to happen, in that the complexities of Nazi philosophy were never discussed. Nobody paid much attention to what the Germans thought the war was for. Göring's refusal to admit that the genocidal policies of the Third Reich were fundamentally wrong caused the court to make a ruling that there should be no further explanation of Nazi policies.[34] Leon A. Jick suggests that the trials 'were designed to forestall continuing analysis rather than to initiate ongoing inquiry'.[35] The ideas that had led millions of ordinary human beings to participate in such fantastic barbarism were too dangerous to discuss. What happened at the Nuremberg Trials was the construction of 'the grand public memory' of the Second World War. The memories which did not fit the story were quietly hidden away and forgotten.[36]

The American government began seizing Nazi Party documents and related material from all over Germany and shipping them wholesale to the USA. In 1949 the *Library of Congress Quarterly* reported that 'Military intelligence teams scoured every likely spot in the occupied territory in their search for documents subject to confiscation as Nazi files, or as the property of Nazi officials, or because of their militaristic or Nazi content'.[37] The Library of Congress organized a 'Mission to Europe' in order to collect vast amounts of 'Nazi material', including documents from the Nazi Party archive, rare books and photographs, 'several thousand films', 'twenty-five hundred German sound recordings', including radio broadcasts and public addresses by Nazi Party officials, forty-seven personal photo albums of Herman Göring, and seventy photo albums belonging to other Nazis. Other confiscated material included several thousand photographs, posters, anti-Semitic material, the private photographic collection of Heinrich Hoffmann and even an 'exhaustive photo report on the Daimler-Benz automobile complex of manufacturing plants', which amounted to 5,000 photographs in forty-three albums.[38]

For the Western democracies to have continued to remind Germany of its evil past would now have been counter-productive. The evil was no longer Nazism, but communism. 'Communism meant one thing,' said critic Gulie Ne'eman Arad, 'marginalizing the Holocaust and rebuilding a new Germany.'[39] In the USA, according to author George H. Roeder, 'some officials worried that the death camp pictures would make it harder to convince the American public of the need to rebuild postwar Germany to counter Soviet influence in Europe'.[40] Seizing the pictures and documents was a way of getting rid of the evidence. With the spotlight off Germany, former Nazis were able to take seats in power and, in some cases, in government.[41] 'The only winners from this Cold War', as Simon Wiesenthal said, 'were the Nazis.'[42]

In the West, the many thousands of photographs taken by resisters, Jews, Nazis and perpetrators, along with photographs of the liberations, would be scattered throughout personal and public archives where they would gather dust for the next fifty years. At Dachau camp in early 1955, an exhibition of Nazi atrocity photographs, which had been erected by the Americans at the end of the war, was taken down after local civic leaders 'complained bitterly that the display was not only offensive to good taste but also damaging to international relations'. The Americans closed the exhibition and posted a sign on the door, 'Closed until further notice'.[43]

National Memories Take Shape

How the world remembered the Second World War was to vary. Each nation had its own memories and images to construct. Just as the Western message was the triumph of liberal democracy, in the Soviet Union it was the victory of communism over fascism. The way in which the memory of the destruction of European Jewry was represented was diverse, not least among the Jews themselves.

In the Soviet Union, the memory of the 2 million Jews murdered on Soviet territory was generally incorporated into the memory of the 27 million citizens who died in what became known as the Great Patriotic War. In Soviet-controlled Poland the story was the same. The 3 million murdered Polish Jews were subsumed into the national memory of the 3 million murdered non-Jewish Poles, which took precedence. The decree by which the Auschwitz-Birkenau State Museum was established in July 1947 stated: 'On the site of the former Nazi concentration camp a Monument of the martyrdom of the Polish Nation and of Other Nations is to be erected for all times to come.'[44] Although the Jews were not specifically mentioned by name, James E. Young suggests that Poles were not so much neglecting Jewish memory, 'but only recalling the Jews' experiences through the images of their own remembered past. That the death camps were located on Polish soil suggests to the Poles not their national complicity, but their ultimate violation: it was one thing to be ravaged outside one's land, another to be occupied and enslaved at home. In this view, the killing centers in Poland were to have begun with the Jews and ended with the Poles.'[45]

For Jewish survivors returning to their pre-war homes in Eastern Europe, the situation was increasingly tense, sparking hostility. In August 1945 a 'pogrom' was reported in Slovakia and 'anti-Jewish riots' in Hungary and in Poland.[46] The following year, in July 1946, forty-two Jews were murdered in a pogrom in Kielce, Poland,[47] and by the end of that year approximately 77,000 Jewish survivors had left the country. In the early post-war years it was left primarily to the Jewish organizations in Poland to preserve the memory of the Polish Jews. In 1945, the Central Jewish Historical Committee, founded in 1944, produced an album of atrocity photographs, said to have been taken by Germans, Poles and Jews, entitled *Zagłada Żydostwa Polskiego, Album Zdjęć* (The Extermination of Polish Jews, an Album of Photographs). It was said to be 'the first publication of its kind'. In it were copies of six pages of the album which Arie ben-Menachem had made in the Łódź ghetto.

Britain, like the Soviet Union and the Eastern Bloc countries, had its own national memory of the Second World War to construct. There were war heroes, the Blitz, the Battle of Britain, the 'Dam Busters' and the daring escapes from Colditz. These gripped the popular imagination and were absorbed into popular culture. There were dozens of feature films made about the war but in them the Nazis were portrayed as persecuting gallant British heroes, never Jews or other prisoners. Jewish refugees and Holocaust survivors who came to Britain kept quiet about their experiences in Nazi-occupied Europe. In the USA the story was the same. Belsen survivor Josef Rosensaft described how 'American Jews did not grasp the full scope of the tragedy which I tried to describe to them'. He further wrote about the lack of interest in the survivors of Belsen among the Jewish communities:

From a psychological viewpoint the years 1945 and 1946 were very bitter. In an ironical sense they were more oppressive to our souls than the years in the hell of *Auschwitz and Belsen*. Before liberation, a hope kept us alive. We dreamed about the day of liberation and had our ideas of what it would look like … And when the free Jews arrived at last, they looked upon us as objects of pity. All offers of help in the first month after liberation invariably contained the question whether we needed psychiatrists. They even sent us some without being asked … It is a fact that in the whole of Jewry there was not one famous children's specialist, surgeon or gynaecologist who was willing to come and work with us … despite all our appeals … There does not seem to have been any ordinary Jews with the desire to come over and see the few survivors of the greatest catastrophe in Jewish history. Why did they not come?[48]

In the 1950s the insecurity of Jews in American society, and their 'striving to enter the mainstream', made them reluctant to identify themselves with what Jick describes as 'this ultimate experience of victimization'.[49] In 1953 Gerald Reitlinger's book *The Final Solution* was published but received little coverage in Britain or the USA. In 1954 American Jewry celebrated the 300th anniversary 'of the settlement of the first group of Jews in America', but, as Jick points out, 'no mention of the recent fate of closer relatives was allowed to mark the festivities'. Even more shocking, writes Jick, was 'the inclusion of songs expressing attachment to the *Shtetlach*', while the fact that they had been all but destroyed was 'totally repressed'.[50]

Norman G. Finkelstein, in his book *The Holocaust Industry*, argues that the silence was in line with the US government's Cold War policy. The Final Solution was a 'taboo topic', he writes, for the reason that leftist Jews who were opposed to the Cold War alignment with Germany against the Soviet Union 'would not stop harping on it'. In Finkelstein's view, 'remembrance of the Nazi holocaust was tagged as a Communist cause'.[51] The primary reason for this, according to Peter Novick, was that in the USA the majority of communists were also Jews and the striking feature in communist rhetoric of these years 'was the frequency with which that rhetoric invoked the Holocaust'. It became one of the main arguments among Jews in favour of 'opposition to Cold War mobilisation'. In 1948 a campaign leaflet for Henry A. Wallace, presidential candidate of the Progressive Party, a newly organized third party with a pro-Soviet platform attacking the Marshall Plan and calling for disarmament, showed 'stacked corpses at Buchenwald' with the question to President Truman, 'Did You Forget This? … This is the kind of Western Germany to which you give Marshall Plan billions … A vote for Truman is a vote to rebuild Nazi Germany.'[52]

In Israel the memory of the millions of murdered Jews was no less complex.

As early as 1942, the year the Final Solution was implemented, Mordechai Shen-havi, a member of Kibbutz Mishmar Ha'emeq, proposed to 'collectively com-memorate' the destruction of European Jewry. The Kibbutzim began to collect documents and photographs of the disappearing Jewish communities in Europe. In 1945, when the scale of the destruction became clear, Shenhavi submitted his proposal renamed, 'Yad Vashem Foundation in Memory of Europe's Lost Jews: An Outline of a Plan for the Commemoration of the Diaspora'.[53]

The fact that the struggle for the independent Jewish state of Israel had been won only three years after the end of the war in Europe, and had been fought for in part by survivors, meant that from the outset there was an 'immense emotional intensity' in the relationship between the Holocaust and Israel. But to ask how it was possible that so many millions could have gone to their deaths 'like lambs to the slaughter' raised feelings of anger, shame and disappointment which did not entirely fit with the image of the new state. In 1953 the Knesset passed the Yad Vashem Law, which established Yad Vashem Martyrs' and Heroes' Remembrance Authority as the 'national centre of memory and commemoration' in Jerusalem. This was an important step in the process of incorporating the memory of the Holocaust into the symbolic structures of Jewish sovereignty in Israel and, as the name suggests, remembering all those who died as Martyrs.[54] Furthermore, in 1959, the Knesset designated the Remembrance Day for European Jewry as 'Holocaust and Heroism Remembrance Day', which signified the extent to which heroism had been ingrained in national memory. At the end of Israel's War of Independence, a number of Kibbutzim were established which honoured the heroes. Beit Lohamei Haghetaot (Ghetto Fighters' Kibbutz) was among them. It was founded on 19 April 1949 by 220 participants in the Warsaw Ghetto Up-rising and other survivors. At the foundation ceremony a 'modest exhibition', including photographs from the *Stroop Report* of the Warsaw Ghetto Uprising, marked the establishment of a Holocaust museum – the first of its kind. At the ceremony, pioneering Zionist and ghetto fighter Antek Zuckerman's explana-tion of the photographs not only provided a narrative frame but 'transformed the original story which the images were meant to convey – the story of the liquidation of the Warsaw Ghetto as a Nazi victory – into a heroic story of resistance and revolt'.[55]

The Zionist memory which celebrated heroism and martyrdom and marginal-ized the millions who had died angered some in Israel. In 1958 Yaacov Shelhav wrote in an article in *Yad Vashem Bulletin*: 'The immense tragedy which over-took Jewry in the past generation is fading from the memory of the broad Israel public.' According to Shelhav, the Holocaust was being 'increasingly ignored'. This, he wrote, was both 'deliberate' and 'official' for the purpose of building a new state of Israel.[56]

While Israel remained divided on how to remember the Jews of Europe, a new wave of anti-Semitic purges was gripping Germany. On Christmas Eve in 1959 a newly built synagogue in Cologne was defaced with huge swastikas and anti-Semitic slogans. This signalled outbursts of anti-Semitism, not only in Germany but in other European countries, and Jewish cemeteries and synagogues were daubed with swastikas.[57] Throughout the 1950s there had been increasing neo-Nazi activity in Germany. According to author and journalist T. H. Tetens, in his book *The New Germany and the Old Nazis*, the years 1950–51 'must be marked as the time when Hitler's old officers, SS leaders, and party function-aries returned to positions of power and influence'. In 1955, a rally organized by eminent former Nazis took place in Goslar, near the East German border. The Social Democrats, who saw this as a provocative act, appealed to the government to stop it. They were ignored. A 'Munich newspaper man', who saw several dozen photographs of the rally, remarked, 'we have seen these pictures once before … when the nationalistic Right went all out to attack the Weimar Republic'. In 1958, Bonn cancelled the allied occupation law which had banned the Nazi Party and all its affiliates. According to Tetens, the directorate of the Central Council of Jews in Germany said that the outbursts 'evoke pictures that bring to mind the November days of 1938', that is Kristallnacht. Rarely were these events reported in the Western press and, if they were, Konrad Adenauer's government was quick to counteract the criticism by declaring the incidents were communist-inspired.[58]

The rise of neo-Nazism, the formation of NATO[59] and the rearmament of Germany prompted the Soviet Union and Eastern Bloc countries to direct stories and photographs of Nazi atrocities at the West as reminders of the horrors of Nazism. In the Soviet Union a new interest was shown in the memoirs of Soviet POWs interned in Nazi camps, who had been largely ignored in the immediate post-war years.[60] In Poland in 1959 the first edition of *1939–1945, We Have Not Forgotten* was published in English, Russian and French. Two further editions in English, Spanish, Portuguese and German followed in 1960 and 1961. All three editions consisted principally of Nazi atrocity photographs – among them, public hangings, the executions at Bochnia and mass execu-tions, including at Mizocz and Liepaja, those taken at the ramp at Birkenau, the photographs taken by the Sonderkommando at Birkenau, photographs from the *Stroop Report* of the crushing of the Warsaw Ghetto Uprising and the Soviet liberation of Auschwitz-Birkenau, which served as a reminder of what Nazism had meant during the war and of 'Poland's martyrology under Nazi occupation'. The Introduction to the 1960 edition stated that 'in the light of recent events', Nazism had taken on a 'special meaning'. The authors saw it as necessary to remind the world about the 'Nazi barbarity in Poland' and 'to warn the young generation against the recurrence of genocide'. Its message was unambiguous: 'A wave of anti-Semitism is spreading in various directions and young people in schools are presented with a false picture of the past that is insulting to the memory of the victims of fascism.' In an attempt to 'disseminate the truth' about the Third Reich a detailed account of the extermination of Jews in the death camps of Poland was also included.[61]

During the early 1950s at Auschwitz-Birkenau, much to the dismay of some of the former prisoners who had been custodians of the museum since 1946, the Polish communist authorities expanded the displays to promote contemporary Cold War political themes which had little connection with the camp itself. Among the displays were depictions of the British concentration camps in South Africa during the Boer War. As the Nazis had used information about these camps in 1939 to highlight British hypocrisy and to undermine its criticism of German concentration camps, at Auschwitz the communist-led government was using them to discredit imperialism. In addition 'Impoverished black districts in New York were shown as the first ghettos and epitomized the evils of the capitalist system ... Space was also found for the October Revolution and the counter-revolution.'[62]

In 1967, the memory and images of Nazi atrocities were used as a battering ram against what was regarded in the Soviet bloc as Western aggression in Israel and Vietnam. In Poland, the introduction to an exhibition catalogue of contemporary photographs and art-works on the theme of Majdanek, organized by Majdanek State Museum, was titled 'An Exhibition Which Accuses ... ' It made a direct reference to the Six-Day War in Israel and the Vietnam War and seized the opportunity to draw parallels between 'American crimes in Vietnam', the 'cruelties of Israelite soldiers committed on Arab civilian population', and the 'mass homicide' of 'The Hitlerites'.[63] Following the Six-Day War there were renewed anti-Semitic purges in Poland which led to further emigration and expulsions of the Jewish population. Film-maker Aleksander Ford, whose film *Majdanek, Cemetery of Europe* had helped bring attention to Nazi crimes committed at the camp, and who had achieved prominence in the Polish film industry as the first director of Film Polski, began to encounter difficulties in realizing his projects and was accused of 'anti-Polish tendencies'. He was refused a visa to the USA and in 1969 emigrated to Israel.[64]

In Israel, the Six-Day War had its own effect on the memory of the European Jews. The war is frequently cited as one of the 'triggers' which brought back the memory of the extermination of European Jewry into public consciousness, as a reminder of the threat of annihilation. Finkelstein argues that this doesn't wholly make sense, as the 1948 war, in which the fledgling state had fought off an invasion from neighbouring states, had posed more of a threat to Israel than the 1967 war. The new interest in the extermination of European Jewry, he argues, was more to do with the USA's incorporation of Israel as a strategic asset in the Middle East.[65] Remembrance of the Holocaust could be used to raise fears of a new threat to annihilate the Jewish people and to justify the massive supply of arms to Israel. According to Peter Novick, 'for many years' it was official Israeli policy that diplomatic visitors to Israel first be taken on a tour of Yad Vashem.[66] When I visited in 2000 the story told in the 'historical museum' section began with photographs of humiliations and the ghettos of Poland and ended with a photograph of a group of people, including two men in what look like concentration camp uniforms, holding an Israeli flag. The text above the photograph reads, 'May 14 1948 Israel Independent'.

There had, however, been other 'triggers' before the Six-Day War, notably the Civil Rights movement in the USA, which raised the consciousness and confidence of ethnic minorities, as well as the trial of Adolf Eichmann in 1961 and his execution in May 1962. On 24 May 1960 Israeli Prime Minister David Ben-Gurion announced that Adolf Eichmann, former chief of the Department for Jewish Affairs in the Gestapo and main organizer of the Wannsee Conference of January 1942 which focused on issues related to the 'final solution of the Jewish question', would be tried in Israel for his crimes against the Jewish people. Eichmann was abducted in Argentina by Israeli agents. It was known to many that any number of senior Nazis had been living freely in Latin America, and indeed in Germany, for years so why Ben-Gurion chose to hunt down Eichmann at this time was something of a mystery. But it was the first time that the Holocaust had been represented as a distinct phenomenon in the Second World War, and the trial marked the beginning of a popular awareness of the extermination of European Jewry, not only in Israel but throughout the world. Throughout the trial Eichmann occupied world headlines and the image of him with his glasses and headphones on his bald head in the bullet-proof witness box became firmly entrenched in the memory of the Western world. The term 'Holocaust', first used in 1957 in the *Yad Vashem Bulletin* to refer to the extermination of the Jews, began to be used more frequently, even though, according to Jick, its use was still limited. When Raul Hilberg's book *The Destruction of the European Jews* was published in 1961, he was not apparently aware of the term and did not use it. In 1968 the Library of Congress in Washington, DC created a new major entry card, 'Holocaust-Jewish, 1939–1945'.[67]

Coinciding with the passing of Eichmann's death sentence in December 1961, an American film, *Judgment at Nuremberg*, based on the trials of leading Nazis, premièred in Berlin. It received an 'unprecedented volume of publicity', with 200 European and American journalists flown in as guests of United Artists.[68] The film, produced and directed by Stanley Kramer and featuring such stars as

Spencer Tracy, Burt Lancaster, Marlene Dietrich, Richard Widmark and Judy Garland, is a courtroom melodrama in which footage taken at the liberation of Dachau, Buchenwald and Bergen-Belsen is shown as prosecution evidence. Only once is the murder of 6 million Jews formally acknowledged; otherwise Jewish suffering is passed over. Much hangs on a fictionalized version of a *cause célèbre* in which an elderly Jew had been executed for his friendship with a German teenage girl. As Judith E. Doneson points out in her book *The Holocaust in American Film*, all its sympathy is for the girl: 'The viewer may believe this film is about the Holocaust ... but the Jew has been removed from his own history to become a prop for suffering Germans.'[69]

Judgment at Nuremberg is a film of some political and philosophical depth. Not only were Nazi war criminals on trial, it is argued in the course of the film, along with the German people, but also those countries, notably Britain and the USA, whose appeasement policies had allowed the Third Reich to build its apparatus of repression. But the film's resolution places responsibility firmly on the individual – particularly, in this case, on a liberal judge who collaborated with Nazi 'justice'. This conclusion led Doneson to criticize *Judgment at Nuremberg* for setting up America as 'the exemplar and guardian of justice ... America teaches Germany and the rest of the world a lesson in democracy'. But as Doneson acknowledges, the film is not quite as straightforward as that, for when pressure is applied to the tribunal by the US military to be lenient with the defendants in the interest of Cold War expediency, it is sharply rebuffed.[70]

The Inadmissible Past

Although Americans may have been replaying images of the concentration camps to teach the world a lesson in liberal democracy, they were at least showing them. In Britain there was resistance to dragging up the Nazi past and showing atrocity images. In February 1960, former Buchenwald prisoner Maurice Bolle was busy promoting a Belgian exhibition, 'Life in the Concentration Camps', organized by two groups of camp survivors, Fraternelles des Amicales des Camps (the Brotherhood of Friends of the Camps) and the Belgian National Confederation of Political Prisoners and their Dependants.[71] The success of the exhibition in Belgium prompted Bolle, president of the exhibition committee, to propose that the British city of Coventry host the exhibition. Coventry, a centre of the motor and engineering industries, had suffered severe bombing during the war, and it was thought that its population would better understand the suffering of others.[72] To the organizers the message of the exhibition was clear – 'forgive, but do not forget'. According to Dr Walter Deveen, the national president of Fraternelles des Amicales des Camps, the intention was not to foster hate or stir up bitterness but to show 'objective facts' to younger people so to 'avoid in the future the repetition of the past'. Deveen said the exhibition was all the more important in the light of what he referred to as 'a revival of racism'.[73]

On 3 May 1960 Coventry City Council officially agreed to stage the exhibition in June the following year, but from the outset the church authorities in Coventry were vehemently opposed to it. Throughout May and June 1961 angry letters and articles appeared in the local and national press condemning the exhibition, inspired, not least, by the Provost of Coventry the Very Reverend Harry C. N. Williams. An article by the Provost in the *Coventry Evening Telegraph* on 1 May was headlined, 'Message of Hate Does Not Belong to the City: CHRISTIANS SHOULD BOYCOTT THIS EXHIBITION.' It stated: 'To attempt to justify this exhibition on the grounds that to remember these horrible events will ensure that they do not happen again, is the reverse of the truth.'[74] The following day, in an article in *The Times* headlined, 'AN EXHIBITION OF BITTERNESS', the Provost wrote that 'the aims of the exhibition were diametrically opposed to the Cathedral's policy of fostering peace and international reconciliation'.[75] The Reverend E. Lincoln Minshull of Coventry Methodist Central Hall joined in the debate in support of the Provost, suggesting that to remind Germany of the 'sins of their predecessors' would do no good and 'could cause hatred, suspicion and resentment that may militate against the international friendship we are trying to build up. I cannot see that one can forgive without making some attempt to forget.'[76] In the May edition of *Coventry Cathedral Review*, the Provost warned the public against seeing the exhibition, particularly the young, and concluded by asking that 'no sincere Christian person in Coventry will give any support to this disruptive voice which looks to the past, or to any other voices like it, but will support the vision of Hope for all men, which seeks to reconcile all human divisions by our dependence upon the forgiveness and mercy of God'.[77]

Despite the Provost's fine words, he and the church authorities were strangely quiet about the hostility shown towards the exhibition by the British National Party (BNP), led by Coventry school teacher Colin Jordan, Britain's leading fascist in the 1960s. The day before the exhibition opened, the Lord Mayor of Coventry, Alderman William Callow, received an anonymous telephone call from a man who was reported to have said: 'If you and your stinking Jewish friends open this exhibition you and your family will suffer.' The message ended with the words, 'friends of Eichmann; Zieg Eichmann'.[78] Despite the large amount of national press coverage this incident received, the church made no comment and the mayor dismissed the caller as a 'crank'. Nor was there public condemnation when the BNP plastered graffiti and anti-Semitic posters on the walls and doors of St Mary's Hall where the exhibition was to be held. In fact, rather than being concerned by the neo-fascist activities of the BNP, in some quarters there seemed to be more concern about whether the exhibition

50·Former concentration camp prisoners arriving at the opening ceremony of the exhibition 'Life in the Concentration Camps', at St Mary's Hall, Coventry, June 1961. They are bearing banners of the various camps. (Dr Hélène Mair)

was aligned with left-wing groups. A few days before the exhibition was due to open, 'a minor storm' apparently broke out at Coventry City Council when Councillor Mrs Stoneman asked whether a 'Left-wing section' was sponsoring it.[79] The Provost had mentioned the Soviet Union in the *Coventry Cathedral Review* when he sardonically asked 'whether the existing concentration camps beyond the Iron Curtain figure in this exhibition'.[80]

Despite the controversy, the exhibition went ahead. The exhibits included arte-facts and atrocity photographs from the main concentration camps. In the press, terminology similar to that used in 1945 was used again to describe those in the photographs – the *Coventry Evening Telegraph* referred to the 'piles of bodies or living camp inmates who resemble walking skeletons'[81] – but in contrast to 1945, none of these was published in the press. There were photographs of the open-ing ceremony: the Lord Mayor delivering his speech and concentration camp survivors carrying banners of the various camps (see Figure 50). In spite of the bad press, and the fact that the teachers' panel of the council's joint consultation committee followed the Provost's advice and voted unanimously against the organization of school parties to visit the exhibition, approximately 8,000 people attended.[82] The organizers had intended that the exhibition should travel to ten other venues in Britain, but due to lack of support and funds its only other show-ing was at Houldsworth Hall in Manchester in March 1962, where Canon Hedley Hodkin said the exhibition administered to 'sadism and morbid curiosity'.[83]

Constructing the Post-war Memory

At both the Coventry and Manchester exhibitions, Alan Resnais's film *Nuit et Brouillard* was shown. Although it included footage of people in the ghettos wearing the yellow star, it did not mention Jews by name. The film combined contemporary colour images of Auschwitz-Birkenau with black and white newsreel footage of the liberation of the western camps in 1945. But when, on 2 February 1960, Gala Film Distributors received certification for *Nuit et Brouillard* from the British Board of Film Classification (BBFC) a number of shots which showed naked women, burned or charred bodies or piles of corpses were removed. It wasn't until 1990 that the film was again submitted to the BBFC, for release on video. This time it was passed in its entirety.[84] By then the world order had changed again and the horrors of the Nazi concentration camps had become an 'acceptable' part of the history of the Second World War.

Nuit et Brouillard was not the only film about Nazi Germany subjected to censorship. In the late 1950s a number of films were made about former high-ranking Nazi officials living freely in West Germany, but the fact they were East German productions made them suspect in the eyes of the British authorities. Stanley Forman of Plato Films (later to become Educational & Television Films Ltd, ETV), who was largely responsible for securing their release in Britain, came under fire from the authorities on a number of occasions. In 1959, according to Forman, the BBFC refused a certificate to a film which showed the appalling conditions in the Warsaw ghetto. The 20-minute two-reel silent film, apparently commissioned by Göbbels, had been found by the Soviet army in the Reich archives when they liberated Eastern Germany. It was later deposited in the East German State Archive. In the early 1950s East German film-makers Annelie and Andrew Thorndike discovered it 'in a puddle of water on the archive floor'.[85] They restored it as best they could and used some of the footage in their film *Du und mancher Kamerad* (The German Story, 1956). In 1959 the first copy of the Warsaw ghetto film to reach Britain was brought in by Stanley Forman. It showed some of the worst evidence of Nazi crimes that he had seen. For this reason, he told me, he had intended to show it as a part of his defence in a libel action sparked off by the controversy surrounding two other Thorndike films, *Urlaub auf Sylt* (Holiday on Sylt, 1957) about former SS officer Heinz Reinefarth who had played a leading role in the crushing of the Warsaw Ghetto Uprising and who was currently the Christian Democrat Mayor of the North Sea island of Sylt, and *Operation Teutonic Sword* (1958), which revealed the Nazi past of General Speidel who was a commander of NATO Allied Land Forces in Europe from April 1957 to September 1963. For various reasons the court case did not materialize.[86] The BBFC's decision not to certify the Warsaw ghetto film made it impossible for Forman to show it commercially. According to Forman, ITV, the British commercial television network which had tentatively agreed to broadcast it, withdrew its offer under pressure from the Foreign Office. In 1960 it had a limited run in the Compton Cinema in Soho, London, but received little press coverage.[87] The fact was that any film which levelled criticism at West Germany and which came from communist-controlled countries was viewed with suspicion. Thirty years later in a different political climate, this Nazi footage from the Warsaw ghetto became one of the most widely shown films in Holocaust museums and exhibitions throughout the world.

In the same year as the Warsaw ghetto film was refused a certificate, the BBFC also failed to certify *Action J*, another East German film submitted by Plato Films. The documentary was a revealing portrait of Dr Hans Globke who, under the Nazi regime, had served as a top official in the Office for Jewish Affairs in the Ministry of the Interior and had been 'a key administrator' in the Final Solution, working directly with Adolf Eichmann. At the time the film was made, Globke was serving as Secretary of State in Chancellor Konrad Adenauer's government.[88] *Action J* dealt almost exclusively with the Jewish question and used a compilation of Nazi photographs, including those of the partially clothed women taken at Liepaja, photographs from the Lili Jacob album and the liberations of Majdanek and film footage from both the *Chronicle of the Liberation of Auschwitz*, and the Nazi film of the Warsaw ghetto. According to the *Jewish Echo*, the BBFC said about *Action J*: 'The film appears to have been made for the purpose of damaging the reputation of an individual and for these reasons the Board takes the view that it would not be in the public interest to show the film commercially.'[89]

Sections of the Nazi film of the Warsaw ghetto emerged again in 1961, this time as stills in an exhibition, 'The Life and Death of the Warsaw Ghetto' which opened in July at the Herbert Samuel Hall in Bayswater, London. The aim of the exhibition was to 'depict the fate of the Jews in Poland under the Nazis' and was timed to take advantage of the 'Eichmann trial atmosphere'.[90] It was organized by five sponsors: the World Jewish Congress (British Section), the Polish Jewish Ex-Servicemen's Association, the Board of Deputies of British Jews, the Association of Jewish Ex-Servicemen and the Memorial Committee, which included Stanley Forman of Plato Films. The exhibition included paintings, 'relics' and around sixty photographs of 'Jews being marched to their death, Jews branded, Jews starving, Jews before the firing squad'.[91] The organizers also considered it important that 'exhibits' be acquired from the Jewish Historical Museum in Warsaw. Yet the Polish embassy would apparently allow them to be released only if a number of conditions were met: that the exhibition should make reference to non-Jewish Polish victims and that acknowledgement should be given to the assistance of the non-Jewish Polish underground. These points were accepted by the organizations involved.

51 · Front cover of
the catalogue for the
'Warsaw Ghetto'
exhibition which
opened in London in
July 1961. (Wiener
Library, London)

In June 1962 the exhibition moved to a second venue at Hackney Town Hall, although by that time the Board of Deputies were beginning to distrust the Memorial Committee, which they said was 'an extreme left-wing group' which incorporated 'remnants of the Jewish section of the Communist Party'. They suspected that they were using their association with the board as a 'respectable' front and the exhibition as a way to 'collect funds for their own political ends'.[92]

Despite the Board of Deputies' mistrust of the Memorial Committee, the exhibition was considered a success and even drew positive remarks from the church authorities. The Bishop of Southwark, Mervyn Stockwood, made none of the damning allegations about 'The Life and Death of the Warsaw Ghetto' that the Provost had about the Coventry exhibition. In fact, he took quite the opposite view and said: 'By giving us an accurate account of what happened, it should inspire us to work more thoughtfully and energetically for a way of life which will enable people of all nations and colours to live together in harmony and peace.'[93]

There were no doubt several reasons for this changed viewpoint, but one fundamental difference between the two exhibitions seems to have been that while one mourned victims the other celebrated heroes. Throughout the 1950s, particularly in the USA, there was a general unease about promoting the Jewish-victim image which produced feelings of 'pity mixed with contempt'. During this period the World Jewish Congress had encouraged Jewish groups world-wide to commemorate the Warsaw Ghetto Uprising as the prime act of resistance shown by the Jews.[94] This stance was notably similar to that of the Zionists in Israel. 'The Life and Death of the Warsaw Ghetto' placed emphasis on the heroism and martyrdom of the ghetto fighters, whereas 'Life in the Concentration Camps' explicitly focused on the evils of Nazi crimes, which was not only at odds with government policy towards West Germany but, more importantly, represented the Jews primarily as victims. This was a crucial difference. The heroic image used on the exhibition leaflet (Figure 51) of a raised arm with the star of David holding a gun, is in stark contrast to the press picture of the solemn elderly camp survivors taken at the opening ceremony of the Coventry exhibition in Figure 50. The former image also echoes the style used in the Eastern Bloc countries where, in portrayals of the Second World War, heroism and martyrdom were pivotal. For example, in 1963 the Polish film *Requiem for 500,000*, made by Jerzy Bossak, who filmed at the liberation of Majdanek, and Wacław Kaźmierczak, remembered the Jews in the context of the resistance. The opening of the film states: 'In memory of the Polish Jews, murdered by the Nazis, in memory of the Polish underground Fighters, who fell trying to save them.'[95]

Exhibitions also celebrated resistance. In the 1960s at Auschwitz State Museum some displays emphasized resistance over defeat, as did the permanent exhibition, 'The Martyrdom, Struggle and Destruction of the Jews 1933–1945', which opened at the camp on the anniversary of the Warsaw Ghetto Uprising in 1968.[96] In 1963 New York hosted an exhibition called 'Life, Struggle and Uprising in the Warsaw Ghetto'.[97] The ironic fact was that, during the Cold War, the Warsaw Ghetto Uprising became a symbolic event for both East and West, albeit for different political reasons. No nation wanted victims but everyone wanted heroes, a point exemplified by the large number of books and pamphlets published about the ghetto fighters on both sides of the Iron Curtain.[98]

Apart from these commemorations of the Warsaw Ghetto Uprising, there were to be no more displays of Nazi atrocity photographs in the West for two decades. Only when, as communism crumbled and the world order began to change again, did the murder of the 6 million Jews in the Western world, by then unambiguously referred to as the Holocaust, become of prime importance. The Jewish question, which Western nations had colluded in suppressing for thirty years, would become central to memories of the Second World War and, crucially, its representation would shift from one of heroes to that of victims.

EIGHT

Commercializing the Holocaust: 'There's No Business Like Shoah Business'

Establishing a Holocaust Memory

By the early 1980s the commemoration of the Holocaust as a uniquely Jewish event was gaining momentum in the Western democracies. The winding down of the Cold War had a decided influence on the way the new Holocaust memory was constructed. With the decline of communist power, the USA needed a new symbolic evil to affirm the values of liberal democracy and the spectre of Nazism was temporarily revived. In 1982, the USA revised its visa form for foreign applicants. Instead of asking if the applicants had ever been members of a Communist Party, as it had done since 1952, a new question was added: 'Were you involved, in any way, in persecutions associated with Nazi Germany or its allies?'[1]

Images of Nazi atrocities were widely displayed to shock the public once again. In addition to images of the camps liberated by the Western allies, now there were images of Auschwitz-Birkenau, notably those from the Lili Jacob album, together with atrocity pictures taken by Nazis and collaborators and ghetto photographs taken by Jews and members of the German armed forces.

In the USA, museums, memorials, exhibitions and 'Holocaust Centres', and university courses on the Holocaust mushroomed into what Norman G. Finkelstein later referred to as the 'Holocaust Industry'. This 'industry' relied heavily on pictures, and displays were mounted in Holocaust memorial centres. The Holocaust gripped the American imagination and became presented, as Peter Novick points out, as 'not just a Jewish memory but an American memory'.[2] So popular did it become in the USA that there was concern among some that its representation was having a detrimental effect on the memory of the Jews. In an article written in 1981, author Leon A. Jick expressed concern that students who knew nothing else about Jewish culture and history, learned only about the Holocaust: 'Their knowledge of the Jewish experience is limited to victimisation – how Jews died.'[3] But the representation of the Jew as victim may not have been a phenomenon specifically related to the Holocaust. Simon Louvish argues that 'the cult of victimhood' is part of a wider American discourse, that is, a 'politically correct' idea that sees 'everyone as a survivor of some real or imagined trauma'.[4]

In 1981 author Robert Alter suggested that 'serious distortions' of the Holocaust and 'Jewish life' were occurring as a result of the Holocaust being 'commercialized, politicized, theologized, or academicized'. He criticized a 'multi-screen, multi-channel sound, audio visual experience of the Holocaust' at the Wiesenthal Center in Los Angeles, which had been established in 1977, and wondered whether this ' "experience" to sell to the millions' showed an 'abysmal lack of faith in the human imagination to reconstruct the nature of evil from the printed page or even from the photographed image ... The ultimate aim is not to ponder or remember or understand the Holocaust but to simulate it.'[5] Jick agreed. The 'devastating barb', he wrote, ' "There's no business like *Shoah* business", has became a recognizable truth.'[6]

The first major media representation of the Holocaust was a 1978 American NBC television series called *Holocaust*, watched by millions of television viewers around the world. For many, it was the first time they had been confronted with the idea that millions of Jews had been murdered by the Nazis. As the London *Evening Standard* pointed out, 'Americans brought into the open a question which has been virtually taboo for 40 years'.[7] An NBC survey conducted among a group of high-school students in Washington, DC, before the programme was broadcast, proved how neglected the Holocaust had been. When they were asked what the Holocaust was, the majority apparently thought it was 'a Jewish holiday'.[8] In the USA, the seven-and-a-half-hour dramatization of Gerald Green's novel *Holocaust* was an astounding success. It won eight Emmy Awards and was the second most popular series NBC had ever produced, with more than half of all Americans, 120 million people, watching part or all of the series.[9] NBC's most popular TV series had been *Roots*, which just a year earlier had tapped into the increasing awareness of ethnicity in the USA, growing out of the Civil Rights movement. This consciousness was a factor in the 'coming out' of the Holocaust. But the programme had its critics.

The series *Holocaust* begins in Berlin in 1935 and tells the story of the German-Jewish family Weiss and their fight for survival throughout the war years. The opening scene is of the wedding of Karl Weiss to a German called Inga (played by Meryl Streep), some of whose family are supporters of National Socialism. By 1945, only Inga and Karl's younger brother Rudi have survived. Many press reviews were scathing about the use of inaccurate historical data and the trivialization of the Jewish tragedy. In Britain the programme was referred to as 'typical Hollywood' or 'schmaltz'.[10] In one scene, after Karl Weiss has been arrested and interned in Buchenwald, Inga is filmed merrily walking down a country lane on her way to the camp to visit her husband and bargain for his freedom. Outside the camp entrance is a large sign reading 'Buchenwald'. The guards do not seem to notice Inga, who pauses to look through the barbed-wire fence at healthy-looking prisoners, dressed in clean, neat camp uniforms, unconvincingly pulling carts laden with stones through lush green grass. She tells the guards she has come to see a relative who is a camp official, and they let her in.

The London *Daily Express* said that the fictional representation of Buchenwald concentration camp looked 'almost out of "Ideal Homes"', and a review in the *Sunday Times* worried that the inmates looked so 'well-fed and well dressed' that neo-Nazis might reproduce the images in propaganda leaflets to show how 'decent conditions were' in this and other Nazi camps.[11] Certainly the images of the prisoners at Buchenwald are reminiscent of the propaganda photographs taken at the Dora-Mittelbau factory by Walter Frentz, Göring's official photographer, which show prisoners occupied with their work dressed in neat uniforms.[12] At points in the series compilations of historical photographs are shown to the Nazi hierarchy, as proof that their policies are being carried out, a neat device for introducing the historical evidence. But more often than not the images are used wrongly. The first image, incorrectly used to introduce the round-ups in Poland in 1939, is from the Lili Jacob album and shows an old woman with three children walking towards the gas-chamber at Birkenau; this picture is discussed at length in Chapter 10. Other images used in a haphazard way include scenes of harassment, hangings, the execution at Bochnia in December 1939, the half-naked women at the execution site at Liepaja, the naked women before their execution at Mizocz and pictures taken by the Sonderkommando at Birkenau.

The series had political repercussions. For some American and Israeli Jews it confirmed the need for a more secure Israeli state. In the USA the Israeli-American Public Affairs Committee sent free copies of the novel to all members of the Washington press corps, suggesting that the extermination of 6 million Jews 'underscores Israel's concerns for security without reliance on outside guaran-tees'.[13] When the same committee was lobbying against the sale of American aircraft to Saudi Arabia, it sent copies of *Holocaust* to every Congress member.[14] Some viewers in Israel, according to the *Jerusalem Post*, suggested that there were two lessons to be learnt from the programme: that '"all Jews must live in Israel, and that Prime Minister Begin mustn't give up an inch of territory" in any peace agreement'.[15] Conversely, an article in *Free Palestine* chose to point out that the horrors shown in the film were not dissimilar to those being inflicted on the Arab population of Israel and that the film did not acknowledge that other peoples had also suffered during the Second World War.[16]

In Europe the political reverberations were no less serious. Initially the intention had been to film in Eastern Bloc countries but permission had been withdrawn due to 'Zionist' elements in the script.[17] As a result the film was shot in Germany and Austria, with Mauthausen used as the concentration camp location. In West Germany, *Holocaust* was shown despite opposition from newspaper and television officials. One critic thought it a 'commercial concoction' and therefore 'unsuitable to adequately commemorate victims'. And Helmut Lamprecht, an official at Radio Bremen, said that instead of broadcasting *Holocaust*, the network should be giving extensive coverage of the Majdanek war crimes trials that had been underway in Dusseldorf for three years.[18] According to the *Spectator*, in France, the last non-Arab, non-communist country to show the series, the authorities were nervous and the decision finally to screen it 'was the result of something approaching a domestic scandal'. The official reason against screening it, the magazine reported, was that 'it would stir up anti-German feelings and thus provide grist for the Communist and Gaullist propaganda mills'. But the real reason, the article claimed, was that it would 'sharpen interest among the new generation as to the role played by the Vichy government … as accomplices in the implementation of the "final solution"'.[19]

In Britain, the National Yad Vashem Committee (NYVC), formed in 1977 under the auspices of the Board of Deputies at the request of the Jerusalem Yad Vashem authorities, was enthusiastic about the film. It hoped that it might give a boost to popularizing knowledge of the Holocaust.[20] In the late 1970s Yad Vashem had been concerned about a lack of interest in the Holocaust. There had been 'a serious fall off in visitors to the memorial' in Jerusalem and a 'slow down' in completing the recording of the names of the victims. One of the 'primary aims' of the NYVC was to establish a 'permanent exhibition' in London which would show 'events of 1933–48 and their context within European Jewish History'.[21] In 1977 it was suggested that the Imperial War Museum be approached 'about having a small section … devoted to the Holocaust'.[22] That idea was shelved. In 1980 the Roundhouse in London was under serious consideration as a suitable site, though by 1983 that plan too had been dropped due to lack of funds.[23] It was not until 2000 that a permanent Holocaust exhibition was established in Britain at the Imperial War Museum.

As plans for a permanent exhibition were stalled, in 1981 an opportunity arose to adapt an exhibition, curated by Teresa Świebocka, from the Auschwitz-Birkenau State Museum. The NYVC showed a great deal of interest in what it called the 'Auschwitz exhibition' which had been brought to Britain by the 'Auschwitz Initiative Group' (which NYVC noted was a Christian group). It consisted of '130 associated items, drawings and paintings, possessions of camp victims, including suitcases and shoes, and sew-on Stars of David' and photographs including a few from the collection of the 2,500 family photographs (referred to in Chapter 5) which had been returned to Auschwitz in 1958 in a suitcase. The committee saw it as 'a basis for a very effective mobile exhibition' but there was one problem: its emphasis was not sufficiently Jewish. The committee realized that 'a great deal of work would have to be done in order to mount the exhibition in a proper manner and give a specifically Jewish, as compared with Polish, emphasis to it'.[24]

In September 1981, members of the committee with the leading Holocaust historian Martin Gilbert went to see the exhibition while it was being assembled by a designer in Birmingham. Gilbert suggested six additions: pre-war Jewish life in Poland, pre-war anti-Jewish acts, deportation to Auschwitz, Jews in the camps, Jewish resistance and the scale of the Jewish tragedy. By January 1982 the committee had taken the decision to 'adopt' the modified exhibition as a part of their educational programme, so that it would 'clearly display the Jewish aspect of the camp and the Jewish Holocaust as a whole'.[25] From the outset, the NYVC frequently stressed that the exhibition should be promoted as a 'Christian initiative' rather than a Jewish one, and that the committee itself should keep 'a low profile'. As a result a new committee was formed with its own charitable status, 'which had the merit of appearing to give Christian groups and organizations the credit for the initiative and promotion of the exhibition'. This arrangement gave the Jewish community 'an assurance that the exhibition would specifically demonstrate that Auschwitz was in the main a Jewish tragedy'.[26] But there were some who were not entirely convinced of this version of history. One committee member reported back to the NYVC that 'it was only after hours of argument' that a teachers' committee in east London had been convinced of the 'special importance of the Jewish aspect of the Holocaust'.[27] To promote the exhibition, and attempt to overcome any difficulties, it was suggested that NYVC committee members should 'feel obliged' to buy between ten and a hundred copies of Martin Gilbert's *Atlas of the Holocaust* so that they could be distributed free to 'young people, students, libraries etc.'.[28]

The NYVC version of the Auschwitz exhibition opened on 23 February 1983 at the Church of St George in the East End of London, under the auspices of the Bishop of Stepney, the Right Reverend Jim Thompson.[29] NYVC minutes noted that Martin Gilbert gave a forty-minute lecture in which 'he touched on the suffering of the Gypsies, Poles and other non-Jewish victims, but made it clear that the Holocaust was a uniquely Jewish event'.[30] The exhibition was a success, and other 'non-Jewish' venues in Britain were sought. But by the time it was due to open at a venue in Newcastle, in 1984, the NYVC was no longer associated with it. The Polish embassy had made 'last minute demands for textual alterations', which although 'unsatisfactory', had been accepted by the organizers. The result was that the committee had disassociated itself from the project.[31] However, in 1984 any plans for future showings were quashed when a fire broke out at the warehouse in Birmingham where the exhibition was being stored and original documents, paintings and some suitcases of former prisoners were destroyed. The fire was thought to be the work of fascist groups.[32]

The London exhibition, however, had had 'permanent' benefits. By 1984 the Inner London Education Authority was instructing teachers on how to teach the Holocaust and producing video tapes which were being widely distributed through the country.[33]

In the same year, as the fortieth anniversary of the liberation of the camps drew near, the film which Sidney Bernstein had been working on in 1945 resurfaced. An NYVC committee member who went to see the film reels at the Imperial War Museum said that they had 'disclosed horror worse than anything he had seen before'. The NYVC requested a copy of the film. According to a committee report, the Imperial War Museum was not prepared to arrange for the film to be publicly shown but would make the film available for 'copying and editing' at the NYVC's expense.[34] The NYVC and the Board of Deputies agreed on a 'limited showing' for their members, of what they referred to as the 'Hitchcock film about the Holocaust' and hoped that it might be widely shown for the fortieth anniversary of the liberation of the camps.

That year another film stole the limelight: Claude Lanzmann's marathon project *Shoah*. This much acclaimed and much criticized nine-and-a-half-hour film consists of interviews with perpetrators, survivors and witnesses of the Holocaust. Although *Shoah* has been called documentary, Lanzmann has been quoted as saying: 'My film is absolutely not documentary; the scenes were selected solely on the basis of their artistic merit.'[35] There were no atrocity images in this film. Instead Lanzmann uses harrowing and penetrating interviews cut with repetitive silent eerie and desolate images of contemporary Poland. Recurrent images of steam trains cutting through the landscape, pulling in and pulling out of depots and close-ups of rail tracks are juxtaposed with a hand-held camera probing the sites of the former death camps. In a repeatedly used shot, the camera moves slowly in and out of the gateway of the watchtower at Birkenau, the bleakness of the camp accentuated by its snow-covered landscape. Sometimes these images have no accompanying sound, other times an interviewee tells a chilling story in voiceover. One death camp survivor, Abraham Bomba, recalls how he was ordered by the Nazis to cut women's hair in the gas-chambers of Treblinka immediately before they were gassed. Lanzmann films Bomba telling the entire story while cutting a customer's hair in a busy barber's shop in Israel. As he recounts the occasion when he was faced with having to cut the hair of women he knew from his home town of Częstochowa, he breaks down.

Commercializing the Holocaust   177

Lanzmann uses the moment to move the camera to a close-up of his face. 'It's too horrible,' said Bomba. 'You must go on,' insists Lanzmann.

A recurring theme in *Shoah* is that the Poles were complicit in the extermination of the Jews. During carefully manipulated interviews with Polish peasants, he elicits answers which make them seem less than remorseful about the Jewish tragedy. During a presentation of the film at the Institute for Polish-Jewish Studies, according to Stefan Nowicki who was present, Lanzmann apparently infuriated some Poles when he said that if anyone had survived Auschwitz it was at the expense of those Jews who had died. Nowicki, himself angry at the comments, pointed out that no mention was given to the French Gendarmes and the Dutch police who rounded up and deported the Jews to the camps.[36] In *Shoah* Lanzmann also interviews former Polish underground courier Jan Karski who begins by saying, 'I will now go back thirty-five years', then abruptly adds, 'No I do not go back', and leaves the frame, distressed. The camera stays on the empty chair and then follows him back into the room as he returns to continue his story. According to Karski's biographers E. Thomas Wood and Stanisław M. Jankowski, Lanzmann spent eight hours interviewing Karski at his home. When the final cut was made the only topic covered was Karski's meeting with the Jewish leaders and what he had witnessed in the Warsaw ghetto. There was no account of his efforts to alert the world to the Jewish catastrophe, efforts for which he risked his life. Karski was not bitter about this. He supported the film, but hoped that another film would be made, 'equally great, equally truthful', to present 'a second reality of the Holocaust ... not in order to contradict that which *Shoah* shows but to complement it'.[37]

Such a film might have told the same story as the exhibition 'Polish Help for the Jews (1939–45) Documents' curated by the Polish Underground Movement (1939–45) Study Trust and Polish Institute and Sikorski Museum in London. It was assembled in 1988, possibly in response to *Shoah*, but publicly to celebrate the forty-fifth anniversary of the 'heroic and tragic Uprising of the Warsaw Ghetto'. Its aim was to show that 'The Polish Secret State' and the 'Polish Government in London' had 'tried to alert' the world to the 'terrible truth of the HOLOCAUST' and that 'the Poles did what was humanly possible under the conditions of the German terror in Poland'.[38]

Making the Holocaust 'Real'

Throughout the 1980s and 1990s, increasing public consciousness about the Holocaust – as a unique Jewish tragedy – had paved the way for the opening in 1993 of the world's largest Holocaust memorial, the multi-million-dollar US Holocaust Memorial Museum in Washington, DC. President Jimmy Carter had set the wheels in motion for the museum through a commission to establish a national memorial 'to the six million who were killed in the Holocaust'. It is now widely accepted, writes Peter Novick, that the memorial was 'an attempt to placate American Jews, who were increasingly alienated by what they saw as the President's "excessive evenhandedness" in dealing with Israelis and Palestinians'.[39]

In less than a year more than one and a half million people had filed through the doors of the museum. From the outset its principal aim was to provide visitors with an experience they could identify with. In 1991 exhibition designer Ralph Appelbaum said of the museum: 'We're aiming to create an atmosphere where people will feel close to the events, therefore, barriers between the viewer and the viewed must be minimized.'[40] This was a device Philip Gourevitch later called a 'gimmick for audience participation in the Holocaust narrative'.[41] After visiting the exhibition, a fourteen-year-old wrote in the visitors' book: 'I think this museum is great. It makes you feel like you're there.'[42]

As visitors enter the museum the identification process begins. Everyone is issued with an ID card with a passport-sized photograph of 'a real person who lived during the Holocaust' or prematurely died in it, which can be kept as a souvenir. The person I unwittingly adopted was Eszter Mendel Braun. According to her card, she was born in 1903 to religious Jewish parents in the small town of Hidegkut in eastern Hungary. Each of the four pages of the identity card reveals a little more about her life and corresponds to the four floors of the exhibition. The final page, to be read at the last stage of the exhibition, reveals the fate of Eszter Braun: she was gassed with her youngest daughter, Aranka, on arrival at Auschwitz in May 1944.

As well as identifying with a real person, visitors are invited to associate with the real artefacts and experiences; the museum has collected around 50,000 artefacts since 1979. The fall of communism gave 'numerous opportunities' to acquire what was referred to as 'unique and critically important' Holocaust artefacts from Eastern Europe, allowing the Americans to re-create the Holocaust in their own back yard. An 'authentic German railcar ... which was used to transport thousands of Jews from the Warsaw Ghetto to their deaths in Treblinka' was the first artefact to be set in place; in fact, the five-storey museum was built around it. Other objects followed: the milk can in which historian Emmanuel Ringelblum placed the Warsaw ghetto archives, 'tattered concentration camp uniforms', 'toothbrushes, tea strainers, mirrors', 'the sleeve of a Gypsy woman's burgundy velvet jacket touching an array of shimmering jewelry', 'an accordion from Rumania', 'a wooden gypsy caravan from Czechoslovakia', 'the wrought iron gates of Tarnow cemetery', 'cobblestones from the Warsaw ghetto', 'the barracks from Birkenau' and 'a Majdanek Table – a special table for removing gold from corpses'. More than 5,000 items were chosen for display.[43] Visitors are encouraged to interact with these objects.[44]

Part of 'the experience' is the walk though the railcar. Visitors emerge to see a sign which reads 'WHO SHALL LIVE AND WHO SHALL DIE', surrounded by a selection of photographs from the Lili Jacob album. Among the people who squeezed through the railcar with me was a middle-aged man who commented that he now knew what it must have been like to be in a transport. Other visitors seemed enthralled with the idea that the railcar they had just passed through might be 'real'. Having 'experienced' the selection process, the crowds surge towards THE CONCENTRATION CAMP UNIVERSE and pass beneath the sign ARBEIT MACHT FREI ('Work gives freedom'), a replica of the gateway at Auschwitz, to see bunks taken from the barracks. Next a walk through an enormous photograph of the 'entrance at Birkenau' where there is a moment to pause and listen to taped stories of Auschwitz survivors.

Near the end of the exhibition, having seen thousands of photographs of humiliations, ghettos, deportations, executions and public hangings as well as pictures taken by the liberating armies, there is more. On three television screens, horrific images of dismembered bodies, corpses and 'medical experiments' unfold behind a 4-foot-high wall intended to dissuade young people from looking. The reverse happens. The 'peep show' tactics attract dense crowds, young and old, craning over each other to watch the spectacle. The crowd might groan, twitch or tut, but they still watch.[45]

Amid this macabre fantasy there is a history lesson, albeit an American one. The exhibition begins with the story of the American liberations which, as Gourevitch notes, serves 'as a means of orienting visitors who may have no knowledge whatever of history'.[46] In this history lesson the Americans are the heroes who liberated the Jews in the camps. The first image in the exhibition, over two metres high, shows a pile of twisted naked bodies at Ohrdruf concentration camp in Germany, liberated by the Americans in April 1945. On the same wall is projected a colour film of horrific scenes filmed at the liberation of Dachau, said to have been taken by Lieutenant Colonel George Stevens, 'one of America's leading film directors'. Even before visitors encounter these images, the voice of an American soldier transmitted through a speaker in the lift tells the captive audience: 'Things like this don't happen.' In one sentence, the extermination of European Jewry is separated from the events of the Second World War in which 40 million lost their lives. Ironically, photographs of the liberations, which in 1945 had been exhibited without mentioning the Jews, were now being used to centralize their tragedy. The Soviet Union, the nation without which the war could not have been won and whose army liberated the death camps, has been written out of the story. At the museum the first line of Martin Niemöller's frequently quoted confession written in the 1930s – 'First they came for the Communists, but I was not a Communist' – has been left out.[47] It may not be surprising that in a recent survey to establish the extent of the American public's knowledge of the Second World War, only 49 per cent knew that the Soviet Union was an ally. Additionally, a third 'either didn't know that the Holocaust took place during World War II or "knew" that it didn't'.[48]

By the mid-1990s the US Holocaust Memorial Museum had become the authoritative centre on the Holocaust, surpassing, in the view of some, that of Yad Vashem. Jeffrey Feldman, in his 1995 essay about the shifting aesthetic of Holocaust museums, suggests that since the US Holocaust Memorial Museum opened, both Yad Vashem and the Auschwitz-Birkenau State Museum have been struggling to keep up with its 'technological and epistemological innovations'. It is the increasing emphasis on artefacts to commemorate the Holocaust which, Feldman says, 'has catalysed a crisis of authority' at Yad Vashem, which had previously cultivated an 'archival-documentation model of historical evidence'. Feldman also further considers 'that this crisis of authority (at Yad Vashem) might signify the displacement of ideological capital with financial capital as the shaping force of Holocaust commemoration'.[49]

The Holocaust Tourists

The fall of communism made large-scale tourism and the commercialization of the Holocaust in Poland not only possible but desirable. Spurred on by *Holocaust* and *Shoah*, and by renewed interest in ethnicity and 'roots', increasing numbers of American and Israeli Jews were inspired to visit. In a volatile economy the Holocaust became a business opportunity. Jack Kugelmass describes it as a marriage between 'the Eastern European thirst for cash and the Jewish search for roots'.[50] In December 1993, the year the US Holocaust Memorial Museum opened, Steven Spielberg's blockbuster film *Schindler's List*, based on Thomas Keneally's novel *Schindler's Ark*, opened in the USA. The film has popularized the Holocaust more than any other single project, and the number of Holocaust tourists visiting Poland multiplied. An article by Jack Matthews in the *Guardian* reported that 'Spielberg has made sure that neither he nor the Holocaust will ever be thought of in the same way again'.[51]

Spielberg had first visited Kraków in early 1992 to look at 'authentic' places relating to the life of Sudeten German businessman Oskar Schindler, who moved to Kraków at the outbreak of the war to make money from the Nazi war machine. In the process Schindler saved more than 1,000 Jews by having them work in his enamelware factory. According to Franciszek Palowski, Spielberg's Polish guide during his first visit to Kraków, it took Spielberg only thirty-six hours to decide that he would make the film in Poland. There were a number of advantages to this location. Poland has a well developed film industry which could offer top-quality 'American standard' technicians and actors, with no union-regulated wages or demarcation, at a 40 per cent saving on Western costs.[52] In addition, the pre-war appearance of some parts of Kraków greatly impressed Spielberg. In an interview with Palowski, Spielberg said: 'I am looking at the town as if it were a stage. A stage we didn't have to build … We are using ready scenes, we are filming authentic places where events depicted in *Schindler's List* really happened. Cracow has presented us with its history and opened its history handbooks for us so that we could dance on their pages.'[53] Spielberg had offered Roman Polanski the director's chair on *Schindler's List*, but the renowned Polish-Jewish film-maker, a survivor of the Kraków ghetto, turned it down on the premise that 'it would be too close to him' – though ten years later he was to make his own, very different film about the suffering of the Jews in war-time Poland.[54]

With few Jews left in Poland to fill out the cast, Spielberg brought survivors and children of survivors from Israel. Spielberg mused on what he called their 'really great Eastern European Jewish faces'.[55] In many published interviews, he was keen to stress the discovery of his own Jewish roots (although his accounts about how that happened varied), which fitted perfectly with the American mood at the time. In one interview he confessed: 'I was so ashamed of being a Jew, and now I'm filled with pride. I don't even know when that transition happened.'[56] Not everything went according to plan, however. There was protest from the World Jewish Congress and the International Council for Christians and Jews over his plan to film, with 1,500 actors, at Birkenau, and to rebuild the crematoria chimneys demolished by the Nazis before they fled.[57] Consequently, the camp scenes were filmed outside Birkenau, and the train apparently steaming into the camp under the famous archway is in fact pulling out.

For many the details of history did not seem to matter. So successful was *Schindler's List* that some people seemed to believe that the film *was* the Holocaust and that Spielberg had just recorded it as it was. In the USA, the Jewish Federation Council of Los Angeles issued psychological guidelines, the *Viewer's Guide to Schindler's List*, to help viewers to cope with the experience of watching the film, which included the recommendation that consuming refreshments was not suitable.[58]

Spielberg exploited the reality angle of his film with some curious comments. In one interview he said, 'there were whole weeks when I wasn't really aware of the camera'.[59] In another he pondered on the cinema-vérité touches to his film: 'The worst mistake I could have made with this film was to have involved myself with some kind of style and drama that would have been antithetical to the presentation of the story.'[60] Preposterous as these declarations from a top Hollywood director renowned for his skill at emotional manipulation might have seemed, some appeared to be convinced. An article in *The Economist* stated: 'There is no striving for effect, no crude manipulation, no artificial drama. Mr

Spielberg just tells it how it was ... He lets the horror of history speak for itself.'[61] Spielberg is essentially a showman, but this film does have a political value, in its openly Zionist conclusion: the film goes from black and white to colour as the Schindler Jews walk literally into the Promised Land.

The fact that many imagined *Schindler's List* to be 'real' was to have serious consequences not only because it distorted historical fact but because of the way it affected the lives of individuals. In Kraków one woman reportedly approached Spielberg while he was filming and said that she was horrified to see 'Nazis' again on the streets, bringing back her own memories of the ghetto. To Spielberg this was what it was all about. 'They see the stars on the clothes and the armbands, and the costumes, and they go white. That's what it's all about. Creating an opportunity to remember. What is that famous line?' he said, 'Lest We Forget.'[62] A Polish female extra in the film objected to a scene where she was asked to shout abuse at the Jews on the premise that this was not how she remembered the occupation in Kraków to be. In 1994 a seventy-five-year-old Czech Jew, haunted by the death of her family in Auschwitz, committed suicide after watching the film.[63]

Some compared it to a documentary film. 'Schindler Jews', Richard and Lola Krumholtz, thought that the film should be nominated for an Oscar in the 'documentary' category.[64] Other reviews compared it to the revolutionary films of Sergei Eisenstein, or the Polish post-war realist films of Andrzej Wajda and Aleksander Ford. One article suggested that if the film stock had been grainier, and some scratches added, it could have passed for newsreel.[65] This was undoubtedly Spielberg's aim. Filming in black and white, often using a hand-held camera, he set out to exploit the audience's familiarity with black and white archival footage, documentaries and still photographs of the Holocaust. Reference was made not only to the melancholy images of Roman Vishniac – the film's director of photography Janusz Kamiński was inspired and influenced by Vishniac's photographs – but to Nazi films and photographs. Still images of Jews having their sidelocks cut surrounded by amused Nazis, of Jews made to shovel snow and of Jews carrying their belongings through the streets during the deportation from the ghettos, were re-enacted with precision. Spielberg gave to those static images movement, sound and emotion, and constructed a narrative around them; in other words, he filled the gaps previously left to the imagination. When we next see a photograph taken by the Nazis of Jews shovelling snow, we will no doubt think of the one-armed man in the film who was taken from the group and shot.

Spielberg pushed the reality angle further when he filmed a group of naked women with shaven heads packed tightly in what we, the audience, believe to be a gas-chamber. Even the Nazis, as far as we know, drew the line at filming in the gas-chambers.

The success of *Schindler's List* reverberated around Kraków and specifically the district of Kazimierz. Although in 1978 UNESCO listed Kazimierz as a World Heritage Site (as was Auschwitz-Birkenau in 1979), little attention had been paid to it until Spielberg came along. For the millions around the world who had come to believe that *Schindler's List* was the Holocaust, then Poland was where it happened. The picturesque city of Kraków and Auschwitz-Birkenau, approximately 50 kilometres away, became a winning combination, with Kazimierz a symbol of a Jewish past which has been destroyed, and Auschwitz a symbol of the forces responsible for that destruction.

Within weeks of the film opening, American tourists began to pour into Kraków in search of the movie sites. The *Jarden* Jewish bookshop and tourist agency in Szeroka Street in Kazimierz was inundated with tourists brandishing newspaper and magazine articles about the film, requesting assistance in locating the sites. But far from relying on the authenticity of his locations, Spielberg in fact manipulated them. Many assumed that Szeroka Street, a scenic square with an old synagogue and other buildings little changed since before the war, which featured in *Schindler's List* as the Kraków ghetto, was the real war-time ghetto. This was not the case. Spielberg no doubt chose Szeroka Street because it is picturesque, but in 1942 the Jewish residents were forcibly moved across the river Wisła to the actual ghetto in Podgórze. Today few tourists venture to this less photogenic suburb even though the *Pod Orłem* ('Under the Eagle') pharmacy, which stands on the corner of what had been the entrance to the ghetto, featured in *Schindler's List*. Now the premises is a small museum of ghetto photographs in memory of its former Polish owner Tadeusz Pankiewicz, who throughout the occupation gave assistance to the Jews in the ghetto.

Such was the demand to see the locations featured in Spielberg's film, that *Jarden* organized tours and by 1994 'The Schindler's List Tour' of Kraków was a part of the official city tourist programme. *What, Where, When*, the city's cultural guide, published a special pull-out supplement to the tour less concerned with historical events than with Spielberg's film locations. Where fiction meets fact is unclear. The guide lists the locations where memorable scenes from the film were filmed: the 'Jews Forced to Shovel Snow' scene, the 'Jewish Ghetto Liquidation' scene, the 'Little Girl in the Red Coat' scene and the 'Oskar and Ingrid Riding Horses' scene.[66] The tour simply gives more weight to the delusion that Spielberg had simply recorded the Holocaust as it was. The evidence of history has been replaced with the dramatization of history.

With the influx of tourists the city authorities made Kazimierz a priority for development. Throughout the 1990s Jewish cafés, restaurants, bookshops and exhibitions were opened, sometimes by non-Jewish Poles, to cash in on the new trade. In 1993, the Centre for Jewish Culture was established in Kazimierz. In 1997 the Isaac synagogue, dating back to the seventeenth century, opened its

52 · A poster advertising 'The Memory of Polish Jews' exhibition at the Isaac synagogue, Kraków, 2000. (Copyright Janina Struk)

doors to the public to promote Jewish history and culture, and two years later an exhibition of films and photographs entitled 'The Memory of Polish Jews' was displayed (see Figure 52). The compilation of films include *Kazimierz Krakowski* (Kazimierz in Kraków) made by American photographer and cameraman Julien Bryan during one of his trips to Europe in 1936, Nazi footage taken in the ghettos in Dąbrowa Górnicza, Będzin and Warsaw, and of the removal of Jews to the Kraków ghetto and subsequent deportations to the camps. The silent footage is accompanied by a melancholy adaptation of the music from *Schindler's List*. In an adjoining room a photographic exhibition has been made up entirely of stills from Nazi films. Almost all are portraits. Among them is the face of a young boy which is used as the poster image advertising the exhibition. His peaked cap covers one eye, the other eye looks warily to the camera. The photograph has a striking resemblance to the photograph of the young boy with his arms raised taken during the destruction of the Warsaw ghetto (see Figure 26). Who is he? Did he die in the ghetto, in the camps, or did he survive? It doesn't seem to matter; like the boy in the Warsaw ghetto his innocence has become a symbol of the destruction of the Polish Jews. But for the little more than a hundred Jews who still live in Kazimierz, the Jewish revival – a theme park representation of their past – has given them little more than an opportunity to appear as real-life exhibits for the passing tourists and their cameras.[67]

In 1939 the Jewish population of Kraków had included the family of the then six-year-old Roman Polanski, who through youthful ingenuity was to survive the Holocaust and become a film-maker. In early 2000 Polanski began his own film about the Holocaust, *The Pianist*, about which he said: 'I wanted to re-create my memories from childhood. It was also important for me to remain as close to reality as possible, and not make a film that was typically Hollywood.'[68] A film about the Holocaust by Polanski was long awaited and had been the subject of much speculation. When it came, it was not about Kraków but the Warsaw ghetto. Polanski had no problem raising the $41 million budget, reportedly the highest ever for a European movie.

The Pianist won the Palme D'Or at Cannes, Europe's most prestigious film festival, in 2002, and in 2003 won Polanski an Oscar for Best Director. It is based on Polish-Jewish musician Władysław Szpilman's book *The Pianist* (originally published as *Death of a City* in 1946), a dispassionate account of his struggle for survival in the Warsaw ghetto, and is faithful to the book in style and content. Szpilman's story, written shortly after the end of the war, is both a harrowing account of his life in the ghetto and in hiding in the ruins of Warsaw and a complex story about good Jews, bad Jews, good Poles, bad Poles, and not least a good Nazi, an officer who finally secures Szpilman's survival. In the first edition Szpilman was obliged to pretend that the good Nazi was an Austrian as, at the time, it was not acceptable to present a German officer as sympathetic and helpful.[69]

Szpilman's book was not translated and published outside Poland until the late 1990s and it was then that Polanski recognized it as, he said, 'the story I was seeking', through which he could portray what he called 'this painful chapter in Polish history'. Polanski's film is a remarkable exercise in self-restraint, for-going open emotion and the lurid representation of horror. Instead he films in a detached and matter-of-fact style. For instance, the two Warsaw uprisings, by Jews in the ghetto in the spring of 1943 and by Poles in the city in the autumn of 1944, are seen and heard only from a distance, from the perspective of Szpil-man in his hiding place. Although Polanski makes reference to an image from the *Stroop Report*, filming a person jumping from a burning building, there are no gruelling close-ups. As journalist Jay Rayner wrote in the *Observer*, 'There are no overcrafted edits from terrified faces to revolvers, to trigger fingers. For the most part the horrors are played out in single shots, as if you were simply there to witness ... The corpses of the dead in the street pass by at the bottom of the frame, unremarked, as Szpilman ... steps over them.'[70] *The Pianist* contains no post-war politics and no sentimentality, and could be seen as a long-awaited antidote to the emotive and sometimes simplified good-versus-evil accounts of both *Schindler's List* and *Shoah*.

The Battle for Memory

In the early 1990s, as awareness of the Holocaust grew in the West, attention turned to Auschwitz-Birkenau as a symbol of the destruction of European Jewry. Auschwitz had been largely neglected by the Western democracies during the

Cold War. For the Poles, the camp was the principal memorial to the Second World War and a site commemorating not only the thousands of Poles who had died there but also the millions of Poles who had died during the occupation. Throughout the 1960s, 1970s and 1980s those countries which had lost nationals at Auschwitz-Birkenau were invited to erect their own national exhibitions at Auschwitz. The first country to be represented was Czechoslovakia, followed by the Soviet Union, the German Democratic Republic (GDR), Yugoslavia, Bulgaria, Austria and France, Holland, Italy and Poland.[71]

During the Cold War, when Western democracies paid little attention to Auschwitz-Birkenau, the Auschwitz authorities made links with Hiroshima, the city that suffered the cataclysmic effects of an atom bomb dropped by the USA in August 1945. In 1972 the first Auschwitz exhibition of photographs to be exhibited outside the Eastern Bloc was staged in Japan.[72] In December 1985 another Auschwitz Museum exhibition, 'Auschwitz: A Crime Against Humanity', opened at the United Nations headquarters in New York on International Human Rights Day. It was curated by Teresa Świebocka, who had brought the Auschwitz exhibition to England in 1983. The American authorities were initially nervous about hosting the exhibition, unsure about the 'line' it would take. Before it opened, around thirty American historians went to see it to give their verdict. Only one minor change was considered necessary: that a photograph of the Jewish resistance be included.[73]

At Auschwitz in 1989 the contentious GDR exhibition was dismantled as East Germany collapsed. As other former Soviet-controlled countries began to rewrite their post-war histories, the memory which had been enshrined at Auschwitz for fifty years was changed. The numbers of those who had died at the camp, which had previously been estimated at 4 million, was reassessed by historians and estimated at 1.5 million. The victims, who had previously been generally referred to as 'people', were now defined by race. The museum acknowledged that 'the very great majority of them were Jews'.[74]

In 1994 a Polish worker carved a new message on the memorial stone tablets at Birkenau (see Figure 53). The previous message, in twenty different languages including Yiddish and Hebrew, had read: 'Four million people suffered and died here at the hands of the Nazi murderers between the years 1940 and 1945.' The new message reads: 'Forever let this place be a cry of despair and a warning to humanity, where the Nazis murdered about one and a half million men, women, and children, mainly Jews from various countries of Europe.'

By 1995, the fiftieth anniversary of the liberation of the camps inspired numerous television documentaries and newspaper and magazine articles written about the Holocaust. Central to the narrative was Auschwitz-Birkenau and the Jewish tragedy. During the anniversary year a battle ensued between the Jews

53 · A worker renewing the message on the memorial stones at Birkenau, 1994. (Copyright Janina Struk)

and Catholics over how the liberation of Auschwitz should be commemorated but the Soviets, who had liberated the camp, were no longer contenders in the battle for memory. The USSR state exhibition, still defined as such, stands as a testimony not only to the past but the present. The photographs, once displayed here in memory of the heroism of the Soviet victory, symbolize a country whose war effort and millions of dead have been marginalized. In the dingy exhibition area, unchanged since 1985, hang faded and discoloured photographs of Red Army soldiers in battle overlaid with photographs of Soviet prisoners and the liberation. Three photographs on display were taken by Soviet photographer Dymitr Baltermanc at Kerch. One of them shows a woman searching among the dead. This image had been published on 20 June 1942 in *Picture Post* and was also included in the exhibition in Doncaster in the north of England in 1943 referred to in Chapter 2. Then the Soviet Union was an ally and the photograph was propaganda for the war effort.

During the mid-1990s controversy surrounding the camp intensified. In April 1996, a group of around 100 neo-Nazis made world headlines as they marched with their right arms raised in a Nazi salute through the gates bearing the in-scription 'ARBEIT MACHT FREI'.[75] In 1998 there were more protests as Yad Vashem objected to the presence of 300 crosses outside the perimeter of the camp. The Institute of the World Jewish Congress issued a statement: 'World Jewry will not tolerate this blatant attempt at "Christianisation" of the site.'[76] By the late 1990s it had become commonplace to see young Israeli tourists in the camp wrapped in, or waving, Israeli flags (see Figure 54).

Neither *Shoah* nor *Schindler's List* referred to the fact that Poles – not to mention Russians and other Eastern European peoples – had also suffered under the Nazis. In fact, both interpretations of the Holocaust seem to have helped inflame the relationship between the Poles and the Jews. Polish guides at Auschwitz-Birkenau are sometimes harangued by Israeli and American tour groups for what they see as Poland's collaborative role in the extermination of the Jews. This fashionable folly (there was less collaboration in Poland than any other non-communist country occupied by the Nazis) has even led to tour groups of young Israelis being warned by their guides of the 'constant danger' of being on Polish soil.[77] As a result Auschwitz-Birkenau has become a symbol not only of the destruction of European Jewry but also of Western moral authority over Poland for its anti-Semitism and supposed collaboration with the Nazis and for its failure to centralize the Jewish tragedy in its post-war memorials. What has been conveniently forgotten is that the West did not centralize the Jewish tragedy either. Is this simply an opportunity for the West to shift the blame? James E. Young suggests that rather than accord blame for the wrong memory, Western memory might be reassessed. He writes: 'We might ask to what extent our own sympathies and memories have been shaped by the alliances forged after the war. If Poles seem to have displaced the Germans as the first enemies of the Jews, it's time we asked why: not to diminish the spectre of anti-Semitism in Poland, but to remember what our postwar alliances ask us to forget.'[78] Meanwhile, Auschwitz-Birkenau, the very symbol of the Holocaust, seems to have become not a place of reconciliation, but a site at which to demonstrate nationalism, separatism and intolerance. If there are lessons to be learned in remembering those who died in the Holocaust, they are being submerged beneath political and ideological struggles to this day.

With more than a half a million visitors annually (approximately 50 per cent Poles), the state exhibitions at Auschwitz are gradually being updated by their respective countries. The same photographs are common to all of them: the selection at the ramp at Birkenau, the three photographs taken by the Sonderkommando, Nazi images of executions, hangings and ghettos, and the 'death pit' photograph (Figure 1). Auschwitz is a black hole into which all images of the Holocaust are drawn. As if seeing the horrifying photographs is not sufficient, visitors take their own photographs. The now famous gate to the Auschwitz camp has become a bottle-neck as crowds pause to photograph or video each other under the sign 'ARBEIT MACHT FREI'. Everyone wants to be pictured here. Not to be photographed under these gates would be like leaving Pisa without having been photographed with the leaning tower; it's a kind of establishing shot, a way of making sure friends and family back home know that you were really there. Inside the camp barracks, visitors line up to take more photographs.

54 · Young people wrapped in Israeli flags at Auschwitz museum, 2000. (Copyright Janina Struk.)

How many photographs must there now be of the glass display cases of human hair, the suitcases, the shaving brushes, footwear and other belongings of those who lived and died in the camp? Or photographs of photographs of emaciated prisoners, the camp orchestra, the crowds arriving at the ramp at Birkenau and the naked children photographed for Mengele's experiments? As visitors gasp with horror at the way the victims were photographed, they photograph them again. Why photograph an atrocity photograph? Perhaps a camera puts a distance between the person taking the photographs and an otherwise distressing experience. Or maybe it is simply because for the majority of tourists taking photographs of places of interest is part of the experience, as it was for some members of the Wehrmacht. Sontag writes: 'Most tourists feel compelled to put the camera between themselves and whatever is remarkable that they encounter. Unsure of other responses, they take a picture. This gives shape to experience: stop, take a photograph and move on.'[79] What becomes of these tourist photographs taken at Auschwitz? Will they be placed in family albums next to an evening out in Kraków, a group photograph taken outside the hotel, or maybe alongside the synagogues and relics of Kazimierz? Is this not uncomfortably reminiscent of the photo albums the Nazis made?

While Auschwitz-Birkenau is awash with tourists and tour buses, only the more adventurous seek out other death camp sites. A few tour itineraries include the purpose-built death camps at Sobibór, Treblinka, Chełmno and Bełżec, where now there are only memorials to those who died. Few outside Poland, even now, have heard of Bełżec, where 600,000 were murdered. Near Lublin,

Majdanek concentration camp museum is well off the tourist track. It has none of the trappings of Auschwitz-Birkenau – no carparks full of tour buses, no souvenir shops and no ideological battles over memory. The bleak camp at Majdanek consists of a few of the original wooden huts housing the shoes and other belongings of former murdered prisoners.

The only sign of contemporary life at Majdanek is a Coca-Cola drinks machine and the chilling graffito, etched into one of the camp watchtowers, of a hangman's noose, from which hangs a Jewish star. There seems to be little public concern from the international Jewish communities about how Majdanek represents itself. As with Auschwitz-Birkenau, historians have recently reassessed the numbers of those who died at the camp. The estimate made in Aleksander Ford's film, *Majdanek, Cemetery of Europe*, which is still shown in the museum, is 2 million, although the English-language version, made in 1960, estimates 360,000. The most recent assessment is 235,000; 48 per cent are thought to have been Jews.[80] In 1997 the exhibition of photographs and text which traces the history of Majdanek was updated and reassessed, but with little financial support the opportunities were limited. The management has tried to attract international funding for exhibition and research purposes, but there has been little response. Archivist Janina Kiełboń suggests one reason is that whereas Auschwitz has Kraków, Majdanek has only Lublin, which has fewer hotels and tourist facilities. 'Auschwitz is a world symbol, Majdanek is not.' said Kiełboń. The faded grandeur of Lublin has changed little since the Red Army marched on the cobblestones in July 1944 to liberate the city. There are no bus tours to the camp, nor indeed any indication that Majdanek is just a few kilometres down the road. Kiełboń suggests that another reason for its lack of popularity may be because there are few pictures. Although the Nazi administration made some photographs of the construction of the camp, and a handful were taken clandestinely from outside the fence by unknown members of the Polish resist-ance, there was no organized system of photographing prisoners as there was in Auschwitz and elsewhere. Majdanek doesn't have anything like the photographs taken at the ramp in Birkenau. In the camp museum hang photographs taken at the liberation – the same ones that were sent to the West in 1944 – but these are generally of poor quality. It is possible that the originals were taken to the Soviet Union, as were other documents relating to the Polish Committee of National Liberation which collected evidence of German crimes at Majdanek, but they have not resurfaced.[81] This apparently was the fate of the first part of Aleksander Ford's film, *Majdanek, Cemetery of Europe* which is still missing. The museum was refused access to it by authorities in Moscow, but no one there is quite sure why, or what the film contains.[82] The lack of visual documentation at Majdanek means that the majority of photographs in the exhibition were taken elsewhere, including the arrivals at the ramp in Birkenau and the liberation of Auschwitz-Birkenau.

Artefacts and Fakes

Although few may visit the Majdanek State Museum, there is no end to requests for its 'artefacts'. In 1999, in preparation for Britain's first Holocaust museum, 800 pairs of shoes arrived at the Imperial War Museum for a painstaking conservation process. The 'post war ... dirt' of each shoe was removed while 'mud and polish' was left, on the premise that 'it was part of its history'.[83] Carefully and subtly lit photographs of these shoes were used on posters and leaflets to advertise the exhibition. Why Britain needed a Holocaust exhibition was questioned, but in an article by Madeleine Bunting in the *Guardian* both Professor Dick Geary and Dr David Cesarani urged that the museum should 'face up' to Britain's failure to condemn Nazi anti-Semitism, its policy of appeasement and reluctance to accept refugees.[84] The exhibition, which opened in June 2000, is loosely based on the design of the US Holocaust Memorial Museum, though on a smaller scale and without the gimmicks. The centrepiece is a large white model of Auschwitz-Birkenau surrounded by photographs of the arrivals at the ramp at Birkenau from the Lili Jacob album. In other parts of the exhibition the videoed testimonies of survivors are intercut with Nazi film, the same film footage of the Warsaw ghetto which in 1959 was refused certification in Britain and which now plays in museums around the world. But the emphasis is on artefacts. Apart from the shoes from Majdanek, there are displays of the belongings of those who died: combs, rusty pans, bent rusty spoons and broken glass. There are buttons from the camp at Chełmno, a 'telephone from Sobibór railway station', a 'railway lamp from Bełżec railway station', and a 'sign from Bełżec death camp'. Imperial War Museum curator, James Taylor, said that there was never any doubt about using artefacts. In his opinion, 'one has to have striped uniforms, shoes and personal belongings of people who were murdered in the gas-chambers and a yellow star'.[85]

Perhaps not surprisingly, the increase in Holocaust museums and their growing demand for 'authentic' artefacts has led to fakes appearing on the market. When a team from the Imperial War Museum went to Hamburg to look at Holocaust artefacts being offered for sale, including a tail-coat with a yellow star sewn on it and a watercolour ghetto scene made on a page of a 1940 diary, they could tell at once that they were fakes; the owner was asking around £20,000 for them. When the same team went to an auction in Lewes, England, a female prisoner's concentration camp uniform was also suspect. A white star had been sewn on to the uniform instead of a yellow star. The consensus was that it had probably been made for a film. Similarly, it is now reckoned that Nazi photo albums, which occasionally turn up in auction houses, will fetch higher prices if they contain atrocity photographs. Predictably, 'extra atrocity photographs' are copied from books, aged and added to albums before being offered for sale.[86] The desire to cash in on the Holocaust industry may mean that more of these faked artefacts and photographs will appear on the market. Should criticism be levelled only at those who are cashing in on producing them, or is it a sign that the display of relics of the dead and atrocity photographs has simply gone too far?

Is it time to ask what purpose is served by moving the belongings of those who died in the camps in Poland to museums in Europe and the USA? What can we learn from looking at the shoes of those who died at Majdanek in London, or from walking on cobblestones from the Warsaw ghetto in Washington, DC? What difference does it make to our understanding of history whether or not a tea-strainer we are looking at really belonged to a prisoner? Young writes: 'That a murdered people remains known in Holocaust museums anywhere by their scattered belongings, and not by their spiritual works, that their lives should be recalled primarily through the images of their death, may be the ultimate travesty.'[87]

By the 1990s, it had become commonplace in Holocaust museums to include family photographs of those who had died during the Holocaust and of those who had survived, among the plethora of atrocity images and artefacts, adding extra poignancy to the way in which the Holocaust is understood.

NINE

Interpretations of the Evidence

A Tower of Faces

There seems to be a consensus in Holocaust museums that the public is no longer interested in exhibitions made up entirely of atrocity photographs. In Western societies predisposed to soap opera culture, the stories and photographs of individual people are considered more appealing, adding personal drama to an otherwise incomprehensible event. As a result, pre-war family photographs are now being added to Holocaust collections. These photographs, previously considered private mementos without documentary value, are becoming central to the Holocaust narrative; no visual memorial seems complete without them.

The Holocaust exhibition at the Imperial War Museum begins with a display of more than twenty family photographs. Curator James Taylor told me they had included them because 'We didn't want to show people as victims but we wanted to show those who were murdered.'[1] These, like all such family collections, are idealized versions of family life: births, marriages, holidays, birthday parties and family outings. Family albums never directly feature conflict, misery, poverty or death; the family photo album is a linear narrative of happy moments which lend themselves unequivocally to nostalgia and longing. Implicit in such photographs of happy moments are feelings of sadness and loss. Family photographs are not only a recognition of the continuity of life but also of the inevitability of death. Roland Barthes wrote that every photograph represents 'the return of the dead'.[2]

Besides being intensely personal, family photographs are universal; they are unique but at the same time ordinary. Everyone can 'read' a family photograph, regardless of whom it belongs to, projecting on to the image their own memories, longings or desires. In the context of the Holocaust, placing family photographs beside those of shootings, hangings, death pits and piled tangled skeletal bodies increases their poignancy. The juxtaposition of images of serene moments alongside images of brutal death taps into our complex and contradictory associations of family, nostalgia and mortality. The ordinariness of the family photographs is accentuated by those which show extraordinary deaths. We cling to the familiar rather than alienating, terrifying and sometimes incomprehensible images.

One of the major exhibits at the US Holocaust Memorial Museum is the Tower of Faces (Figure 55), a three-storey-high exhibit of 1,500 family photographs. The photographs were taken between 1890 and 1941 in Ejszyszki, a small town near Vilno, then in Poland, now in Lithuania. They were donated to the museum by Yaffa Eliach, Professor of History and Literature at Brooklyn College, who was born in the town. Many were taken by her grandparents, local photographers Yitzhak Uri Katz and Alte Katz. They show fragments of the lives of more than 100 families in Ejszyszki who were murdered in September 1941 by the Einsatzgruppen. 'The only way we can remember the past in Ejszyszki', said Professor Eliach, 'is through photographs. There is no other evidence, no gravesites, no childhood friends – only photos.'[3] In her book, *There Once was a World*, Yaffa Eliach wrote: 'I wanted to create a photographic exhibit depicting every man, woman, and child of twentieth century Eishyshok, bringing them all back to life, and all together in one place.'[4] The idea that photographs could (metaphorically) bring them back to life indicates the powerful presence photographs can have. According to the US Holocaust Memorial Museum, the Eliach photographs 'will help tell the story of the massacres carried out by the Nazi mobile killing squads'.[5] The photographs, of course, do not tell that story. It is the museum that creates it.

As museums create narratives in the way they display photographs, so archives create narratives by the way they file them. In the computerized search system at the US Holocaust Memorial Museum photo archive, photographs are divided into topics under particular headings. One such heading is 'Babi Yar'. Here are not only images of the ravine in Ukraine where thousands were murdered, but dozens of family photographs – of couples, babies, family groups and children – interspersed with photographs of the ravine. Where there were once only photographs of a deserted ravine, now there are faces and names. The juxtaposition creates a poignant narrative, not because of what the photographs show, but because of what is known about the massacres that took place.

Roman Vishniac's photographs of pre-war Jewish communities have also become central to Holocaust remembrance. Meanings are now given to them with hindsight. When Jane Hughes reviewed an exhibition of these photographs in London in 1998, she referred to them as 'harrowing'. She was not describing the images, so much as what we now know about the fate of those photographed.[6] Although they are not family photographs in the general sense of the term, they have come to represent the larger family of Eastern European Jewish communities that were lost. We bestow on the faces of those he photographed beauty, serenity and tragedy in an exemplary vision of the past. Polish-Jewish

55 · Detail of one
of the models of
the permanent
exhibition at the US
Holocaust Memorial
Museum, showing
the Tower of Faces.
(Courtesy USHMM
photo archives)

writer Rafael F. Scharf recalls that before the war the Orthodox Jews did not 'appear to us to be attractive. On the contrary,' he writes, 'I am shamed to admit – many of us looked on these people with a sense of embarrassment. Those beards, side-locks, crooked noses, misty eyes, what do our non-Jewish fellow citizens make of this?'[7] Vishniac's intimate representation of Jewish poverty is seen as the quintessence of the pre-war Jewish Eastern European communities, as though they were one homogeneous mass. This was not, however, the case. Scharf is keen to stress that Vishniac's view was 'very partial', representing only one layer of the Jewish community. He writes that Vishniac focused 'almost entirely' on Jewish poverty and the Orthodox. 'As a photographer he found them more picturesque and as a man he felt a greater affinity with them – it is his prerogative.'[8] In Scharf's opinion, Vishniac was as much a stranger in other people's realities as German soldier-photographer Willy Georg was when he visited the Warsaw ghetto.[9] It is not the photographs which are problematic for Scharf so much as some of the captions. The photograph showing an elderly Jew peering from behind a door, supposedly hiding from the Endecja (Polish National Party), Scharf said, is slightly absurd, in that they would not have been in a Jewish area. 'He was probably a door keeper' (see Figure 4).[10]

On 6 July 1995 Sharon Muller, photo archivist at the US Holocaust Memorial

Museum, put out a press release concerning the 2,500 family photographs which had apparently been returned to Auschwitz-Birkenau State Museum in 1958 by a museum worker (referred to in Chapter 5). Although some had been exhibited in Eastern Europe and a few at the Auschwitz exhibition which was shown in London in 1983, no special attention was paid to them in Western Europe or the USA. But in the mid-1990s the increasing interest in personal Holocaust stories propelled them from relative obscurity into significant additions to the Holocaust archive. At the request of US Holocaust Memorial Museum, in 1995 Barbara Jarosz, then a chief archivist at Auschwitz-Birkenau State Museum, personally brought the collection of photographs to the USA for duplication. The attempt to identify those in them began, and the US Holocaust Memorial Museum staff set to work translating the captions on the back of the photographs, which were mostly written in Polish but occasionally in Yiddish or Hebrew.

In mid-1995 Muller sent the press release, with a pre-war photograph of a young mother and child in the foreground, and a car with a Canadian number-plate in the background, to the *Canadian Jewish News*, hoping that someone might recognize the family. The newspaper ran a front-page story with the headline 'Auschwitz photos a mystery'.[11] On 20 July the newspaper ran a response to the article from Jennie Lipson. She was the young mother in the photograph and had sent it to her parents in Poland almost sixty years earlier. Mrs Lipson's son said of the photographs that they were the 'first objective verification' that his grandparents 'met their end in Auschwitz'.[12]

With the help of survivors, relatives and historians, others in the photographs have also been identified. To Muller, the importance of these photographs has been not only in matching names to faces, but in providing an alternative to photographs of anonymous corpses. 'This collection of photographs', wrote Muller in the press release, 'will serve as an important corrective to the impression created by pictures of emaciated, typhus-ridden survivors at Bergen-Belsen and piles of corpses stacked like cordwood in front of the crematoria at Buchenwald. The people that were victimized by the Nazis were not some barely recognizable form of the human species devoid of life and consciousness.'

It was established that a large majority of those in the pictures were from Będzin and surrounding areas in Silesia, south-west Poland. In Będzin the pre-war population numbered around 50,000, of whom half were Jewish. Most of the inhabitants of the Będzin and nearby Sosnowiec ghettos were deported to Auschwitz-Birkenau in August 1943. A few hundred of the photographs are known to have belonged to well-to-do Jewish families. Among them are studio photographs, groups on holiday in the fashionable Polish mountain resort of Krynica, beach and skiing holidays and group family portraits. Not all were taken before the war. In a studio portrait of fashionably-dressed Benjamin Cukierman and his wife, both are wearing armbands with a star on their left arms. Although the vast majority of the photographs in the collection portray Jews, about two dozen photographs are of uniformed Nazis. In 2001 two books were published of these photographs: *Before They Perished ... Photographs Found in Auschwitz* compiled by the Auschwitz-Birkenau State Museum and *The Last Album: Eyes from the Ashes of Auschwitz-Birkenau* by Ann Weiss. In the opinion of Weiss, it is possible that the images of Nazis were used as an outer 'cover' to help hide the images of the Jews and so save them.[13] It is impossible to know. Neither Weiss, nor the Auschwitz-Birkenau State Museum chose to publish the images of the Nazis. In the opinion of Auschwitz-Birkenau State Museum curator Teresa Świebocka, they were not considered important to the collection.[14]

By 2001 a large number of these photograph were on display at Birkenau. In April, the building previously known as the 'Sauna' was opened to the public for the first time. It was here that from 1943 prisoners were registered and de-loused. Now visitors follow the same route that the prisoners did. In the penultimate room is an exhibition of these photographs.[15] In Świebocka's opinion the 'Sauna' exhibition has been a huge success and has received a positive response from the public, who find it easier to relate to family photographs than to the prisoners' identity photographs, which picture them in three mug-shot poses in camp uniforms with shaved heads; in other words, after they have been, says Świebocka, 'dehumanized'.[16] Implicit in Świebocka's comment is the fact that people are also responding to two distinct photographic genres. We do not react to an identity photograph, such as a present-day police mug-shot, in the same way as we do to a family photograph. In his Foreword to *The Last Album*, Leon Wieseltier defines the photographs as 'supremely cruel documents of the reality of the world', a 'busy universe of bourgeois dreams and Jewish dreams' inhabited by 'ferociously normal' people.[17] It would be hard to imagine these sentiments being applied to the identity photographs, a difficulty that has less to do with the dehumanized images and more to do with the language of photography. 'Identity' photographs were first utilized by the state in the nineteenth century (as discussed in Chapter 1), and, as a consequence, came to be understood and 'read' as authoritative documents rather than personal mementos. The Nazis understood this well. We might ask whether the prisoners' dehumanized image – a camp uniform and shaved head – was constructed to fit with the physiognomic criminal 'type'. For a regime obsessed with images of 'types', this may not be a ludicrous proposition.

Photographs and Memories

Recent renewed interest in Nazi crimes and acknowledgement of the destruction of European Jewry have encouraged survivors and their families to come forward with their memories and their photographs. When the US Holocaust Memorial Museum established a photo archive in 1994, archivists had no idea of the importance family photographs would have for their collection, nor the sheer numbers or type of photographs that survivors and their relatives would donate. 'There is no end to these personal collections,' said Sharon Muller.[18] Family collections, it turned out, included not only pre-war family photographs, but images of ghettos, atrocities and deportations as well. In addition, a large number of liberation photographs have been offered to the museum by former GIs, many of whom had secretly kept them as mementos of the horror they witnessed.[19]

A book *And I Still See Their Faces*, published in Poland in 1995, includes over 200 pages of photographs from personal collections. 'The book', states the Introduction, 'has been woven from scattered snatches of memory which clung to old photographs.'[20] The project, initiated by the Shalom Foundation, which was established in Warsaw in 1988 to 'save' the memory of Polish Jews, invited individuals to donate memories and photographs. The Foundation had an overwhelming response to their request and were sent not only family photographs but images of the Łódź ghetto, a round-up of Jews for deportation in Kraków, a transport on its way to Chełmno death camp, and a man posing in front of corpses in the Okopowa Street cemetery in the Warsaw ghetto. There is also a clandestine photograph of Jews preparing to depart for 'resettlement' in Myślenice taken from an upstairs window by Maria Górniesiewicz.[21]

The stories printed alongside some of the photographs reveal the extraordinary lengths that people went to in order to preserve them. Some were hidden in attics, stuffed into sewerage pipes, or even passed on to strangers. On the day of her deportation from a ghetto in 1942, a Jewish woman sent a photograph of herself to a friend inscribed. 'Wandzia, remember Lola as long as you can!! A few hours before the departure for the unknown.' Another donor recalls having met an unknown woman 'on the road'. The woman handed her a photograph of herself and said, 'Maybe some time someone will recognize me and he will know what happened to me.'[22] But whereas some are able to part with their photographs, for others they are so inextricably bound up with memory that parting with them is too painful. In 1999 a woman who had donated photographs of her family, who had all perished in the Holocaust, to the Ghetto Fighters' House, later returned and asked for the originals back. Copies would not suffice.[23]

Some who do not have personal photographs of themselves or relatives who died in the Holocaust hope to find them in public collections or on museum walls. For some, photographs are a way of verifying the past. All major Holocaust archives – Yad Vashem, Auschwitz-Birkenau State Museum, US Holocaust Memorial Museum and the Ghetto Fighters' House – have had visitors who recognize themselves, friends or family in photographs. In 1998 an elderly man visited the Ghetto Fighters' House. He had been a postman in the Łódź ghetto and asked if there were any photographs of the post office. He was shown a few, identified himself and wept. Later he returned with his family, so they could all bear witness to the photograph.[24]

During a visit to the US Holocaust Memorial Museum exhibition in 1998, Rhona Liptzin recognized her mother in a photograph taken by George Kadish in the Kovno ghetto. She wrote in a letter to the museum:

> It meant so much to me to see my mother's photo at the Kovno Ghetto exhibition in the Holocaust Museum in Washington, DC. In my wildest dreams I could never have had imagined this scenario. I hoped I would be lucky enough to see a picture of her. So many times I saw pictures of victims and hoped I'd see her in it. It would make her story real. I never dreamed I would see a full size picture of my mother in the museum. I stood there and stared right back at her. I stood there frozen in a particular space and time. I no longer noticed anything or anyone around me and forgot I was in the museum. I was in Kovno and it was 1941.[25]

In February 2000 a former Signal Corps photographer who had taken photographs at the liberation of Dachau wrote to the US Holocaust Memorial Museum in search of them. He wrote: 'I have carried these scenes in my head for almost 55 years. My main interest in getting these pictures is to have my own personal proof the Holocaust did happen and to leave them to my two children.'[26]

Mistaken Identities

While there are those who genuinely seek to find themselves or relatives in photographs, there are others not associated with the Holocaust who seem to have a need to identify with it. The US Holocaust Memorial Museum photo archive regularly receives visitors who *claim* to have seen themselves or relatives in the photographs displayed in the exhibitions. The same has happened at Yad Vashem and the Ghetto Fighters' House. Both Sharon Muller and Daniel Uziel, photo archivist at Yad Vashem, say it is not always difficult to test the validity of the claim. Sometimes it is a matter of simply asking where the person was during the war. At other times it is not so easy. Although no one is yet known to have positively identified anybody in an atrocity photograph, there are 'favourite' photographs in which many people claim to see themselves. The one which men most want to be associated with is that of the small boy with his hands raised taken during the liquidation of the Warsaw ghetto in 1943 (Figure 26). Yad Vashem, the US Holocaust Memorial Museum and the Ghetto Fighters' House have all had a number of visits, letters or phone-calls from those who claim either to be the boy or to know who he is. One such person was Abraham Zejlinwarger of

Haifa, Israel, who in 1997, aged ninety-five, contacted the Ghetto Fighters' House to disclose what had been until then, he said, his closely-guarded secret: that the boy was his son Lewi Zejlinwarger, who was later exterminated in Treblinka. Abraham Zejlinwarger claimed to be absolutely certain it was him because of the special way the boy had of standing. To substantiate his claim, he sent the archive a family photograph of his son taken before the war.[27] No viable evidence has ever been uncovered about the fate of the boy and none of the claimants has been acknowledged by archivists or historians. The reasons why so many people apparently wish to identify with the boy are difficult to ascertain. Is it a psychological need to find something from the past to identify with? Or is it because in almost every Holocaust exhibition the small boy is centre-stage, made an unwitting hero in a scene most associated with martyrdom and resistance?

The conflicting identifications and accounts of the fate of the boy in the Warsaw ghetto have, not surprisingly, been seized on by Holocaust deniers. The majority of interpretations of this photograph imply that the boy was killed in Treblinka. In 1994 an article in the Holocaust deniers' journal, the *Journal of Historical Review*, referred to it as the 'all purpose' Holocaust illustration and disputed claims that the boy was murdered. It alluded particularly to one claimant and survivor, Tsvi Nussbaum, who, in an article in the *New York Times*, maintained that he was the boy and was presently living in the USA.[28]

The confusing interpretation of photographs, which Holocaust deniers have repeatedly exploited, is something that Sybil Milton frequently refers to in her essays. In her opinion mistakes often begin in the archive where photographs are sometimes filed under loose and misleading headings, for example, 'victims', 'atrocities' and 'concentration camps'.[29] For Uziel the question of wrongly identified photographs is a 'painful one'. He, like chief librarian Rosemarie Nief at the Wiener Library and Sharon Muller, is one of a number of archivists who are concerned that photographs should be used correctly and are attempting to secure precise identifications for them. This long-awaited reassessment of photographs as evidence has been prompted partly by Holocaust deniers but also by the increased interest in photographs and their acknowledged value as historical documents. Only in 1983 did Yad Vashem create a separate section for film and photographs and in the last decade the Ghetto Fighters' House has given particular attention to its photo archive. Some of this research has been successful. For instance, it was established in 2000 that one photograph taken in Olkusz in July 1940 does not show what it was previously believed to show. In the background is a row of German policemen humiliating a rabbi in the foreground. At the feet of the rabbi is a row of bodies. Commonly the photograph has been described as showing the rabbi standing among the bodies of his congregants immediately after their murder. It has now been established, through matching historical data with the photograph, that in fact the Jews were alive, having been forced to lie face-down on the ground while the police and the SD members registered them.[30]

Attempting to correct captions and identify photographs can be difficult and sometimes impossible. More often than not, the authors of atrocity photographs are anonymous and there are no recorded data. But there are small steps that can be taken. For example, Uziel explained that it was previously assumed that all perpetrators in photographs of atrocities, hangings or executions were SS men. Now, simply by identifying the uniforms of perpetrators in the photographs it is possible to deduce that not only members of the SS took part in these crimes, but also members of the police, the Wehrmacht and non-German collaborators. For many this has been a breakthrough. Uziel says that many in Israel were surprised by the claims of Christopher Browning in his book *Ordinary Men: Reserve Police Battalion 101 and the Final Solution in Poland* published in 1993, that members of Police Battalion 101 had not only taken part in atrocities in Poland but had also taken photographs which they distributed among themselves.[31] Now the facts behind many more photographs are being established in this way. For example, one widely-used photograph taken in the Ukraine of a German in uniform – previously assumed to be an SS man – pointing a gun at a woman holding a child, has now been confirmed as being of a German policeman.[32]

In Poland, historian Krzysztof Tarkowski at Majdanek State Museum said that photographs previously accepted as having been taken at Majdanek camp were probably taken elsewhere.[33] He is not surprised by the fact that some photographs were wrongly captioned, since after the liberation, photographs were generally centralized in Warsaw where the captions were written. Some photographs, in his opinion, are fabrications. A well-known and widely distributed photograph said to have been taken in 1944 shows piles of footwear of those murdered at Majdanek. According to the caption it shows '820,000 pairs of footwear', found on liberation of the camp. The photograph is in fact a montage of three separate photographs. On close examination it is easy to see the lines where the three images are joined. Tarkowski is doubtful that there would have been so many shoes left after liberation, as the local population who came in search of valuables would have looted many of them;[34] but at the time of liberation, the impact of the image was more important than the absolute truth.

Besides the reassessment of pictures, captions are being revised for questions of style as well as accuracy. At the US Holocaust Memorial Museum, captions considered to be written in a 'flowery' style – the reporting style of the 1930s and 1940s – are sometimes rewritten 'according to our style', said Sharon Muller. One example shows a close-up of a group of prisoners dressed in camp uniforms. The caption written at time of the original release of the photograph reads:

The men in convict's garb whose crime might not have been more than preaching the Bible in its true sense, or listening to foreign radio transmissions, or just being an 'Intellectual' who thought himself beyond the Nazi propaganda and consequently was termed 'anti-social'. And none of them knew if he would ever be released. Later in the war when the labor shortage became acute, prisoners were pressed into so-called 'Convicts Companies' and sent to one of the fronts. These photographs were taken in one of Hitler's notorious concentration camps: the camp at Sachsenhausen at Oranienburg in the district of Potsdam near Berlin in February 1941. They were not released at the time and have come to light only recently. After the Soviet occupation of the district they used the camp for the same purposes until 1950.[35]

In 2000 the caption was rewritten by Muller to read: 'Close-up of prisoners standing in the Appelplatz during a roll call at the Sachsenhausen concentration camp.'[36] Muller concedes that there are problems in rewriting captions, but she nevertheless thinks it's unnecessary to stick with an 'out-of-date' style. The original captions are sometimes preserved but not always. It is unlikely that historians would change the way in which historical documents are written because they do not fit the style of the institution in which they are kept, and it could be argued that the original captions on historical photographs are historical documents in their own right.

The sheer number of photographs relating to the Holocaust, which run into hundreds of thousands if not millions, makes the task of correctly identifying them all the more difficult. The current collection at Yad Vashem numbers approximately 130,000; at the Ghetto Fighters' House, 60,000; at the Auschwitz-Birkenau State Museum, 40,000; the US Holocaust Memorial Museum, 70,000; and at Majdanek State Museum, 20,000.[37] At Yad Vashem a further 80,000 photographs have been collected as a part of the Hall of Names project, which is attempting to identify and register all 6 million Jews who died during the Holocaust.[38] In all of these archives are many of the same photographs, indicating both their wide distribution during the war and their frequent copying since. One of the largest collections at both the US Holocaust Memorial Museum and Yad Vashem are photographs taken by the Americans at the camps they liberated. Following the liberations they were circulated widely throughout Europe, the USA and Israel. Many of these which have been donated to the US Holocaust Memorial Museum are without captions or locations. To locate them correctly, said Muller, can be a painstaking procedure which often comes down to 'the gruesome thing of comparing piles of corpses', which, she said, 'we do all the time'.[39]

The Holocaust archives are being expanded not just by photographs donated by individuals, but also by fresh discoveries of those taken by Nazis or collaborators. As recently as 1998 a set of colour photographs taken by Herman Göring's official photographer, Walter Frentz, were discovered in a suitcase by his son. They were taken in mid-1944 at the Dora-Mittelbau factory near Nordhausen where the V2 rocket project was underway and show men neatly dressed in camp uniforms busy at work. In reality 20,000 people died at the camp in the most appalling conditions.[40] Uncovering such unique collections is, however, likely to be increasingly rare.

The number of photographs in archives seems set to multiply as both the US Holocaust Memorial Museum and Yad Vashem are actively engaged in seeking out and copying material from smaller archives and personal collections. Both intend to amass *the* most comprehensive collection of Holocaust photographs. Daniel Uziel considers that Yad Vashem is better equipped to facilitate such a collection, while Sharon Muller says that the US Holocaust Memorial Museum has a better system than many smaller archives for filing and organizing pictures. The aim, Muller says, is to have the biggest collection under one roof, as a kind of 'one-stop shopping'.[41] It is as if archives have fallen into a competition, like trading empires, to acquire the biggest stockpile of a valuable commodity.

With so many photographs in circulation, is there a limit to the number that archives are prepared to take? Opinions are divided on this question. Uziel says that there are no limits to the number of atrocity photographs Yad Vashem will take and considers it imperative that they be included in the archive. In Sharon Muller's opinion there are some photographs which would not be acceptable to the archive and would serve no purpose as historical documents. These include photographs of cannibalism among POWs. On a few occasions photographs which show rape scenes have been offered to the archive, but Muller has turned them down on the premise they are 'basically pornographic'. In this 'pornographic' category Muller also places the set of photographs, referred to in Chapter 3, of the savage assault on women, thought to have been taken in the streets of Lvov in 1941. Some historians allege it was a Jewish pogrom, others claim that the women were the mistresses of the retreating Soviets and were being humiliated and punished by the Nazis or that the Germans had incited the incident in order to make a propaganda film. One of the still photographs in the set shows three German soldiers with movie cameras (see back cover). Apart from still photographs of this incident, film footage was also taken; this film was shown at the International Military Tribunal at Nuremberg, referred to in Chapter 7, and called 'Original German 8-millimeter Film of Atrocities against Jews'.

Although the photographs are currently in the archive's collection, Muller is unsure whether they should be, partly because of their pornographic nature but also because, she said, 'We don't really know what we are looking at.' Curator James Taylor has a different view. He agrees that the photographs are horrific, but says it is for this reason, and the fact that he considers them educational, that two have been included in its Holocaust exhibition. 'They are', said Taylor, 'the worst photographs of the Holocaust and for this reason they *should* be shown.' They have a 'raw fear' which 'you don't often get in Holocaust photographs … the fact that they are women makes them all the more affecting'.[42]

It is because they show women that they shock in the way that pornography can, and so might, presumably, be arousing to some people. They could even be a source of amusement. At the Imperial War Museum during preliminary discussions about the Holocaust exhibition one person wondered whether children might 'giggle' at the partially clothed women. Another person considered that would in fact be acceptable, on the premise that it would be a 'displacement activity'.[43] In Holocaust exhibitions it has become acceptable to display abhorrent images, challenging us not to turn away but swallow the horror wholesale because they are representative of what is considered to be the apex of evil: Nazism.

In 2001 a set of twenty-four of these photographs was sent anonymously from Hamburg to the Wiener Library in London with a covering letter stating that they had been stored for safe-keeping in a psychotherapy practice for over thirty years. It noted that the soldiers visible in the photographs were members of the Wehrmacht, not the SS, and, although there are no 'direct hints' as to who the photographer was, the 'haunting documents' were 'probably made in Poland or Latvia'. As a result of receiving this letter, the chief librarian at the Wiener Library, Rosemarie Nief, advised the *Scotsman* magazine, which proposed to use one of these photographs to accompany a story about an alleged Lithuanian war criminal, Anton Geceas, who was living in Scotland, to caption the pictures as having been taken in Poland or Latvia. When published the caption read: 'Balkan Jews are rounded up in the streets.'[44]

The publication of these photographs has frequently been contentious. On 22 February 1993 *Time* magazine used one of those now exhibited in the Imperial War Museum which shows a distressed, partially clothed young woman, sitting in a street, shouting angrily, with her arm outstretched towards the person behind the camera. Next to her is an elderly woman attempting to cover her exposed body. It accompanied an article on rape and the war in Bosnia to 'illustrate the long time use of rape as a weapon in warfare'. The caption read: 'Traditions of atrocity: A Jewish girl raped by Ukrainians in Lvov, Poland in 1945.' The *Journal of Historical Review* contested the truth of the caption on the basis that there is, indeed, no evidence that the woman was raped.[45]

Time's use of the photograph was also contested by angry Ukrainians. In Canada Professor Danylo Struk (no relation to the author), editor of the

Encyclopaedia of Ukraine, wrote a letter to *Time* disputing its interpretation on a number of points, including the fact that in 1945 'Lvov' was not in Poland but in the Soviet Union. If one fact is wrong, stated Struk, then maybe other facts are also wrong.[46]

Amid the controversy, the cruel nature of these photographs is overlooked. But are they more affecting than other Holocaust photographs? When I was researching at the US Holocaust Memorial Museum, filing through frame after frame of photographs, I found the constant repetition of low-level harassment – taunting, jeering, pushing, poking – sometimes more difficult to look at than more overtly horrific images. Photographs of the dead are definitive, images of humiliation show protracted rather than summary cruelty.

Public Memory, Private Profit

As the 'post-modern' world becomes more and more mediated through representation, Holocaust images are increasingly being woven into other cultural forms, their iconographic status exploited for profit. On 27 January 2001, the fifty-sixth anniversary of the liberation of Auschwitz-Birkenau, Britain held its first Holocaust Day. A press release issued by the Holocaust Educational Trust echoed the sentiment of Holocaust remembrance world-wide. It was a day which would 'offer everyone the opportunity to reflect on the Holocaust and more recent crimes against humanity. It will promote a society that opposes racism, anti-Semitism and discrimination.' The idea, however ill-founded, that 'understanding' the Holocaust can set right the evils of the world has become increasingly popular, and, based on this premise, a variety of causes have utilized the Holocaust for their own purposes. In the USA, Finkelstein points out that 'one is hard-pressed to name a single political cause, whether it be pro-life or pro-choice, animal rights or states' rights, that hasn't conscripted The Holocaust'.[47] One visitor to the US Holocaust Memorial Museum exhibition chose to write anonymously in the visitors' book: 'Abortion! Abortion! is another holocaust and it is right in our neighborhoods.'[48]

In January 1995 the *Independent on Sunday* in London published a front-page photograph from a Paris fashion show of a gaunt-looking model with close-cropped hair dressed in a striped pyjama outfit. The article which accompanied the photograph was headlined, 'Outrage at "death camps" pyjama fashion'. The French fashion house Comme des Garçons was condemned by the World Jewish Congress for including in the show two men with shaved heads modelling 'striped pyjamas bearing numbers'. The fact that the fashion show opened on 27 January, the fiftieth anniversary of the liberation of Auschwitz-Birkenau, was, said the head of the fashion house, a 'terrible coincidence'.[49] The designer of the outfit, Rei Kawakubo, said: 'The meaning; there is no meaning.' Perhaps her comment is less ridiculous than it might sound. Maybe the saturation of Holocaust images *has* rendered them meaningless.

In 1979 an international photographic exhibition 'Fotografia Polska' (Polish Photography) included a picture of a group of naked women being driven to the gas-chambers, taken by members of the Sonderkommando at Birkenau. This, however, is a widely circulated blown-up version of the original (see Figure 37). In the exhibition catalogue *Fotografia Polska* it is contextualized as being among 'original masterworks from public and private collections in Poland 1839–1945'.[50] Twenty years later it was included in the first anthology of Polish photography. The editor of the collection, Polish photographer Jerzy Lewczyński, chose to include the image, first, because he claimed that it was taken by a Pole and, second, he told me, because there is 'an inherent beauty in the women'. The caption reads: 'Worth noticing is the upward (heaven-bound?) movement, on the diagonal line of the photo. The face of the beautiful woman in front can be almost clearly seen!' To emphasize what he refers to as the beauty of the woman he has enlarged her face and inserted it in the top right-hand corner of the frame of the photograph.[51] Perhaps Lewczyński was not to know that the camera shutter was most probably pressed by a Greek Jew; nor that the diagonally angled blurred image is indicative of its being taken clandestinely and not for aesthetic reasons; nor that the facial features of the women, in this blown-up version of the photograph, are the result of crude retouching.

The caption does refer to the historical origins of the image, stating that 'the photograph was taken from hiding by a Sonderkommando prisoner', but this is overridden by the context in which it is placed. The danger of using photographs which are historical documents uncritically, as Allan Sekula points out, is that they 'are transformed into esthetic objects … the pretense to historical understanding has been replaced by esthetic experience'.[52] To the ideological, commercial and propaganda use of these images we must apparently add the aesthetic. A photograph taken at incredible risk as evidence of genocide has been accorded the status of an art-work. The women, stripped naked before their deaths, have been transformed from victims of Nazi genocide into objects of desire.

Although the photo archive at Auschwitz-Birkenau owns the publication rights to this photograph, plus the two other extant photographs taken by the Sonderkommando, when I spoke with archivist Halina Żdziebko at Auschwitz-Birkenau State Museum shortly after its publication, she was not aware of its inclusion in the anthology.[53] But as these photographs can be found in numerous exhibitions, archives and on websites, it is not difficult to acquire them. The widespread use of these and other overused Holocaust photographs has begun to raise questions, not only about the contentious way they are used, but also about their ownership. During the fifty years of silence in the West about Nazi atrocities and the extermination of the Jews, they were considered of little value outside specialist archives. Copyright and ownership was not an issue. But increasing demand for photographs for exhibitions, books, museums and television programmes has meant that some Holocaust photographs have become valuable commodities.

Technically, as the authors of the overwhelming majority of these photographs are anonymous, the images are in the public domain. The most elementary of copyright laws states that the creator must be identified before copyright can be held. But many archives and photographic agencies are charging fees for reproduction rights of the photographs and some are making a great deal of money out of doing so. The photograph of the boy in the Warsaw ghetto with his hands raised, taken from the *Stroop Report*, is a case in point (Figure 26). The original *Stroop Report* is kept at the Instytut Pamięci Narodowej (IPN) in Warsaw. The National Archives and Records Administration (NARA) in Washington, DC, hold a microfilm copy, made in September 1945 and used as evidence in the Nuremberg Tribunal. Both the IPN and NARA consider that photographs from the *Stroop Report* are in the public domain. This means that, apart from paying a fee for a print, anyone can reproduce them free of charge.

Around 1993, however, Corbis, the largest commercial photo-agency in the world, owned by Bill Gates, the founder of Microsoft, indirectly acquired photographs from the *Stroop Report* after buying the New York-based agency Bettmann. It is alleged that Bettmann originally procured these photographs from NARA. Corbis are now licensing these photographs and charging commercial rates for the right to reproduce them. On the Corbis website are three photographs of the small boy with his hands raised in the Warsaw ghetto. Stamped across the images is a Corbis 'digital watermark' to prevent unauthorized use.

One is credited: '© Bettmann/Corbis (BE064730)'; the second: '© Hulton Deutsch/CORBIS (HU007442)', the third: '© CORBIS' (NA002806)'.[54] The NA code, according to a manager at the London Corbis office, means that the photograph has most probably originated from NARA. A legal representative of NARA stated that they would 'be concerned' if Corbis were to claim that it owned copyright of public domain photographs obtained from them.[55] Although Corbis do not claim publicly to have exclusive rights to the photographs, all three of the images referred to are accompanied by a copyright symbol.

Kate Flaherty, archive specialist at NARA, said that it is not only photographs from the *Stroop Report* that are being sold for commercial gain, but also US Signal Corps photographs. NARA, as the official repository for US military photographs, states categorically that these are also in the public domain. 'Researchers can come to our research room and copy anything,' said Kate Flaherty. 'We don't copyright the photographs, they belong to the American people.' But, adds Flaherty, if an agency sends researchers to copy photographs at NARA, once copied, there is nothing to stop them from copyrighting their own version of it.[56] As Corbis continue to acquire archives, it is possible that other Holocaust photographs will also be included in the collection. On Corbis's current website collection are some of the early smuggled photographs from Poland, Nazi photographs of executions and an image of the Warsaw ghetto wall – the image that was sent to the Ministry of Information in 1941, which one official claimed was not genuine. This particular image was previously part of the Hulton Deutsch collection, although it is also in the Public Record Office in London, the Imperial War Museum, the Polish Institute and Sikorski Museum and no doubt in many other public archives.

NARA, like many other major photo archives, has much of its collection on a website. As the photographs are in the public domain anyone can download them without authorization. On the majority of archive websites, downloading photographs is acceptable for research purposes only. But almost anyone can download images from a site, either to use on their own web pages or even for publication (although the technical quality of pictures on a website is not usually of a high enough resolution for publication). There is evidence that this activity is widespread.

Most Holocaust archives see the Internet as a double-edged sword. While it gives the public wider access to their collections, the archives have less control over how their images are used. In July 2002 a web search revealed 1,143,237 sites relating to 'Holocaust', many of them using photographs. A search for 'Auschwitz' alone found 315,133. Some sites are almost exclusively made up of Holocaust photographs. A search for 'Holocaust photographs' found 65,000 sites. Many of these sites trade on the idea that the photographs will tell a story. On some websites the story is enhanced by the inclusion of pre-war family photographs of survivors interspersed with atrocity photographs. Many sites include the same photographs, frequently incorrectly captioned and categorized under generalized headings: 'Ghettos', 'Einsatzgruppen', 'Executions' and so on. On *The Holocaust History Project* website, the heading 'Einsatzgruppen' is sub-divided into 'Undressing and Waiting', 'The Shooting' and 'After the Killing'. The distressing images, one of which is of the massacre at Mizocz, showing the naked bodies of executed women strewn in a ravine (Figure 21), are accompanied by a constant flow of advertisements: 'Boost your business', 'Take $100 off your utility bills!', buy a mobile phone or a discount airfare. If you want further distraction from the atrocity photographs you can press the 'yes' button by the side of a photograph of a pouting blonde woman and a text which asks: 'Do you want to date me? Press yes or no.'[57]

It is difficult to look at these disturbing juxapostions without being reminded of the Nazis' photo albums – photographs of hangings and executions juxtaposed with photographs of places of interest and social gatherings. The Nazis took these photographs for personal gratification and to support Nazi ideology. They are now being used for commercial gain, for entertainment or to sell pornography. Are we educating ourselves or entertaining ourselves?

TEN
Dying for Eternity

§ In 1999 a new display of photographs was erected at various points around the camp at Birkenau. The photographs are from the Lili Jacob album of the arrivals at the ramp. Unlike the main Auschwitz camp, Birkenau had previously been left as a barren memorial, devoid of photographs and artefacts. Fewer visitors came to Birkenau, but of those who did, many found its bleak landscape more affecting than the ordered professional displays at Auschwitz. It was a place for reflection. Now there are billboards with photographs. One shows a bent elderly woman carrying a bundle under her arm. Trudging along beside her are three young children. In the original album it was placed on a page with three other uncaptioned photographs of women and children. In one photograph a group are walking carrying bundles of their belongings. In the other two they are grouped next to the barbed-wire fence posed for the camera.[1] We know that the photographs were taken at Birkenau. We also know that a large majority of those arriving at the ramp – particularly the young and the elderly – were sent straight to the gas-chambers. We believe the old woman and the three children were walking towards them. The captions bestowed on this picture have said so a thousand times.

It is a poignant image, a professional image. It could be a contemporary image made by a photojournalist in Bosnia or elsewhere of displaced persons or refugees. It would not be out of place in a newspaper or magazine. It is a photograph that would adapt to many stories. Images of the elderly and the young amid tragedy are particularly affecting; they represent the vulnerability of humankind. The Nazis equated their vulnerability with weakness; unfit for work, they were condemned to death. It was evidence of Nazi supremacy and of the efficiency of the selection process. To those who opposed the Nazi regime the same image was evidence of the Nazis' barbarism or a symbol of the destruction of European Jewry. Is there a correct interpretation? A photograph, Barthes said, proves little more than that the scene has actually existed. Any other meaning is extraneous. To know more we must look not at the photograph, but beyond it.[2]

The popular sentiments expressed about photographs – 'every picture tells a story' or 'a picture is worth a thousand words' – are meaningful only if the context or story has already been established, whether in a museum, an archive, a newspaper, a family album or even a death camp. Ulrich Keller, in his introduction to *The Warsaw Ghetto in Photographs, 206 Views Made in 1941*, writes: 'How we perceive and interpret a given photograph is largely a matter of the specific context in which we find it embedded, as well as the specific historical situation in which we are rooted ourselves.'[3] In addition to the context, a caption directs us how to 'read' an image and tells us what we should see. Anchoring meaning with captions was prevalent not only in Nazi propaganda or the personal photo albums made by the Nazis, who recognized that the image itself did not adequately reflect their ideology, but also in the Judenrat albums and in the photographs of those who opposed the Nazi regime. As Walter Benjamin asked in 1931, 'Will not the caption become the most important part of the photograph?'[4]

Whether or not a photograph is captioned, instinctively when we look at the framed image we want to *see* more. The captured moment intrigues us and disappoints us. What happened before or after the photograph was taken? We cannot know. The limitations of what a photograph can show prompt us to ask questions but can rarely answer them. Our imaginations, informed by the context of the photograph, complete the narrative of that which we don't see, that which lies outside the image. As Leon Wieseltier said of the family photographs found at Auschwitz, 'we must complete the story of every picture'.[5] This we do automatically. We do not show a family photograph or a family album to someone else without describing it; on the contrary, we tell stories that do not necessarily describe what the photographs show, but rather the associations and memories triggered by them.

When, as a lecturer in photojournalism, I would ask students to describe an image they had taken on assignment, their descriptions did not directly relate to the image but to the event itself. The photograph triggered recollections of a bigger picture. It wasn't so much that the students had not captured the essence of the event in their photograph, but that a photograph is a woefully inadequate way of imparting information. So empty is the two-dimensional image that we can fill it with meanings. Like memory, photographs are ephemeral, subject to change according to whom the memory belongs. But unlike memory, a photograph is evidence that a moment in time did indeed exist. As people learn to interpret photographs, they can also learn to interpret memory. At Yad Vashem, survivors are tutored in 'testimony classes', trained in vocabulary and how best to bring order to their fragments of memory and the confusion of the past.[6] Photographs, like memory, can reveal evidence of a moment-in-time but they can also conceal the story that lies outside the image.

Like many other repeatedly used images, this photograph of the elderly woman and the children has become not only an icon of the destruction of European Jewry but of Auschwitz-Birkenau. As very few people have direct memories of the camp, we 'know' it only through its relics and photographs. So familiar have these images become that we imagine that photographs – of the elderly woman and the children, the crowds on the ramp at Birkenau and the inscribed gates at Auschwitz – give us an unmediated access to the past. We imagine that this is how it was. Convinced that photographs reflect the reality of the past, we have entered the realm of fiction.

The images have become the sum total of what most people 'know' about the Holocaust. Pictures, often of unrelated events, sometimes taken thousands of miles apart, are placed side by side and give us the impression that there was some continuity in the events they portray. The historical facts of the policies of the Third Reich are reduced to easy-to-follow picture stories which can be made appropriate to many different memories. In the US Holocaust Memorial Museum, as in other Holocaust museums, the Holocaust narrative begins with Nazi Germany, then the ghettos, the camps and the liberations. The pictures of anonymous people displayed along the way belong to every story and yet are specific to none. In an episode of the BBC's *World at War* documentary series, made in 1975, Jews from Poland, Czechoslovakia, Hungary and Holland and an SS Lance-Corporal tell of their own experiences of Auschwitz-Birkenau.[7] The photographs taken at the ramp are used to authenticate their stories. We listen to each story and look at the photographs as a seamless account of what it was like. But the juxtaposition of their stories and the photographs cannot be their memory, or the memory of the photographer, or the memory of those on the ramp but, in effect, created 'memory'. It is, in effect, a fiction. Fiction invites fantasy.

The justification for looking at these images is that they will help to educate and act as a deterrent to racism and war, but nobody has ever produced any evidence for this. We do not commonly display images of war in the hope that the world can be rid of wars. On the contrary. The idea that atrocity photographs have an educational value is anathema to Zvi Oren, who has been involved in educating young people about the Holocaust for over a decade at the Ghetto Fighters' House. 'We try not to use horrendous photographs to teach about the Holocaust,' he said. 'The Holocaust is much more than mass graves.' In his opinion, rather than educate, atrocity photographs are more likely to alienate and discourage young people from learning about the Holocaust.[8] A young person at the exhibition at the US Holocaust Memorial Museum wrote in the visitors' book, 'I didn't like the exhibition as I don't like seeing my friends cry.' This may be a more cogent response than the young person, referred to in Chapter 8, who wrote that the exhibition was 'great'.[9]

These two responses highlight the dichotomy of looking at atrocity images. They prompt us to recoil or express futile generalized responses of disgust, as shown by those who peer at the horrific images behind the wall at the US Holocaust Memorial Museum, and yet they are compelling, as proved by the crowds who gather to look. And maybe images gratify. It is a disturbing fact that there are those who seem to derive some kind of satisfaction from looking at atrocity photographs. After visiting the US Holocaust Memorial Museum exhibition, there are some who get 'hooked on horror' pictures and call in at the photo archive asking to see more. The archivists usually show them a binder containing the liberation images of Buchenwald taken by Signal Corps photographers, which they consider to be some of the most horrific. The majority turn a few pages and leave. Occasionally, someone will spend a long time looking at them and ask to see more, although this is rare. US Holocaust Memorial Museum historian Ann Millin said that they have never been able to figure out why people do this. At best they think that people need to see additional evidence to absorb the shock of what they saw and try and make sense of it.[10] But looking at a graphic photograph of piles of corpses at Buchenwald cannot make sense of what happened. If acts of atrocity are beyond the comprehension of most of us, then little can be achieved by looking at images of them. So why display them? *Are* the effusive displays of photographs really teaching us about the Second World War and the Nazi genocide? Or has 'The Holocaust' – as represented by these photographs – proven to be, as Finkelstein suggests, 'an indispensable ideological weapon'.[11]

The emphasis on victimization and atrocity photographs has produced visual casualties – for example, the albums of the Łódź Judenrat and Arie ben-Menachem discussed in Chapter 4. Their messages are much harder to comprehend than images of anonymous emaciated people dying in the ghetto streets. They challenge our preconceptions of the ghetto. To appreciate their significance requires an understanding of the complex politics involved, and a depth of analysis that few want to undertake. Maybe this is where the problem lies. The Judenrat was a particularly difficult memory for many Jewish communities to contend with. Compliance with Nazi authority was not a phenomenon they wanted to consider – though during recent years the role of the Judenrat has been reassessed and judged less harshly, based on the premise that it is impossible to know how others might have acted in similar circumstances. Some of the photographs taken by Mordechaj Mendel Grosman or Henryk Rozencwajg-Ross, however, are used because like the photographs the Nazis took they show the victims.

The majority of photographs displayed as evidence of the Holocaust were made by the Nazis as proof of their power. It could be said that the Nazis' obsessive visual documentation is in part responsible for making the Holocaust unique. If there were no pictures, what would the public memory of the Holocaust

56 · A photograph from the Lili Jacob album erected at Birkenau, 1999. (Copyright Janina Struk)

be, and how would the plethora of museums and exhibitions represent it? How many perpetrators of genocide have left behind such a detailed documentation of their crimes? How many intended to display them? If the Nazis' intention to memorialize the destruction of European Jewry in a museum in Prague had been realized, what would their exhibition have looked like? Their narrative would undoubtedly have used some of the same photographs of the ghettos, public hangings and mass executions and those produced by the Erkennungsdienst photographers at the camps. Same photographs, different story.

The Nazis took photographs of their victims to humiliate and degrade them. Are we not colluding with them by displaying them ourselves? Do we have a right to show people in their last moments before facing death, to support propaganda, for whatever purpose? Must the torment and deaths of millions be replayed on museum walls around the world for millions to watch? It seems time to call a halt to the repetitive and frequently reckless use of these photographs, out of respect for those who died. Consider if *you* would want your last moments of a degrading and unimaginably cruel death to be flaunted world-wide to support any amount of causes, let alone to sell cars, pornography, or even books? Should we not return these photographs, and those unfortunate enough to be in them, to the status of historical documents, instead of flaunting them?

The photograph of the old woman and the children has been erected so that they face down a long track which once led to the gas-chamber (see Figure 56). Whoever they were, they have been condemned to tread the path for ever. Returning their image to Birkenau may be their final humiliation. They had no choice but to be photographed. Now they have no choice but to be viewed by posterity. Didn't they suffer enough the first time around?

Notes

Introduction

1. Susan Sontag, *On Photography* (London, 1979), p. 111.

2. Ibid., p. 19.

3. I have consulted a number of historians about the identity of the perpetrators in this photograph and no one is able to identify their uniforms.

4. US Holocaust Memorial Museum (USHMM) photo archives worksheet 19359.

5. Sybil Milton and Roland Klemig (eds), *Archives of the Holocaust: An International Collection of Selected Documents*, vol. 1, *Bildarchiv Preussischer Kulterbesitz, Berlin*, Part 2, 1939–1945 (New York and London, 1990), photo no. 414.

6. Jewish Historical Committee *Zagłada Żydostwa Polskiego, Album Zdjęć* (The Extermination of Polish Jews, an Album of Photographs) (Łódź, 1945), photo nos 195, 196. The juxtaposition of these two photographs is also displayed in 'Martyrology of the Jews', at Auschwitz-Birkenau State Museum and Yad Vashem Martyrs' and Heroes' Remembrance Authority in Jerusalem. In the latter it is captioned 'Extermination by Einsatzgruppen' and is flipped left to right. See also USHMM photo archives worksheets nos 43195 and 43196 where in both the photograph of the women and the photograph of the 'death pit' the location is given as Śniatyń. The caption of the former reads, 'German police and Ukrainian collaborators in civilian clothes look on as Jewish women are forced to undress before their execution, 11 May 1943', and the latter, 'German police and Ukrainian collaborators in civilian clothing'.

7. Tadeusz Mazur, Jerzy Tomaszewski and Stanisław Wrzos-Glinka (eds), *1939–1945, We Have Not Forgotten* (Warsaw, 1959), p. 71.

8. *Action J* (Walter Heynowski, GDR, 1959).

9. Jakub Poznański, *Pamiętnik z Getta Łódźkiego* (Łódź, 1960), p. 240.

10. Adam Rutkowski, *Męczeństwo, Walka, Zagłada Żydów w Polsce 1939–1945* (Warsaw, 1960), photo no. 321.

11. Fédération Nationale des Déportés et Internés Résistants et Patriotes, *La Déportation* (Paris, 1968), p. 50.

12. The Hebrew word for Holocaust is 'Shoah', which is preferred by some Jewish historians, and which means 'desolation'.

13. Martin Gilbert, *The Holocaust: Maps & Photographs* (London, 1978), p. 51. The Polish name is incorrectly spelt – the town is called Śniadowo.

14. Gerhard Schoenberner, *The Yellow Star: The Persecution of the Jews in Europe 1933–1945* (London, 1978), pp. 224, 89.

15. Michael Berenbaum, *The World Must Know: The History of the Holocaust as Told in the United States Holocaust Memorial Museum* (Boston, Toronto and London, 1993), p. 97.

16. *The World at War*, no. 20, 'Genocide', BBC Television, 1975.

17. Ernst Klee, Willi Dressen and Volker Riess (eds), *'The Good Old Days': The Holocaust as Seen by Its Perpetrators and Bystanders* (New York, 1991), p. 97.

18. *Executions*, directed and produced by David Herman, Arun Kurmar and David Monaghan (1995).

19. Hamburg Institute for Social Research (eds), *The German Army and Genocide, Crimes Against War Prisoners, Jews, and Other Civilians, 1939–1944* (New York, 1999), p. 129.

20. Yitzhak Arad (ed.), *The Pictorial History of the Holocaust* (New York, 1990), p. 195. See also <http://mod.owe.lug.a.be/Schmitt/Holocaust/eg3.html>.

21. Udo Walendy, *Forged War Crimes Malign the German Nation* (Hull, 1979), p. 48.

22. Allan Sekula, 'Photography Between Labour and Capital', in B. H. D. Buchloh and R. Wilkie (eds), *Mining Photographs and Other Pictures 1948–1968* (Nova Scotia, 1983), p. 194.

23. The term Holocaust is in wide general use in Western Europe, Israel and the USA but not necessarily in Poland.

24. USHMM photo archives worksheet no. 43196.

25. James E. Young, *The Texture of Memory: Holocaust Memorials and Meanings* (New Haven and London, 1993), p. 2.

1. Photography and National Socialism

1. See generally: John Willett, *The New Sobriety: Art and Politics in the Weimar Period 1917–1933* (London, 1978).

2. Walter Benjamin, 'New Things About Plants', in D. Mellor (ed.), *Germany: The New Photography 1927–33* (London, 1978), p. 20.

3. For an essay about the German workers' photography movement see: W. Körner and J. Stüber, 'Germany: Arbeiter-Fotografie', in Photography Workshop (eds) *Photography Politics: One* (London, 1979), pp. 73–81.

4. Benjamin, 'New Things About Plants', p. 20.

5. David Green, 'On Foucault: Disciplinary Power and Photography', in J. Evans (ed.), *The Camerawork Essays: Context and Meaning in Photography* (London, 1997), p. 127. For a general discussion see: John Tagg, *The Burden of Representation: Essays on Photographies and Histories* (London, 1988), pp. 66–102; David Green, 'Classified Subjects', *Ten.8*, no. 14 (1984), pp. 30–7; David Green, 'A Map of Depravity', *Ten.8*, no. 18 (1985), pp. 36–43; Allan Sekula, *Photography Against the Grain: Essays and Photo Works 1973–1983* (Nova Scotia, 1984), pp. 77–101.

6. A. Kraszna-Krausz, 'Exhibition in Stuttgart, June 1929, and Its Effects', in Mellor (ed.), *Germany: The New Photography 1927–33*, p. 35.

7. For an critique of Sander's work see Anne Halley, 'August Sander', in J. Liebling (ed.), *Photography: Current Perspectives* (Rochester, NY, 1978), pp. 35–51.

8. August Sander, 'From: "The Nature & Growth of Photography": Lecture 5: "Photography as a Universal Language"', in Liebling (ed.), *Photography*, p. 50.

9. Walter Benjamin, 'Extract from *A Short History of Photography*', in Mellor (ed.), *Germany: The New Photography*, p. 71.

10. *Głos Gminy Żydowskiej*, Year I, August 1937, no. 2, p. 43. Year I, September 1937, no. 3, pp. 65–6; Year I, November 1937, no. 5, p. 116; Year I, December 1937, no. 6, p. 140.

11. Halley, 'August Sander', pp. 40–3.

12. Tagg, *The Burden of Representation*, pp. 8–12.

13. Tim Gidal, 'Modern Photojournalism – The First Years', *Creative Camera*, no. 211 (July/August 1982), p. 573.

14. Walter Benjamin, *Illuminations* (London, 1979), p. 226.

15. Peter Reichel, 'Images of the National Socialist State. Images of Power – Power of Images', in K. Honnef, R. Sachsse and K. Thomas (eds), *German Photography 1870–1970, Power of a Medium* (Cologne, 1997), p. 70.

16. Hanno Loewy, '" … without masks": Jews Through the Lens of "German Photography" 1933–1945', in Honnef et al. (eds), *German Photography 1870–1970*, p. 101. For a short history of German anti-Semitism see Matthew Stibbe, *Nineteenth Century German Antisemitic Propagandists*, Holocaust Educational Trust Research Papers, vol. 2, no. 1 (2000–01).

17. Loewy, ' " … without masks"', p. 103. For images from 'The Eternal Jew' exhibition see: MOI files/Jew (AUT), Department of Photographs, Imperial War Museum (IWM).

18. Reichel, 'Images of the National Socialist State', p. 79.

19. Sybil Milton, 'The Camera as Weapon: Documentary Photography and the Holocaust', *Simon Wiesenthal Center Annual*, vol. 1 (New York, 1984), p. 47.

20. *The Yellow Spot: The Extermination of the Jews in Germany* (London, 1936), pp. 225, 227.

21. Milton, 'The Camera as Weapon', p. 47.

22. Rolf Sachsse, 'Photography as NS State Design/ Power's Abuse of a Medium', in Honnef et al. (eds), *German Photography 1870–1970*, p. 92.

23. Martin Gilbert, *The Holocaust: The Jewish Tragedy* (London, 1987), pp. 32–6.

24. Gidal, 'Modern Photojournalism', pp. 572–83 and 'Working for *Picture Post*', pp. 602–9, *Creative Camera*, no. 211 (July/August 1982).

25. Institut für Auslandsbeziehungen Stuttgart, *Photography in the Weimar Republic* (Stuttgart, 1983).

26. Gisèle Freund, *Photography & Society* (London, 1980), pp. 131–5.

27. Sachsse, 'Photography as NS State Design', p. 90.

28. C. A. Kanitzberg, 'Der neue Weg', *Photofreund*, no. 13 (20 July 1933), Berlin, pp. 259–60, quoted in Loewy, '"… without masks"', p. 100.

29. Heiner Kurzbein, 'Reichsverband deutscher Amateurfotografen', *Photofreund*, no. 13 (20 July 1933), pp. 367 quoted in Loewy, '"… without masks"', p. 104.

30. Sachsse, 'Photography as NS State Design', p. 91.

31. Yad Vashem Film and Photo Archives (YVFPA), album FA/161.

32. Library of Congress, lot 11369.

33. The SS, or Schutzstaffel, 'protection squad' was Hitler's personal police force founded in 1925.

34. Library of Congress, lot 11390.

35. Library of Congress, document 3381.

36. Library of Congress, Göring's Library. Album 12.01.1937.

37. *The Library of Congress Quarterly, Journal of Current Acquisitions*, vol. 6, no. 4 (August 1949), p. 21.

38. Gilbert, *The Holocaust*, pp. 47–8.

39. Ibid., pp. 53–4.

40. Ibid., pp. 58–9.

41. Ibid., p. 69.

42. Martin Gilbert, *The Holocaust: Maps & Photographs* (London, 1978), p. 6.

43. *150 Lat Fotografii Polskiej* (Warsaw, 1989), p. 12.

44. 'Kazimierz Krakowski', in *Polish Jews*, a video compiled by Documentary and Feature Film Archive, Warsaw (2000).

45. Marion Wiesal (ed.), *To Give Them Light: The Legacy of Roman Vishniac* (New York, 1993), see Bibliographical Note.

46. Roman Vishniac, *A Vanished World* (New York, 1983), see Preface.

47. Ibid., see notes to photographs, 132, 133.

2. Photographs as Evidence

1. Andrew Sharf, 'The British Press and the Holocaust', in N. Eck and A. L. Kubovy (eds), *Yad Vashem Studies on the European Jewish Catastrophe and Resistance* (Yad Vashem, Jerusalem, 1963). For picture stories see *Picture Post*, 26 November 1938, pp. 13–19; *Life*, 21 August 1939, pp. 22–3.

2. Phillip Knightley, *The First Casualty: The War Correspondent as Hero, Propagandist and Mythmaker from the Crimea to Vietnam* (London, 1975), pp. 80–2. For an account of the British propaganda campaign see Arthur Ponsonby, *Falsehood in Wartime* (London, 1928).

3. PRO FO/371/23105.

4. Ibid.

5. Ibid.

6. Tony Kushner, *The Holocaust and the Liberal Imagination: A Social and Cultural History* (Oxford, 1994), pp. 124–5.

7. *Life*, 25 September 1939, p. 85.

8. PRO FO/371/24227.

9. Knightley, *The First Casualty*, pp. 220–1.

10. PRO INF/1/908, 'Photographs as News', July 1941.

11. *Life*, 18 September 1939, p. 6.

12. *Life*, 2 October 1939, pp. 16–17.

13. R. Hunt and T. Hartman (eds), *Swastika at War. A Photographic Record of the War in Europe as Seen by the Cameramen of the German Magazine Signal* (London, 1975), see Introduction.

14. PRO INF/1/908.

15. PRO FO/371/24227.

16. *Life*, 28 August 1939, p. 9.

17. Andrew Mollo, *The Pictorial History of the SS 1923–1945* (London, 1976), p. 12.

18. Janusz Gumkowski and Rajmund Kuczma, *Zbrodnie Hitlerowskie Bydgoszcz 1939* (Warsaw, 1967), pp. 10–11.

19. Polish Ministry of Information, *The German New Order in Poland* (London, 1942), p. 133.

20. *Life*, 2 October 1939, p. 20.

21. *The Heroic Battle of the Poles: Poland's Fight for Civilisation and Democracy* (Geneva, 1940), p. 10; *Polish*
Acts of Atrocity Against the German Minority in Poland (Berlin and New York, 1940), p. 10.

22. *Polish Acts of Atrocity*, pp. 9–10.

23. *The Heroic Battle of the Poles*, pp. 277–309; *Polish Acts of Atrocity*, p. 11.

24. *The Times*, 18 March 1940, p. 6.

25. PRO FO/371/27031.

26. *Polish Acts of Atrocity*, pp. 77–89.

27. Julien Bryan, *Warsaw, 1939 Siege, 1959 Warsaw Revisited* (Warsaw, 1960), pp. 14–15.

28. Ibid., pp. 14, 18.

29. Ibid., pp. 18, 20.

30. *Life*, 23 October 1939, pp. 73–7.

31. Bryan, *Warsaw, 1939*, p. 21.

32. Klaus Kirchner (ed.), *Flugblätt-Propaganda IM 2. Weltkrieg Flugblätter aus England, G-1943–G-1944* (Erlangen, Germany, 1979), pp. 286, 347.

33. Bryan, *Warsaw, 1939*, pp. 93, 118–21, 159–60. Bryan later states that Kazimiera Mika was twelve years old in 1939.

34. The General Government did not cover the whole of Poland. Western parts of the country, which the Nazis considered German, such as Upper Silesia, Wartheland and West Prussia, were incorporated into the Third Reich.

35. Author's correspondence with Feliks Forbert-Kaniewski, 2002.

36. Henryk Latoś, *Z Historii Fotografii Wojennej* (Warsaw, 1985), pp. 165–78.

37. Andrzej Suchcitz, *Informator Studium Polski Podziemnej 1947–1997* (London, 1997), pp. 159–75.

38. Jan Karski, *Story of a Secret State* (London, 1945), p. 290. For further references to smuggling photographs see: pp. 120, 128–9, 136–7.

39. Jacob Apenszlak (ed.), *The Black Book of Polish Jewry: An Account of the Martyrdom of Polish Jewry Under the Nazi Occupation* (New York, 1943), p. xii.

40. *The War Illustrated*, 5 April 1940, p. 328.

41. See MOI files/Jew (Pol), Department of Photographs, Imperial War Museum (IWM).

42. In Bryan, *Warsaw, 1939*, the caption reads 'Two old Orthodox Jews, helping, like all Warsaw citizens, to defend their city', p. 52.

43. Polish Ministry of Information, *The German New Order in Poland*, photo no. 49.

44. Apenszlak (ed.), *The Black Book of Polish Jewry*, p. 16.

45. There are many examples of photographs copied from German publications in the Polish Institute and Sikorski Museum and the Polish Underground Movement (1939–45) Study Trust photo archive files.

46. For example, the photograph is captioned 'Forced labor in Cracow, Poland' in Yitzhak Arad (ed.), *The Pictorial History of the Holocaust* (New York, 1990), photo no. 96.

47. PRO INF/1/702.

48. PRO INF/1/737.

49. PRO INF/1/702.

50. Ibid.

51. *The War Illustrated*, 16 February 1940, pp. 106–7.

52. *Life*, 26 February 1940, p. 30.

53. *Daily Telegraph*, 19 March 1940, p. 1.

54. *Life*, 29 April 1940, p. 29.

55. *PM*, 5 February 1941, pp. 15–19.

56. Some captions to the 'Labor Battalions' image refer to those in the photograph as Poles, others as Jews. See MOI files/Jew (Pol), Department of Photographs, IWM.

57. See MOI files, Department of Photographs, IWM.

58. PRO INF/1/702.

59. Ibid. A similar photograph of the Warsaw ghetto wall had been published in Britain in *The War Illustrated*, 7 March 1941, p. 251.

60. PRO INF/1/702. The photographs are in PRO CN/11/8.

61. PRO INF/1/702.

62. *The War Illustrated*, 18 April 1941, p. 401; *Illustrated London News*, 22 March 1941, p. 387.

63. Stanisław Kobiela, 'Między Uzbornią a Katyniem', *Wiadomości Bocheńskie* – Spring, 1996, pp. 3–7. The album is in Instytut Pamięci Narodowej (IPN). See Izabela Gass, 'Zbiór Fotografii Głównej Komisji Badania Zbrodni Hitlerowskich w Polsce – Instytut Pamięci Narodowej', *Fotografia*, vols 3–4, nos 49–50 (1988).

64. Author's conversation with Janina Kęsek, Curator of Photographs, Muzeum Im. Stanisława Fischera in Bochnia, Poland, 1999.

65. Five of the Bochnia photographs are captioned as 'Palmiry Forest outside Warsaw 1940', in Sybil Milton and Roland Klemig (eds), *Archives of the Holocaust: An International Collection of Selected Documents*, vol. 1, *Bildarchiv Preussischer Kulterbesitz, Berlin*, Part 2 1939–45 (New York and London, 1990), see photo nos 368, 370–3.

66. Apenszlak (ed.), *The Black Book of Polish Jewry*, p. xiii.

67. Karski, *Story of a Secret State*, pp. 290–310.

68. Ibid., pp. 310–18.

69. Ibid., pp. 273–7.

70. PRO FO 371/34549, January 1943.

71. PRO FO/371/34549.

72. Vernon McKenzie, 'Atrocities in World War II – What We Can Believe', *Journalism Quarterly*, vol. 19, no. 3 (September 1942), p. 269.

73. PRO FO/371/34551.

74. Gerald R. Reitlinger, *The Final Solution: The Attempt to Exterminate the Jews of Europe, 1939–1945* (London, 1953), p. 242.

75. Judith Levin and Daniel Uziel, 'Ordinary Men, Extraordinary Photographs', *Yad Vashem Studies*, no.

XXVI (Jerusalem, 1998), p. 282.

76. See Polish Institute and Sikorski Museum photo archive files.

77. *Daily Mirror*, 28 July 1941, p. 5.

78. Mass-Observation Archive (M-O A): FR 771, 'Invasion of Russia and the Press-survey', 23 July 1941, p. 8. Mass-Observation was founded by Charles Madge and Tom Harrison in 1937; its archive is housed at the University of Sussex, England. All quotations from the archive are reproduced with permission of Curtis Brown Group Ltd, London, on behalf of the Trustees of the Mass-Observation Archive; copyright © Trustees of the Mass-Observation Archive.

79. M-O A: Mary Adams Papers 4E, pp. 15, 16; PRO FO/371/32967, 'Russia at War' exhibition; PRO INF/1/133, 'Red Army' exhibition, 1943; see *Soviet War News Weekly*, 21 January 1943, p. 6; *Anglo Soviet Journal*, vol. IV, no. 1 (January–March 1943), p. 59.

80. M-O A: Mary Adams Papers, Box 4, File 4G 'Morale in 1941', p. 35.

81. M-O A: TC Films 17/7/1, 1936–50, Captured German War Films, 11 September 1941.

82. M-O A: TC Films 7/1, Captured German Propaganda Films, Cricklewood, 8 September 1941, pp. 1–4.

83. M-O A: TC 17/7/1/1936–50, Captured German War Films, 11 September 1941.

84. *Soviet War News*, 27 November 1941; PRO FO/371/32942, April 1942, 'Special Bulletin' on German Atrocities in the Soviet Union.

85. *Soviet War News Weekly*, 19 November 1942, p. 6.

86. PRO FO/371/32942.

87. Ibid.

88. PRO FO/371/34549, 26 January 1943.

89. PRO FO/371/32942.

90. *Daily Sketch*, 11 February 1942, p. 8.

91. *Soviet War News Weekly*, 19 February 1942, p. 3. The photographs are also in MOI files, Department of Photographs, IWM.

92. *Picture Post*, 20 June 1942, pp. 7–9. The photograph of the mother searching for her son was taken by Soviet photojournalist Dymitr Baltermanc in Kerch although he was not credited. See Kazimierz, Seko, 'Dymitr Baltermanc', *Fotografia*, vol. 1, no. 39 (1986).

93. M-O A: FR 25/4, file A, 'Political Attitudes and Behaviour'.

94. M-O A: FR 1378, p. 3.

95. *Doncaster Gazette*, 23 July 1942, p. 4.

96. PRO INF/1/133.

97. *Doncaster Gazette*, 18 February 1943, p. 5.

98. PRO INF/1/778.

99. *Doncaster Gazette*, 11 February 1943, p. 1.

100. Some of the original exhibited photographs are in the MOI files, Department of Photographs, IWM. The

exhibition text is in: PRO INF/1/778.

101.   *Doncaster Gazette*, 18 February 1943, p. 5; PRO INF/1/133.

102.   See US Holocaust Memorial Museum (USHMM), photo archives worksheet no. 69743; *New York Times*, 18 May 1943, p. 19.

103.   Polish Institute and Sikorski Museum, albums 8/A1, 9/A19, March 1943.

104.   Ibid., albums 8/A1, 9/A1.

105.   USHMM, photo archives worksheet no. 03962.

106.   *Illustrated*, 24 April 1943, pp. 3–7. All of these photographs, with the same captions as in *Illustrated*, are in MOI files, Department of Photographs, IWM, credited to the US agency Black Star.

107.   M-O A: TC propaganda Box 5F and exhibition leaflet, pp. 1–4.

108.   Author's correspondence with Wolfgang Suschitzky, 2002.

3. Armed with a Camera

1.   Judith Levin and Daniel Uziel, 'Ordinary Men, Extraordinary Photos', *Yad Vashem Studies*, no. XXVI (Jerusalem, 1998), p. 276.

2.   Alexander B. Rossino, 'Eastern Europe Through German Eyes: Soldiers' Photographs 1939–42', *History of Photography*, vol. 23, no. 4 (Winter 1999), pp. 315, 316. See the photograph captioned 'A Nazi Mock Mass' published in *Polish Review* (New York), 30 August 1941.

3.   Alexander B. Rossino, 'Destructive Impulses: German Soldiers and the Conquest of Poland', *Holocaust and Genocide Studies*, vol. II, no. 3 (Winter 1997), pp. 353–4; Rossino, 'Eastern Europe Through German Eyes', p. 316.

4.   Levin and Uziel, 'Ordinary Men, Extraordinary Photos', p. 269.

5.   Yad Vashem Film and Photo Archives (YVFPA), albums FA/171, FA/29.

6.   Martin Gilbert, *The Holocaust: The Jewish Tragedy* (London, 1987), p. 656.

7.   Leif Furhammar and Folke Isaksson, *Politics and Film* (London, 1971), p. 116.

8.   Erwin Leiser, *Nazi Cinema* (London, 1974), p. 85; Roger Manvell and Heinrich Fraenkel, *The German Cinema*, (London, 1971), pp. 88–90.

9.   Omer Bartov, *Hitler's Army: Soldiers, Nazis, and War in the Third Reich* (New York and Oxford, 1991), p. 127.

10.   Daniel Jonah Goldhagen, *Hitler's Willing Executioners: Ordinary Germans and the Holocaust* (New York, 1996), p. 245.

11.   Levin and Uziel, 'Ordinary Men, Extraordinary Photos', p. 269.

12.   Rossino, 'Destructive Impulses', p. 355.

13.   Susan Sontag, *On Photography* (London, 1979), pp. 8–10.

14.   YVFPA, album FA/300.

15.   *IKP*, no. 2, Year 1, 10 March 1940; no. 9, Year 1, 16 June 1940.

16.   Charles W. Sydnor Jr, *Soldiers of Destruction. The SS Death's Head Division 1933–1945* (New Jersey, 1977), pp. 37–43.

17.   See US Holocaust Memorial Museum (USHMM) photo archives worksheets nos 50414, 50415, 80965, 50418, 50421. For a description of the action see Rossino, 'Destructive Impulses', pp. 358–9.

18.   Janusz Gumkowski and Kazimierz Leszczyński, *Poland Under Nazi Occupation* (Warsaw, 1961), pp. 53–6. See USHMM photo archives worksheets nos 50850, 50852, 50855, 50858, 81247.

19.   For an example of a narrative sequence see USHMM photo archives worksheets nos 18100–37 which show a massacre of between twenty and twenty-five males carried out in Serbia.

20.   USHMM photo archives worksheets nos 26822–31, 21435.

21.   Wiener Library photo archive.

22.   Goldhagen, *Hitler's Willing Executioners*, p. 246.

23.   Sontag, *On Photography*, pp. 14–15.

24.   Hanno Loewy, '" … without masks": Jews Through the Lens of "German Photography" 1933–1945', in K. Honnef, R. Sachsse and K. Thomas (eds), *German Photography 1870–1970, Power of a Medium* (Cologne, 1997), p. 106.

25.   Ghetto Fighters' House (GFH), photo album 7.

26.   For albums containing photographs of hangings, see: YVFPA, albums FA/30, FA/76, FA/54, FA/279 (the Łódź hanging photographed from a different point of view). See also photo album 9701-17 at the Imperial War Museum (IWM).

27.   Goldhagen, *Hitler's Willing Executioners*, p. 246.

28.   Hamburg Institute for Social Research (eds), *The German Army and Genocide, Crimes Against War Prisoners, Jews, and Other Civilians, 1939–1944* (New York, 1999), p. 150.

29.   Walter Benjamin, 'Extract from *A Short History of Photography*' in Mellor (ed.), *Germany: The New Photography 1927–33* (London, 1978), p. 75.

30.   Ulrich Keller (ed.), *The Warsaw Ghetto in Photographs: 206 Views Made in 1941* (New York and London, 1984), p. xix.

31.   YVFPA, album FA/300.

32.   YVFPA, album FA/76.

33.   GFH, photo albums 51, 52.

34.   Niall Ferguson, *The Pity of War* (London, 1998), images 15–18.

35.   The private photo album of Mr C. Ripley.

36. This photograph was widely publicized during mid-2002. See *Journalist*, April and June/July 2002.

37. Rossino, 'Destructive Impulses', p. 361.

38. USHMM photo archives worksheets nos 28216, 28217.

39. USHMM photo archives worksheet no. 60254.

40. YVFPA, document v-23-A. The Einsatzgruppe were mobile units set up for 'special tasks', including the extermination of Eastern European Jewry. Ernst Klee, Willi Dressen and Volker Reiss (eds), *'The Good Old Days': The Holocaust as Seen by Its Perpetrators and Bystanders* (New York, 1991), pp. 126–8.

41. *Trials of War Criminals Before the Nuernberg Military Tribunals – Under Control Council Law Number 10*, vol. x (Washington, DC, 1951), p. 1209.

42. Hamburg Institute for Social Research (eds), *The German Army and Genocide*, p. 89.

43. Sybil Milton, 'The Camera as Weapon: Documentary Photography and the Holocaust', *Simon Wiesenthal Center Annual*, vol. 1 (New York, 1984), p. 48.

44. YVFPA, document v-23-A.

45. Klee et al. (eds), *'The Good Old Days'*, pp. 196–207.

46. See Norman G. Finkelstein, *Image and Reality of the Israel–Palestine Conflict* (London and New York, 2001), pp. 116–18.

47. Polish Ministry of Information, *The German New Order in Poland* (London, 1942), pp. 103–11; Jacob Apenszlak (ed.), *The Black Book of Polish Jewry: An Account of the Martyrdom of Polish Jewry Under the Nazi Occupation* (New York, 1943), pp. 28–9.

48. YVFPA, album FA/30.

49. USHMM photo archives worksheets nos 19121, 19118; Novosti photo archive photo no. 0013999; Klee et al. (eds), *'The Good Old Days'*, p. 128.

50. USHMM photo archives worksheets nos 17875, 17876, 17877, 17878, 17879.

51. For debate see Rossino, 'Eastern Europe Through German Eyes', pp. 314–15.

52. Philip Gourevitch, 'In the Holocaust Theme Park', *Observer* magazine, 30 January 1994, p. 25.

53. PRO INF/1/702.

54. Phillip Knightley, *The First Casualty: The War Correspondent as Hero, Propagandist, and Mythmaker from the Crimea to Vietnam* (London, 1975), p. 221.

4. Cameras in the Ghettos

1. Raul Hilberg, Stanisław Staron and Józef Kermish (eds), *The Warsaw Diary of Adam Czerniaków* (New York, 1979), p. 5.

2. Jan Karski, *Story of a Secret State* (London, 1945), p. 270. For Karski's account of his visit to the Warsaw ghetto, see pp. 261–77.

3. *IKP*, no. 7, Year 3, 15 February 1942.

4. Erwin Leiser, *Nazi Cinema* (London, 1974), pp. 85–8; Leif Furhammar and Folke Isaksson, *Politics and Film* (London, 1971), pp. 116–20.

5. Hilberg et al. (eds) *The Warsaw Diary of Adam Czerniaków* (30 April and 1 May 1941), p. 227.

6. Ulrich Keller (ed.), *The Warsaw Ghetto in Photographs, 206 Views Made in 1941* (New York and London, 1984), p. x.

7. Danuta Jackiewicz and Eugeniusz Cezary Król (eds), *Warsaw 1940–1941 Photographed by Dr Hans-Joachim Gerke* (Warsaw, 1996), p. xxxiii.

8. Rafael F. Scharf (ed.), *In the Warsaw Ghetto : Summer 1941, with Passages from Warsaw Ghetto Diaries. Photographs by Willy Georg* (London, 1993), pp. 110–11.

9. *A Day in the Warsaw Ghetto. A Birthday Trip to Hell*, a film by Jack Kuper, Kuper Productions Ltd, 1991.

10. Günther Schwarberg, *In the Ghetto of Warsaw Heinrich Jöst's Photographs* (Göttingen, 2001), photo no. 41.

11. Joe J. Heydecker, 'Photographing Behind the Warsaw Ghetto Wall, 1941', *Holocaust & Genocide Studies. An International Journal*, vol. 1, no. 1 (1986), p. 75.

12. Joe J. Heydecker, *The Warsaw Ghetto – A Photographic Record, 1941–44* (London, 1990), p. 18.

13. Heydecker, *The Warsaw Ghetto*, p. 21.

14. Heydecker, 'Photographing Behind the Warsaw Ghetto Wall', pp. 76–7.

15. Hilberg et al. (eds), *The Warsaw Diary of Adam Czerniaków* (4 May 1941), pp. 228–9; (19 May 1941), p. 237.

16. Phillip Knightley, *The First Casualty: The War Correspondent as Hero, Propagandist, and Mythmaker from the Crimea to Vietnam* (London, 1975), p. 221.

17. Jacob Sloan, *Notes from the Warsaw Ghetto. The Journal of Emmanuel Ringelblum* (New York, 1958), (20 May 1941), p. 181.

18. Abraham I. Katsh (ed.), *Scroll of Agony: The Warsaw Diary of Chaim A. Kaplan* (Indiana, 1999), p. 336.

19. M. Zylberberg, *A Warsaw Diary 1939–1945* (London, 1969), p. 31.

20. Hilberg et al. (eds), *The Warsaw Diary of Adam Czerniaków*, pp. 348–50.

21. S. L. Shneiderman (ed.), *Warsaw Ghetto: A Diary by Mary Berg* (New York, 1945), pp. 149–61.

22. Katsh (ed.), *Scroll of Agony*, pp. 334–5. See *Berliner Illustrirte Zeitung*, 24 July 1941, US Holocaust Memorial Museum (USHMM) photo archives worksheet no. 31530.

23. Hilberg et al. (eds), *The Warsaw Diary of Adam Czerniaków*, p. 353.

24. Katsh (ed.), *Scroll of Agony* (14 May 1942), pp. 331–2.

25. Keller (ed.), *The Warsaw Ghetto in Photographs*, p. x.

26. Władysław Szpilman, *The Pianist: The Extraordinary Story of One Man's Survival in Warsaw, 1939–45* (London, 1999), p. 81.

27. Lucjan Dobroszycki (ed.), *The Chronicle of the Łódź Ghetto 1941–1944* (New Haven, CT and London, 1984), p. 203.

28. A film by Dariusz Jabłoński, *Storyville – Photos of Łódź Ghetto* (1998).

29. Dobroszycki (ed.), *The Chronicle of the Łódź Ghetto*, p. 209.

30. Hanno Loewy, '"..without masks": Jews Through the Lens of "German Photography" 1933–1945', in K. Honnef, R. Sachsse, K. Thomas (eds), *German Photography 1870–1970, Power of a Medium* (Cologne, 1997), p. 104.

31. Martin Gilbert, *The Holocaust: The Jewish Tragedy* (London, 1987), pp. 387–401; Szpilman, *The Pianist*, p. 90.

32. *7 Dni*, no. 11, Year IV (13 March 1943), p. 5.

33. *IKP*, no. 41, Year 4, 10 October 1943.

34. Jan Jagielski and Urszula Kobiałka-Fuks (eds), *Getto Warszawskie 1940–1942: zdjęcia wykonane przez ludność żydowską* (Warsaw, 1996), p. 13.

35. The original album is in Instytut Pamięci Narodowej (IPN). Andrzej Wirth, *The Stroop Report: The Jewish Quarter of Warsaw is No More* (London, 1980); Jewish Historical Institute, *The Report of Jürgen Stroop* (Warsaw, 1958).

36. Jewish Historical Institute, *Salvaged from the Warsaw Ghetto: The Archives of E. Ringelblum* (Warsaw, 1993); Jagielski and Kobiałka-Fuks (eds), *Getto Warszawskie 1940–1942*, p. 6.

37. Nachman Zonabend, *The Truth About the Saving of The Łódź Ghetto Archive* (Stockholm, 1991), p. 10.

38. Dobroszycki (ed.), *The Chronicle of the Łódź Ghetto*, pp. x–xiv.

39. Genya Markon, 'The Photo Archives of the United States Holocaust Memorial Museum', *History of Photography* (Winter 1999), p. 344.

40. For Foto-Forbert photographs in the Polish Jewish press see: *Ekspres*, 1932; *Głos Gminy Żydowskiej*, 1937, 1938, 1939; and *Nasz Przegląd*, 1936. Author's correspondence with Katia Forbert Petersen and Feliks Forbert-Kaniewski, 2002.

41. Yad Vashem Film and Photo Archives (YVFPA) albums, FA/33, 34, 35, 36; Jagielski and Kobiałka-Fuks (eds), *Getto Warszawskie 1940–1942*, pp. 5–6.

42. In the exhibition at Yad Vashem the caption reads: 'A Warsaw ghetto orphanage. Orphanages such as the one run by Janusz Korczak struggled to care for the growing number of parentless children.'

43. Shneiderman (ed.), *Warsaw Ghetto*, p. 124.

44. Author's interview with Arie ben-Menachem, Tel Aviv, 2000.

45. Grosman is often spelt with double-s. According to Arie ben-Menachem, this is incorrect.

46. Document courtesy of Arie ben-Menachem.

47. Author's conversation with Nachman Zonabend, 2000.

48. *The Trial of Adolf Eichmann: Record of Proceedings in the District Court of Jerusalem*, vol. 1 (Jerusalem, 1992), p. 381.

49. USHMM photo archives worksheets nos 03353, 03355, 03365, 03264, 03267, 03268, 03270, 03275, 03272.

50. USHMM photo archives worksheets nos 18924, 18919, 01632.

51. Author's interview with Arie ben-Menachem.

52. Dobroszycki (ed.), *The Chronicle of the Łódź Ghetto*, pp. xviii, 190–1, 379.

53. Gilbert, *The Holocaust*, pp. 681, 610.

54. The archive of Arie ben-Menachem.

55. Author's interview with Arie ben-Menachem.

56. Ibid.

57. Ibid.

58. *The Trial of Adolf Eichmann*, pp. 381–3.

59. Author's interview with Arie ben-Menachem.

60. Ibid.

61. Zonabend, *The Truth About the Saving of the Łódź Ghetto Archive*, p. 11.

62. Keller (ed.), *The Warsaw Ghetto in Photographs*, p. viii.

63. Franciszek Piper, *Auschwitz, How Many Perished Jews, Poles, Gypsies …* (Kraków, 1992), see 'Transports of Jews to Auschwitz 1940–1945'.

64. Beit Lohamei Haghetaot, *With a Camera in the Ghetto, Mendel Grossman* (Israel, 1970), p. 109.

65. Author's interview with Arie ben-Menachem.

66. Auschwitz-Birkenau State Museum, Department of Archival Documents, dokument 1064/26a/26b.

67. Author's interview with Arie ben-Menachem.

68. Author's interview with Arie ben-Menachem and Nachman Zonabend.

69. Heydecker, *The Warsaw Ghetto*, p. 11, and 'Photographing Behind the Warsaw Ghetto Wall, 1941', p. 65.

70. Schwarberg, *In the Ghetto of Warsaw*, pp. 3–4.

71. Loewy, ' " … without masks", p. 105.

72. Jackiewicz and Król (eds), *Warsaw 1940–1941*, p. xxxiv.

73. Author's interview with Rafael F. Scharf, 2001.

74. Rafael F. Scharf, *'Poland, what have I to do with thee …' Essays without Prejudice/ 'Co Mnie i Tobie Polsko …' Eseje bez uprzedzeń* (Kraków, 1996), p. 13.

75. Jabłoński, *Storyville – Photos of Łódź Ghetto*.

76. *Electronic Telegraph*, no. 1541, 14 August 1999.

77. Walter Benjamin, 'Extract from *A Short History of Photography*', in D. Mellor (ed.), *Germany: The New Photography 1927–33* (London, 1978), pp. 72–3.

78. Shneiderman (ed.), *Warsaw Ghetto*, pp. 34–7, 44, 159.

79. *Electronic Telegraph*, no. 1541, 14 August 1999.

5. Cameras in the Camps

The 'testimonies' referred to in Chapter 5 are kept at Auschwitz-Birkenau State Museum, Department of Archival Documents.

1. Bernd Naumann, *Auschwitz: A Report on the Proceedings Against Robert Karl Ludwig Mulka and Others Before the Court at Frankfurt* (London, 1966), p. 318.

2. Ibid., p. 320.

3. Testimony of Erich Kulka and Ota Kraus, 22 November 1956.

4. O. Kraus and E. Kulka, *The Death Factory: Documents on Auschwitz* (London, 1966), p. 273. The first edition was published in 1945.

5. *Yad Vashem Bulletin*, no. 3 (July 1958), p. 22; Rudolf Hoess, *Commandant of Auschwitz: The Auto-biography of Rudolf Hoess* (London, 1959), see Notes on the Illustrations.

6. *New York Times*, 14 August 1980, p. A16.

7. Teresa Świebocka, *Auschwitz: A History in Photographs* (Auschwitz-Birkenau State Museum, 1999), pp. 37–8.

8. *The Trial of Adolf Eichmann: Record of Proceedings in the District Court of Jerusalem*, vol. 3 (Jerusalem, 1992), pp. 1280–2.

9. *New York Times*, 14 August 1980, p. A16.

10. *Trial of the Major War Criminals before the International Military Tribunal, 14 November 1945–1 October 1946* (42 vols) (Nuremberg, 1947–49), vol. VI, p. 264.

11. David A. Hackett, *The Buchenwald Report* (Oxford, 1995), p. 131.

12. US Holocaust Memorial Museum (USHMM) photo archives worksheets nos 15078–92.

13. See Walter's statement in: Instytut Pamięci Narodowej (IPN), Sąd Okręgowy w Krakowie (the Regional Court in Kraków) SOKr, Cat. no. 437, pp. 59–59a. Although Bernhardt Walter is referred to by this name in documents at Auschwitz-Birkenau State Museum and in all other available texts, in the witness statement in the above file at IPN he appears to have been registered as Walter Bernhardt. For a definition of SS 'Totenkopf' see Samuel W. Mitcham, *Hilter's Legions: German Army Order of Battle World War II* (London, 1985).

14. Testimony of Wilhelm Brasse, 6 April 1984, statement, vol. 101, pp. 221–30. See Walter's statement in IPN, SOKr, Cat. no. 437, pp. 59–59a; Hoess, *Commandant of Auschwitz*, p. 19

15. Testimony of Wilhelm Brasse, 14 June 1959, statement, vol. 3, pp 377–82, Cat. no. Brasse/96, Inventory no. 29794.

16. See Myszkowski's statement in IPN (NTN), Cat. no. 135, pp. 249–50.

17. Author's interview with Wilhelm Brasse, Poland, 2000.

18. Author's interview with Wilhelm Brasse; statement of Wilhelm Brasse, 1984, and 1 September 1989, statement, vol. 125, pp. 50–53, Cat. no. Brasse/3014, Inventory no. 171182. Testimony of Bronisław Jureczek, 3 July 1961, statement, vol. 19, pp. 28–32, Cat. no. Jureczek/473, Inventory no. 49794.

19. Świebocka, *Auschwitz*, pp. 35–6; testimony of Wilhelm Brasse, 1984, 1989; author's interview with archivists Halina Zdziebko and Wojciech Płosa, Auschwitz-Birkenau State Museum, 2000.

20. Auschwitz-Birkenau State Museum, Department of Archival Documents.

21. Testimony of Bronisław Jureczek, 3 July 1961.

22. Author's interview with Wilhelm Brasse.

23. Testimony of Wilhelm Brasse, 1989; testimony of Alfred Woycicki, 18 November 1946, 'The Höss Trial', vol. 15, pp. 1–18, Cat. no. dpr-Hd/15, Inventory no. 38.

24. Auschwitz-Birkenau State Museum, *KL Auschwitz Seen by the SS: Rudolf Hoess, Pery Broad, Johann Paul Kremer* (Oświęcim, 1998), p. 106.

25. Testimony of Wilhelm Brasse, 1984; author's interview with Wilhelm Brasse.

26. Debórah Dwork and Robert Jan van Pelt, *Auschwitz: 1270 to the Present* (New York, 1996), p. 262.

27. Świebocka, *Auschwitz*, p. 21.

28. Auschwitz-Birkenau State Museum, *KL Auschwitz Seen by the SS*, p. 124.

29. Świebocka, *Auschwitz*, pp. 21–2.

30. Dwork and Jan van Pelt, *Auschwitz*, p. 293.

31. Auschwitz-Birkenau State Museum, *KL Auschwitz Seen by the SS*, p. 124.

32. *Trial of the Major War Criminals*, vol. VI, pp. 271, 277.

33. Ibid., pp. 275–6.

34. Świebocka, *Auschwitz*, p. 41.

35. Author's interview with Wilhelm Brasse.

36. Świebocka, *Auschwitz*, p. 41; testimony of Ludwik Lawin, 8 December 1946, statement, vol. 31, p. 74, Cat. no. Lavin/663, Inventory no. 73927.

37. Auschwitz-Birkenau State Museum, *KL Auschwitz Seen by the SS*, pp. 136.

38. Testimony of Ludwik Lawin, 8 December 1946. Świebocka, *Auschwitz*, p. 41.

39. Testimony of Ludwik Lawin, 8 December 1946.

40. Yad Vashem Film and Photo Archives (YVFPA), album FA/157.

41. Testimony of Alfred Woycicki, 25 November 1959, statement, vol. 9, pp. 1311–24, Cat. no. Woycicki/236, Inventory no. 31059; testimony of Władysław Plaskura, 5 March 1984, k.IV-8520-80/609/84; testimony of Bronisław Jureczek, 1961.

42. Testimony of Wilhelm Brasse, 29 July 1977, statement, vol. W1, pp. 11–14, Cat. no. Brasse/2386, inventory no 166965.

43. Testimony of Wilhelm Brasse 1977; Świebocka, *Auschwitz*, pp. 219–22.

44. Auschwitz-Birkenau State Museum, *KL Auschwitz Seen by the SS*, pp. 169–73.

45. Robert Jay Lifton, *The Nazi Doctors: Medical Killing and the Psychology of Genocide* (London, 1986), pp. 251–3.

46. Author's interview with Wilhelm Brasse; testimony of Wilhelm Brasse, 1989; testimony of Alfred Woycicki, 1959.

47. Author's interview with Wilhelm Brasse; testimony of Wilhelm Brasse, 1984.

48. Testimony of Bronisław Jureczek, 1961.

49. Author's interview with Wilhelm Brasse.

50. Lifton, *The Nazi Doctors*, pp. 251–3.

51. Author's interview with Wilhelm Brasse; testimony of Wilhelm Brasse, 1984.

52. Testimony of Wilhelm Brasse, 1977.

53. Author's interview with Wilhelm Brasse.

54. Testimony of Alfred Woycicki, 1946 and 1959.

55. Testimony of Bronisław Jureczek, 1961.

56. Author's interview with Wilhelm Brasse.

57. Ibid.

58. Testimony of Wilhelm Brasse, 1977, 1989; testimony of Alfred Woycicki, 1959; testimony of Bronisław Jureczek, 1961; author's interview with Wilhelm Brasse.

59. Letter from Tadeusz Myszkowski, 18 February, 1963 to Auschwitz-Birkenau State Museum, statement, vol. 35, pp. 83–4, Cat. no. Myszkowski/724, Inventory no. 106037.

60. Franciszek Piper, *Auschwitz, How Many Perished Jews, Poles, Gypsies* (Kraków, 1992), see table 'Transport of Jews to Auschwitz 1940–1945'.

61. Auschwitz-Birkenau State Museum, *KL Auschwitz Seen by the SS*, p. 138.

62. Dwork and Jan van Pelt. *Auschwitz*, pp. 342–3.

63. Piper, *Auschwitz*, pp. 56–7.

64. Świebocka, *Auschwitz*, p. 25.

65. Testimony of Alfred Woycicki, 1959.

66. Auschwitz-Birkenau State Museum, *KL Auschwitz as Seen by the SS*, p. 163.

67. Testimony of Alfred Woycicki, 1959.

68. Author's interview with Wilhelm Brasse.

69. Testimony of Alfred Woycicki, 1959.

70. Świebocka, *Auschwitz*, p. 37.

71. Kraus and Kulka, *The Death Factory*, p. 143.

72. Auschwitz-Birkenau State Museum, Department of Archival Documents, dokument 1063/35b,c,d.

73. Świebocka, *Auschwitz*, pp. 42–3.

74. Piper, *Auschwitz*, p. 51.

75. Author's interview with Wilhelm Brasse.

76. Ibid.

77. Świebocka, *Auschwitz*, p. 36.

78. See Walter's statement in IPN, SOKr Cat. no. 437, p. 59.

79. Andrzej Strzelecki, 'Day One in the History of the Museum', and Tadeusz Szymański, 'I Had to See Whether I Could Cope with Working in This Place', and 'We were a Big Family', *Pro Memoria Nr. 7* (Oświęcim, 1997), pp. 41, 43–5, 69–83.

80. Author's interview with Halina Żdziebko and Wojciech Płosa.

81. Testimony of Ludwik Lawin, 25 September 1946, statement, vol. 31, p. 79, Cat no. Lavin/663, Inventory no. 73427.

82. Author's interview with Halina Żdziebko and Wojciech Płosa.

83. Ibid.

84. Ibid.

85. Testimony of Wilhelm Brasse, 1959.

86. Testimony of Bronisław Jureczek, 1961.

87. Author's interview with Halina Żdziebko and Wojciech Płosa.

88. Testimony of Władysław Pytlik, 17 October 1960.

89. Author's interview with Dr Piotr Setkiewicz, Auschwitz-Birkenau State Museum, 2002.

90. Naumann, *Auschwitz*, p. 216.

91. See Walter's statement in IPN, SOKr Cat. no. 437, p. 59.

92. Walter was tried during the trial of Walter Schieblich, IPN, SOKr 437, pp. 59, 59a.

93. Letter from Tadeusz Myszkowski to Auschwitz-Birkenau State Museum, 18 February 1963.

94. Martin Gilbert, *Final Journey: The Fate of the Jews in Nazi Europe* (London, 1979), p. 72.

95. Serge Klarsfeld (ed.), *The Auschwitz Album: Lili Jacob's Album* (New York, 1980).

96. Author's interview with Wilhelm Brasse.

97. Hoess, *Commandant of Auschwitz*.

98. *Poznaniak 3*, 21–22 January 1995.

99. Author's interview with Andrzej Gass, 2003.

100. Ibid.

101. Author's interview with Dr Piotr Setkiewicz.

6. Liberations

1. *Daily Mirror*, 28 April 1945, p. 5.

2. Vicki Goldberg, *Margaret Bourke-White, a Biography* (London, 1987), p. 291.

3. Jorge Lewinski, *The Camera at War: A History of War Photography from 1848 to the Present Day* (London, 1978), p. 14.

4. Bert Hardy, *My Life* (London, 1985), pp. 74–6.

5. Sergeant A. N. Midgley's letter, 18 April 1945, Box 84/50/1, Department of Documents, Imperial War Museum (IWM).

6. *Daily Express*, 2 May 1945, p. 3.

7. M-O A: FR 2248, response to the *Daily Express* exhibition in Trafalgar Square, 1 May 1945; German Atrocities, 5 May 1945, p. 4.

8. M-O A: FR 2248, Box 1, File A, Victory Celebrations and Parades: 'Comment from a Welfare Worker back from Brussels', 3 May 1945.

9. Letter of C. J. Charters, 15 May 1945, Department of Documents, IWM.

10. *The Times*, 1 May 1945, p. 8.

11. File 65/17/1–12 (8), Department of Documents, IWM.

12. Paul M. A. Linebarger, *Psychological Warfare* (Washington, DC, 1948), p. 187; PRO INF/1/542.

13. PRO INF/1/623.

14. PRO INF/1/636.

15. Caroline Moorehead, *Sidney Bernstein: A Biography* (London, 1984), p. 162.

16. Ibid., pp. 162–9.

17. File 65/17/1–12, Department of Documents, IWM; Moorehead, *Sidney Bernstein*, p. 167; Notes to 'Memory of the Camps', pp. 1–4, Department of Film, IWM.

18. PRO INF/1/636.

19. *New York Times*, 2 May 1945, p. 3.

20. PRO INF/1/636.

21. M-O A: FR 2263, Atrocity Stories, p. 5.

22. M-O A: FR 2248, Box 1, File A, 2 May 1945.

23. Peter Maslowski, *Armed with Cameras: The American Military Photographers of World War II* (New York, 1993), p. 304.

24. National Archives Administration, *Audiovisual Records in the National Archives of the United States Relating to WWII* (Washington, DC, 1992), pp. 20–1, 65.

25. Maslowski, *Armed with Cameras*, pp. 241–2.

26. Ibid., pp. 241–4; Susan D. Moeller, *Shooting War: Photography and the American Experience of Combat* (New York, 1989), pp. 192–3.

27. Moeller, *Shooting War*, pp. 208–12; see generally, Jack F. Hurley, *Portrait of a Decade: Roy Stryker and the Development of Documentary Photography in the Thirties* (New York, 1977).

28. James Agee and Walker Evans, *Let Us Now Praise Famous Men* (London, 1975).

29. National Archives Administration, *Audiovisual Records*, p. 660; Hurley, *Portrait of a Decade*, p. 166.

30. National Archives Administration, *Audiovisual Records*, p. 5.

31. Martin Caiger-Smith (ed.), *The Face of the Enemy: British Photographers in Germany 1944–1952* (London,

1988), pp. 11, 7.

32. Gianfranco Casadio, *Immagini di Guerra in Emilia Romagna* (Ravenna, 1987), pp. 1–5.

33. 'Birth of a War Picture: Soldiers of the Propaganda Army', *Illustrated*, no. 20 (June 1942), pp. 12–13.

34. Moeller, *Shooting War*, p. 193.

35. Maslowski, *Armed with Cameras*, pp. 241–53.

36. *Picture Post*, 15 July 1944, p. 3.

37. Robert H. Abzug, *Inside the Vicious Heart: Americans and the Liberation of Nazi Concentration Camps* (New York, 1985), p. 128.

38. Anthony Penrose (ed.), *Lee Miller's War: Photographer and Correspondent with the Allies in Europe 1944–45* (London, 1992), p. 187.

39. Abzug, *Inside the Vicious Heart*, p. 138.

40. Sybil Milton, 'Confronting Atrocities', in *Liberation 1945* (Washington, DC, 1995), p. 60; Abzug, *Inside the Vicious Heart*, pp. 128–32.

41. *St Louis Post-Dispatch*, 2 July 1945; *Washington Evening Star*, 23 July 1945; *Sunday Star*, 1 July 1945; *Annual Report of the Librarian of Congress Washington* (Washington, DC, 1946), p. 85.

42. Susan Sontag, *On Photography* (London, 1978), p. 20.

43. Ibid.

44. *Picture Post*, 12 May 1945, p. 25.

45. Sontag, *On Photography*, p. 20.

46. M-O A: FR 2248, 'Responses to a film show in Hampstead of Atrocities in Camps', 2 May 1945; 25/15/C, 5 May 1945.

47. Ian Grant, *Cameramen at War* (Cambridge, 1980), p. 157; Daily Mail, *Lest We Forget: The Horrors of Nazi Concentration Camps Revealed …* (London, 1945), p. 35; J. Reilly, D. Cesarani, T. Kushner and C. Richmond (eds), *Belsen in History and Memory* (London, 1997), pp. 4–5.

48. Penrose, *Lee Miller's War*, p. 12.

49. Library of Congress, *Lest We Forget* (Washington, DC, 1945).

50. Daily Mail, *Lest We Forget*, pp. 5, 7–8.

51. Library of Congress, *Lest We Forget*; Reilly et al., *Belsen in History and Memory*, p. 6. *PM* referred to the 'death factory' of Buchenwald: *PM*, 30 April 1945, p. 9.

52. Goldberg, *Margaret Bourke-White*, p. 291.

53. *Daily Mirror*, 30 April 1945, p. 5.

54. PRO INF/1/636.

55. Caiger-Smith, *The Face of the Enemy*, pp. 15, 77.

56. *Daily Mirror*, 30 April 1945, p. 5.

57. PRO INF/1/636. This comment was made about *KZ*, a government publication which included photographs from the concentration camps.

58. M-O A: FR 2228, 'Special Pre-Peace News Questionnaire', pp. 19–20.

59. *Illustrated London News*, 28 April 1945, p. iv.

60. *Daily Express*, 26 May 1945, p. 4.

61. *The Nation*, 19 May 1945.

62. *Picture Post*, 16 June 1945, p. 11.

63. James E. Young, *The Texture of Memory: Holocaust Memorials and Meaning* (New Haven, CT and London, 1993), p. 288; US Holocaust Memorial Museum (USHMM) photo archives worksheet no. 86822.

64. *Picture Post*, 19 August 1944, pp. 7–9.

65. PRO INF/1/636.

66. *Illustrated London News*, 2 June 1945, p. 581.

67. PRO FO/371/39451.

68. Fedorovich Ignatz Kladov, *The People's Verdict: A Full Report of the Proceedings at the Krasnodar and Kharkov German Atrocity Trials* (London, 1944).

69. *Soviet War News Weekly*, 5 August 1943, p. 3.

70. Kladov, *The People's Verdict*.

71. *Life*, 10 July 1944, pp. 94, 97.

72. Milton, 'Confronting Atrocities', p. 67.

73. *Soviet War News Weekly*, 13 July 1944, p. 7.

74. PRO FO/371/43374.

75. PRO FO/371/43371.

76. Author's correspondence with Feliks Forbert-Kaniewski and Katia Forbert Petersen, 2002.

77. A statement sent to the Majdanek State Museum by Adolf Forbert on 22 October 1986, ref. VII–1143, Majdanek State Museum.

78. Ibid.

79. Anna Wiśniewska and Czesław Rajca, *Majdanek: The Concentration Camp of Lublin* (Państwowe Muzeum na Majdanku, 1997), p. 65.

80. *Soviet War News Weekly*, 21 December 1944, p. 1.

81. Alexander Werth, *Russia at War 1941–1945* (London, 1964), p. 890.

82. Ibid.

83. *Polish Jewish Observer*, 18 August 1944, p. 1.

84. Werth, *Russia at War*, p. 890.

85. *Moscow News*, 12 August 1944, pp. 1, 3–4, 16 September 1944, pp. 3–4; *Soviet War New Weekly*, 17 August 1944, p. 3, 24 August 1944, pp. 6, 31, 28 September 1944, *Special Supplement*. See also Konstantin Mikhailovich Simonov, *The Death Factory Near Lublin* (London, 1944).

86. PRO FO/371/39452.

87. PRO FO/371/39453-POL 1944.

88. Werth, *Russia at War*, p. 890.

89. *Life*, 28 August 1945, p. 34; Barbie Zelizer, *Remembering to Forget: Holocaust Memory Through the Camera's Eye* (Chicago and London, 1998), pp. 50–1.

90. See images in *Moscow News*, 16 September 1944, p. 4, 12 August 1944, pp. 1–4.

91. *Life*, 18 September 1944, p. 17.

92. Zelizer, *Remembering to Forget*, pp. 56, 53, 61.

93. Ibid., p. 61.

94. Wiśniewska and Racja, *Majdanek*, p. 61.

95. National Archives Administration, *Audiovisual Records*, p. 4.

96. Wiśniewska and Rajca, *Majdanek*, pp. 62–3.

97. Statement of Adolf Forbert.

98. Ibid.

99. Teresa Świebocka, *Auschwitz: A History in Photographs* (Auschwitz-Birkenau State Museum, 1995), p. 44.

100. Statement of Adolf Forbert.

101. Świebocka, *Auschwitz*, pp. 44–5.

102. *Przekrój*, no. 2, 23 April 1945.

103. Zelizer, *Remembering to Forget*, p. 50.

104. *Soviet War News Weekly*, 1 March 1945, p. 6.

105. Robin O'Neil, *The Bełżec Death Camp and the Origins of Jewish Genocide in Galicia*, PhD thesis: University College, London, 2002.

106. *Manchester Guardian*, 29 January 1945, p. 5.

107. *Daily Express*, 3 February 1945, p. 4.

108. Michał Gawałkiewicz, 'Polska Fotografia Prasowa w Latach 1944–46', *Fotografia*, 18 February 1980, pp. 30–1.

109. Ignacy Płażewski, *Spojrzenie w przeszłość polskiej Fotografii* (Warsaw, 1982), pp. 375–6.

110. Tony Kushner, *The Holocaust and the Liberal Imagination: a Social and Cultural History* (Oxford, 1994), p. 244.

7. Constructing the Post-war Memory

1 The International Military Tribunal at Nuremberg ran from 14 November 1945 to 1 October 1946, although twelve American trials continued until July 1949. See: Robert Wolfe (ed.), *Captured German Documents and Related Records. A National Archives Conference*, vol. 3 (Ohio, 1974), p. 93.

2. *The War in Pictures*, 6 vols (London, 1940–46).

3. PRO INF/1/542.

4. *Daily Express*, 26 May 1945, p. 4.

5. File 65/17/1–12 (9), Department of Documents, Imperial War Museum (IWM).

6. *Memory of the Camps* (WGBH, Boston, 1985). See Notes on *Memory of the Camps*, pp. 1–4, Department of Film, IWM.

7. *Daily Worker*, 5 December 1945, in PRO FO/371/51079.

8. *Eastern Daily Press*, 6 December 1945, in PRO FO/371/51079.

9. *Yorkshire Post*, 7 December 1945, in PRO FO 371/51079.

10. For a summary of newspaper reviews see: 'Nazi Crimes Exhibition', PRO 371/51079.

11. Wolfe (ed.), *Captured German Documents*, p. 95.

12. Ibid.; *Trial of the Major War Criminals Before the International Military Tribunal, 14 November 1945–1 October*

1946, (42 vols) (Nuremberg, 1947–49), vol. VII, p. 601; 'Films Back Charge of German Crimes, *New York Times*, 20 February 1946, sec. 1. 6, quoted in Lawrence Douglas, 'The Shrunken Head of Buchenwald', in Barbie Zelizer (ed.), *Visual Culture and the Holocaust* (London, 2001).

13.   *Trial of the Major War Criminals Before the International Military Tribunal*, vol. XXX, pp. 359–401.

14.   For an account of the photographic evidence on Lvov presented to the tribunal see: *Trial of the Major War Criminals*, vol. VII, pp. 536, 549, 577. For information about Jews in Lvov (Lwów) see: 'The Slaughter of the Jews in Lwów', *Polish Jew*, vol. IV, no. 21 (March 1944), pp. 5–8. See also V. N. Denisov and G. I. Changuli (eds), *Nazi Crimes in Ukraine 1941–1944, Documents and Materials* (Kiev, 1987), p. 212.

15.   *Trial of the Major War Criminals* , vol. III, pp. 530–5, 553–72. The *Katzmann Report* is in Instytut Pamięci Narodowej (IPN). The *Stroop Report*, also in IPN, was used in 1951 before the District Court in Warsaw in the trial of Jürgen Stroop himself.

16.   *Trial of the Major War Criminals*, vol. III, pp. 536–7.

17.   *The Nazi Plan*, National Archives, Washington, DC, no. NWDNM (m) 238.1.

18.   *The Living Dead. Three Films About the Power of the Past*, BBC television series written and produced by Adam Curtis, 1995.

19.   *Trial of the Major War Criminals*, vol. XXX, pp. 357–8, 459–72.

20.   Paul Rotha and Richard Griffith, *The Film Till Now. A Survey of World Cinema* (London, 1967), pp. 579–80.

21.   For the 'Complete text of narration in "Nazi Concentration Camps"', see *Trial of the Major War Criminals*, vol. XXX, pp. 462–72.

22.   *Memory of the Camps* (WGBH, Boston, 1985).

23.   Peter Novick, *The Holocaust and Collective Memory: The American Experience* (London, 2001), pp. 65–6.

24.   M-O A: FR 2424A, Notes on Nuremberg, 22 September 1946.

25.   PRO WO/309/1650.

26.   PRO FO/939/275 and 273.

27.   PRO FO/947/12, PRO FO/946/1; PRO FO/946/10, PRO FO/946/13.

28.   PRO FO/947/12.

29.   PRO FO/946/1.

30.   PRO FO/946/12.

31.   PRO FO/946/1.

32.   *Soviet Weekly*, 25 October 1945, p. 1.

33.   *Soviet Weekly*, 29 November 1945, p. 1.

34.   Curtis, *The Living Dead* (BBC TV).

35.   Leon A. Jick, 'The Holocaust: Its Use and Abuse within the American Public', *Yad Vashem Studies*, no. XIV (Jerusalem, 1981), p. 304.

36.   Curtis, *The Living Dead* (BBC TV).

37.   *Library of Congress Quarterly, Journal of Current Acquisitions*, vol. 6, no. 4 (August 1949), p. 22.

38.   Library of Congress, *Special Collections in the Library of Congress* (Washington, DC, 1980), pp. 137–8, 143, 348. Barbara Lewis Burger (ed.), *Guide to the Holdings of the Still Picture Branch of the National Archives* (Washington, DC, 1990), pp. 107, 109. *The Library of Congress Quarterly, Journal of Current Acquisitions*, vol. 6, no. 1 (November 1948), pp. 21–40; vol. 6, no. 4 (August 1949), pp. 21–7.

39.   Paul Yule (Director and Producer), *Battle for the Holocaust* (Diverse Productions, 2001).

40.   George H. Roeder, Jnr, *The Censored War. American Visual Experience During World War Two* (New Haven, CT and London, 1993), p. 127.

41.   See, generally, T. H. Tetens, *The New Germany and the Old Nazis* (London, 1961).

42.   Yule, *Battle for the Holocaust*.

43.   James E. Young, *The Texture of Memory: Holocaust Memorials and Meaning* (New Haven, CT and London, 1993), p. 63.

44.   Kazimierz Smoleń, *Auschwitz 1940–1945. Guide Book Through the Museum* (Oświęcim, 1978).

45.   Young, *The Texture of Memory*, p. 123.

46.   *The European Jewish Observer*, 17 August 1945, p. 1; 31 August 1945, pp. 1, 3.

47.   See US Holocaust Memorial Museum (USHMM) photo archives worksheet no. 14390.

48.   Josef Rosensaft, 'Our Belsen', in Irgun Sheerit Hapleita Me'Haezor Habriti (ed.) *Belsen* (Tel Aviv, 1957), pp. 25–6, 41.

49.   Jick, 'The Holocaust', p. 308.

50.   Ibid., p. 306. The Yiddish word Shtetl means a small Jewish town or village formerly found in Eastern Europe.

51.   Norman G. Finkelstein, *The Holocaust Industry: Reflections on the Exploitation of Jewish Suffering* (London and New York, 2000), pp. 14–15.

52.   Novick, *The Holocaust and Collective Memory*, p. 93.

53.   Young, *The Texture of Memory*, p. 244.

54.   Batia Donner and Miri Kedem (eds), *Beit Lohamei Haghetaot: The Yitzhak Katzenelson Holocaust and Resistance Heritage Museum 1949–1999* (Israel, 2000), pp. 113–14.

55.   Ibid., pp. 108–9.

56.   Yaacov Shelhav, 'The Holocaust in the Consciousness of Our Generation', *Yad Vashem Bulletin*, no. 3 (July 1958), p. 2.

57.   Tetens, *The New Germany and the Old Nazis*, p. 149.

58.   Ibid., pp. 85, 113, 119–21, 148–52.

59.   Lord Ismay, *NATO: The First Five Years 1949–1954* (Paris, 1954), pp. 31–5.

60.   Raya Kagan, 'Russians on German Concentration

Camps', *Yad Vashem Bulletin*, no. 4/5 (October 1959), pp. 2–3.

61. Tadeusz Mazur, Jerzy Tomaszewski and Stanisław Wrzos-Glinka (eds), *1939–1945, We Have Not Forgotten* (Warsaw, 1960), see Introduction.

62. Teresa Zbrzeska, 'Bringing History to Millions', *Pro Memoria 7* (Oświęcim, 1997), p. 96.

63. *Majdanek: Katalog Wystawy* (Państwowe Muzeum na Majdanku, 1967).

64. Christopher Lyon (ed.), *The Macmillan Dictionary of Films and Filmmakers* (London, 1984), p. 191.

65. Finkelstein, *The Holocaust Industry*, pp. 11–29.

66. Novick, *The Holocaust and Collective Memory*, p. 168.

67. Jick, 'The Holocaust', pp. 309, 314.

68. Judith E. Doneson, *The Holocaust in American Film* (Philadelphia, PA, New York and Jerusalem, 1987), pp. 94, 104–6.

69. Ibid., pp. 101–2.

70. Ibid., p. 105.

71. Letter from Maurice Bolle to the Lord Mayor of Coventry, 23 February 1960, courtesy of Dr Hélène Mair, Vancouver.

72. Author's correspondence with Dr Hélène Mair, November 1998.

73. Dr Walter Deveen's speech at the exhibition in Malines, courtesy of Dr Hélène Mair.

74. *Coventry Evening Telegraph*, 1 May 1961, p. 8. For the full text see *Coventry Cathedral Review*, May 1961, pp. 2–3.

75. *The Times*, 2 May 1961, p. 7.

76. *Coventry Evening Telegraph*, 16 May 1961, p. 11.

77. *Coventry Cathedral Review*, May 1961, pp. 2–3.

78. *Birmingham Mail*, 10 June 1961, p. 5; *Observer*, 11 June 1961, p. 1; *Daily Express*, 12 June 1961, p. 6.

79. *Coventry Evening Telegraph*, 7 June 1961, p. 6.

80. *Coventry Cathedral Review*, May 1961, p. 2.

81. *Coventry Evening Telegraph*, 9 June 1961, p. 21.

82. *Coventry Evening Telegraph*, 17 May 1961, p. 13.

83. Letter from the Council of Christians and Jews to Dr Hélène Mair, 19 May 1961, courtesy of Dr Hélène Mair.

84. Author's correspondence with BBFC Archive, London.

85. Author's interview with Stanley Forman, ETV Films, London, 2001.

86. For a general study of films from this period and an account of the case see: Bert Hogenkamp, *Film, Television and the Left 1950–1970* (London, 2000), pp. 78–82.

87. Author's interview with Stanley Forman.

88. Tetens, *The New Germany and the Old Nazis*, pp. 37–8.

89. *Jewish Echo*, 14 July 1961, p. 1.

90. The Board of Deputies of British Jews Archive (BDA): Acc/3121/B6/2/43.

91. BDA: BBC Radio Newsreel, 12 July 1961.

92. BDA: Acc/3121/02/031.

93. BDA: C10/5/3.

94. Novick, *The Holocaust and Collective Memory*, pp. 104, 121, 138.

95. Jerzy Bossack and Wacław Kaźmierczak, *Requiem for 500,000* (Poland, 1963).

96. Zbrzeska, 'Bringing History to Millions'.

97. YIVO Institute for Jewish Research, *Life, Struggle and Uprising in the Warsaw Ghetto* (New York, 1963).

98. See for example: Janusz Wieczorek and Stanisław Wroński, *To the Memory of the Heroic Defenders of the Ghetto: On the 35th Anniversary of the Outbreak of the Warsaw Ghetto Uprising* (Warsaw, 1979); Philip Friedman, *Martyrs and Fighters: The Epic of the Warsaw Ghetto* (London, 1954); Mark Ber, *Uprising in the Warsaw Ghetto* (New York, 1975); Tadeusz Pelczyński and Adam Ciołkosz, *Opór zbrojny w Ghetcie Warszawskim w 1943 roku* (London, 1963); Nachum Goldman and Jonas Turkow, *The Jewish Resistance on the 25th Anniversary of the Warsaw Ghetto Uprising* (London, 1968); Isaac I. Schwarzbart, *The Story of the Warsaw Ghetto Uprising. Its Meaning and Message* (New York, 1953); World Jewish Congress, *The Warsaw Ghetto Uprising and Its Historical Significance* (New York, 1963); Wacław Poterański, *The Warsaw Ghetto on the 25th Anniversary of the Armed Uprising of 1943* (Warsaw, 1968).

8. Commercializing the Holocaust

1. Author's correspondence with US government visa department, 2001.

2. Peter Novick, *The Holocaust and Collective Memory: The American Experience* (London, 2001), p. 207.

3. Leon A. Jick, 'The Holocaust: Its Use and Abuse within the American Public', *Yad Vashem Studies*, no. XIV (Jerusalem, 1981), p. 316.

4. *Sight and Sound*, March 1994, p14.

5. Robert Alter, 'Deformations of the Holocaust', in *Commentary*, vol. 71, no. 2, February 1981, pp. 49, 54.

6. Jick, 'The Holocaust', p. 316.

7. The Board of Deputies of British Jews Archive (BDA), Acc/3121/EN/69; *Evening Standard*, 4 September 1978, p. 10.

8. BDA, Acc/3121/EN/69; *Radio Times*, p. 60.

9. BDA, Acc/3121/EN/69; *Evening Standard*, 4 September 1978, p. 10; see also Judith E. Doneson, *The Holocaust in American Film* (Philadelphia, PA, New York and Jerusalem, 1987), p. 145.

10. *Sunday Times*, 3 September 1978, p. 4; *Guardian*, 4 September 1978, p. 8.

11. BDA, Acc/3121/E4/69; *Daily Express*, 4 September 1978; *Sunday Times*, 3 September 1978, p. 4.

12. These images are referred to in Chapter 9.

13. BDA, Acc/3121/E4/69; *Evening Standard*, 4 September 1978, p. 10.

14. Novick, *The Holocaust and Collective Memory*, p. 156.

15. BDA, Acc/3121/E4/69; *Jerusalem Post*, 13 September 1978.

16. BDA, Acc/3121/E4/69; *Free Palestine*, September 1978, p. 9.

17. Doneson, *The Holocaust in American Film*, p. 155.

18. BDA, Acc/3121/E4/69.

19. BDA, Acc/3121/E4/69; *Spectator*, 3 March 1979, p. 9.

20. BDA, NYVC, 29 June 1978.

21. BDA, Acc/3121/C23/1/1.

22. BDA, Acc/3121/C23/1/1, NYVC, 25 June 1979.

23. Ibid., 15 April 1983.

24. Ibid., 4 October 1981.

25. Ibid., 13 January 1982.

26. Ibid., 29 March 1982.

27. Ibid., NYVC, 12 July 1982.

28. Ibid., 9 December 1982.

29. Tower Hamlets Arts Project, *From Auschwitz and East London* (London, 1983).

30. BDA, Acc/3121/C23/1/1, NYVC, 24 February 1983.

31. Ibid., 10 January 1984.

32. Author's interview with Teresa Świebocka, Auschwitz-Birkenau State Museum, 2002.

33. BDA, Acc/3121/C23/1/1, NYVC, 10 January 1984.

34. Ibid., 26 July 1984.

35. Stefan Nowicki, *The Defamation of the Poles* (Victoria, Australia, 1989), p. 56.

36. Ibid., pp. 56–7.

37. E. Thomas Wood and Stanisław M. Jankowski, *Karski. How One Man Tried to Stop the Holocaust* (New York, 1994), pp. 254–5.

38. Polish Underground Movement (1939–45) Study Trust and the Polish Institute and Sikorski Museum, *Polish Help for the Jews (1939–45) Documents* (London, 1988), pp. 2–6.

39. Novick, *The Holocaust and Collective Memory*, p. 216.

40. *United States Holocaust Memorial Museum Newsletter*, March 1991, p. 10.

41. Philip Gourevitch, 'In the Holocaust Theme Park', *Observer* Magazine, 30 January 1994, pp. 21–5.

42. Author's visit to US Holocaust Memorial Museum, February 2000.

43. *United States Holocaust Memorial Museum Newsletter*, March 1991, p. 1; April 1991, pp. 1, 4–5, winter 1992/1993, pp. 4–5.

44. Ludmilla Jordanova discusses the use of artefacts in museums in 'Objects of Knowledge: A Historical Perspective on Museums', in Peter Vergo (ed.), *The New Museology* (London, 1989).

45. Gourevitch writes about his response, 'In the Holocaust Theme Park', pp. 21–5.

46. Ibid., p. 22.

47. Novick, *The Holocaust and Collective Memory*, p. 221.

48. Ibid., p. 232.

49. Jeffrey D. Feldman, 'An Etymology of Opinion: Yad Vashem, Authority, and the Shifting Aesthetic of Holocaust Museums', in Y. Doosry (ed.), *Representations of Auschwitz: 50 Years of Photographs, Paintings and Graphics* (Oświęcim, 1995), pp. 122–6.

50. Jack Kugelmass, 'The Rites of the Tribe: American Jewish Tourism in Poland', in I. Karp, C. M. Kreamer and S. D. Lavine (eds), *Museums and Communities: The Politics of Public Culture* (Washington, DC and London, 1992), pp. 406–7.

51. Jack Matthews, 'A Star is Reborn: Schindler's List', *Guardian*, 16 December 1993, p. 2.

52. *Variety*, 21–27 March 1994, p. 9.

53. Franciszek Palowski, *Retracing 'Schindler's List'* (Kraków, 1996), pp. 7–12.

54. Jay Rayner, *Observer* Review, 3 November 2002, pp. 1–2.

55. *Premiere*, March 1994, p. 58.

56. Ibid., p. 62.

57. Jonathan Romney, 'Auschwitz the Movie', *Guardian*, 29 November 1993, p. 5.

58. *Premiere*, April 1994, p. 26.

59. *Empire*, March 1994, p. 22.

60. Jay Carr, *Guardian*, G2, 16 December 1993, p. 2.

61. *The Economist*, vol. 329, 25 December 1993.

62. *Premiere*, March 1994, p. 58.

63. *Guardian*, 29 July 1994, p. 4.

64. *Empire*, March 1994.

65. *Sight and Sound*, March 1994, p. 47.

66. *What, Where, When, Co, Gdzie, Kiedy*, vol. 1, no. 3 (Kraków, 1994), pp. 4–6.

67. Anne Karpf, 'The Last Jews of Kraków Cringe', *Guardian*, 28 October 1995, p. 27. In mid-2001 it was estimated there were around 150 Jews left in Kraków.

68. *The Pianist*, Press Release, Pathé Distribution, UK, November 2002.

69. Władysław Szpilman, *The Pianist: The Extraordinary Story of One Man's Survival in Warsaw, 1939–45* (London, 1999), p. 221.

70. Jay Rayner, *Observer* Review, 3 November 2002, pp. 1–2.

71. Teresa Zbrzeska, 'Bringing History to Millions', *Pro Memoria 7* (Oświęcim, 1997), p. 98.

72. See: Comité International d'Auschwitz, *Biuletyn*

Informacyjny, nos 5–6 (May–June 1972), Warsaw.

73. Author's interview with Teresa Świebocka. See also 'Exhibition on Auschwitz Makes Return to the UN', *Jewish Week, Inc*, 20–26 December 1991, p. 35.

74. *Auschwitz: A Crime Against Mankind* (Oświęcim, 1991).

75. *Warsaw Voice*, 14 April 1996, p. 7; *Searchlight*, no. 251 (May 1996) pp. 3–5.

76. Institute of the World Jewish Congress, Policy Dispatch no. 31, August 1998.

77. Novick, *The Holocaust and Collective Memory*, p. 160.

78. James E. Young, *The Texture of Memory: Holocaust Memorials and Meaning* (New Haven, CT and London, 1993), p. 150.

79. Susan Sontag, *On Photography* (London, 1979), p. 10.

80. Anna Wiśniewska, Czesław Rajca, *Majdanek: The Concentration Camp of Lublin* (Lublin, 1997), p. 46.

81. Ibid., pp. 63–5.

82. Author's conversation with archivist Janina Kiełboń, Majdanek State Museum, 1999.

83. *Imperial War Museum Report*, summer 2000.

84. Madeleine Bunting, *Guardian*, 19 November 1994, p. 8.

85. Author's interview with curator James Taylor, Imperial War Museum (IWM), 1999.

86. Author's conversation with historian Terry Charman and James Taylor, IWM, 2001.

87. Young, *The Texture of Memory*, p. 133.

9. Interpretations of the Evidence

1. Author's interview with curator James Taylor, Imperial War Museum (IWM), 1999.

2. Roland Barthes, *Camera Lucida: Reflections on Photography* (London, 1982), p. 9. For debate about family albums see for example Jo Spence, *Putting Myself in the Picture* (London, 1986); Jeremy Seabrook, 'My Life is in That Box', *Ten.8* (1989), no. 34, pp. 34–41; Annette Kuhn, 'Remembrance', in L. Heron and V. Williams (eds), *Illuminations: Women Writing on Photography from the 1850s to the Present* (London and New York, 1996).

3. *The United States Holocaust Memorial Museum Newsletter*, March 1991, p. 5.

4. Yaffa Eliach, *There Once was a World* (Boston, 1998), p. 5. Eišiškės is the present-day Lithuanian spelling of the Polish name Ejszyszki. In Eliach's text it is written as Eishyshok.

5. *The United States Holocaust Memorial Museum Newsletter*, March 1991, p. 1.

6. *Independent on Sunday*, 25 October 1998, p. 11.

7. Stanisław Markowski, *Krakowski Kazimierz, Dzielnica żydowska, 1870–1988* (Kraków, 1992), p. 15.

8. Rafael F. Scharf, '*Poland, what have I to do with thee … ' Essays without Prejudice / 'Co Mnie i Tobie Polsko …' Eseje bez uprzedzeń* (Kraków, 1996), p. 151.

9. Author's interview with Rafael F. Scharf, London, 2001.

10. Ibid.; Roman Vishniac, *A Vanished World* (New York, 1983), see commentary to photographs 178, 179.

11. *Canadian Jewish News*, 6 July 1995, p. 1.

12. *Canadian Jewish News*, 20 July 1995, p. 1.

13. Ann Weiss, *The Last Album: Eyes from the Ashes of Auschwitz-Birkenau* (New York and London, 2001), p. 38.

14. Author's interview with Teresa Świebocka, Auschwitz-Birkenau State Museum, 2002.

15. Teresa Świebocka (ed.), *The Architecture of Crime: The 'Central Camp Sauna' in Auschwitz II-Birkenau* (Oświęcim, 2001).

16. Author's interview with Teresa Świebocka.

17. Weiss, *The Last Album*, pp. 13–15.

18. Author's interview with archivist Sharon Muller, US Holocaust Memorial Museum (USHMM), 2000.

19. Author's correspondence with USHMM historian, Ann Millin, 2000.

20. Shalom Foundation, *And I Still See Their Faces: Images of Polish Jews* (Warsaw, 1996), p. 8. See Shalom Foundation website: <shalom.org.pl>.

21. Shalom Foundation, *And I Still See Their Faces*, p. 168.

22. Ibid., p. 8.

23. Author's interview with Zvi Oren, Ghetto Fighters' House (GFH) photo archive, 2000.

24. Ibid.

25. USHMM photo archives worksheet no. 30042.

26. Letter sent to USHMM (name withheld).

27. GFH photo nos 2698 and 25235; author's interview with Zvi Oren.

28. *Journal of Historical Review*, vol. 14, no. 2 (March/April 1994), pp. 6–7. For attempts by Holocaust deniers to discredit other photographs see: Udo Walendy, *Forged War Crimes Malign the German Nation* (Hull, 1989); Wilhelm Staeglich, *Auschwitz: A Judge Looks at the Evidence* (Tübingen, 2000), pp. 101–6.

29. Sybil Milton, 'The Camera as Weapon: Documentary Photography and the Holocaust', *Simon Wiesenthal Center Annual*, vol. 1 (New York, 1984), p. 62; Sybil Milton, 'Images of the Holocaust – Part 1', in Yeuda Bauer (ed.), *Holocaust and Genocide Studies*, vol. 1, no. 1 (Oxford, 1986), p. 32.

30. Author's interview with Daniel Uziel, Yad Vashem Film and Photo Archive (YVFPA), July 2000. See *Monthly Focus*, YVFPA, 9 July 2000. It was allegedly carelessly captioned photographs which led to the German exhibition 'The German Army and Genocide', curated by the Hamburg Institute for Social Research, being withdrawn

from public showing in 1999 when two historians launched legal actions. See website: <www. his-online. de>.

31. Author's interview with Daniel Uziel.

32. USHMM photo archives worksheet no. 63689. Caption reads: 'German police take aim at Jews from Ivangorod who have just finished preparing their own grave.'

33. Author's conversation with Krzysztof Tarkowski, Majdanek State Museum, 1999. Józef Marszałek, *Majdanek: The Concentration Camp in Lublin* (Warsaw, 1986), see photographs 'Emaciated Soviet prisoner of war (1941)', 'The burial of corpses of Soviet POWs ... (1941)' and 'Jews being led to execution on 3 November 1943'.

34. Author's conversation with Krzysztof Tarkowski.

35. USHMM photo archives worksheet no. 76017.

36. Ibid.

37. The archive's own estimates in 2001.

38. Up to July 2000, 80,000 had been recorded. Author's interview with Daniel Uziel.

39. Author's interview with Sharon Muller.

40. Yves Le Maner and André Sellier (eds), *Images de Dora 1943–1945* (La Coupole, France, 1999).

41. Author's interview with Sharon Muller.

42. Ibid., author's interview with James Taylor, 2001.

43. Author's interview with James Taylor, 1999.

44. *Scotsman* Magazine, 8 September 2001, pp. 12–14.

45. *Journal of Historical Review*, vol. 14, no. 2 (March/April 1994), p. 8.

46. This is correct: the name of the city is Lwów in Polish, Lvov in Russian, L'viv in Ukrainian. Lvov was liberated by the Soviet army in July 1944. For further discussion see: <http://ukar.org/struko3.shtml>.

47. Norman G. Finkelstein, *The Holocaust Industry: Reflections on the Exploitation of Jewish Suffering* (London and New York, 2000), p. 144.

48. Author's visit to USHMM, February 2000.

49. *Independent on Sunday*, 5 February 1995, p. 1.

50. International Center of Photography, *Fotografia Polska* (New York, 1979), p. 45.

51. Author's conversation with Jerzy Lewczyński, Poland, 1999. See Jerzy Lewczyński, *Antologia Fotografii Polskiej 1839–1989* (Poland, 1999), p. 79.

52. Allan Sekula, 'Photography Between Labour and Capital', in B. H. D. Buchloh and R. Wilkie (eds), *Mining Photographs and Other Pictures 1948–1968* (Nova Scotia, 1983), p. 199.

53. Author's interview with archivist Halina Zoziebko, Auschwitz-Birkenau State Museum, 2000.

54. There are also other images from the *Stroop Report* on the Corbis website. See ref: Warsaw ghetto. Some are dated 1940, others have 'location information' given as 'Nuremberg'. All were taken in Warsaw in 1943. See, for example: BE029334, BE029332.

55. Author's correspondence with legal department of National Archives and Records Administration (NARA), Washington, DC.

56. *Journalist*, April 2001, pp. 16–17.

57. See <http://history1900s.about.com>. For examples of other websites see: <photo http:/holocaust survivors. org>. Gallery of Holocaust images: <http://coedu.usf.edu>. Holocaust Pictures Exhibition: <http://modb.oceulg.acbe/schmitz/holocaust.html>.

10. Dying for Eternity

1. Yad Vashem Film and Photo Archives (YVFPA), see album FA/268, photo nos 118–21.

2. Roland Barthes, *Camera Lucida: Reflections on Photography* (London, 1982), p. 82.

3. Ulrich Keller (ed.), *The Warsaw Ghetto in Photographs: 206 Views Made in 1941* (New York and London, 1984), p. xviii.

4. 'Walter Benjamin 1931: Extract from *A Short History of Photography*', in D. Mellor (ed.), *Germany: The New Photography 1927–33* (London, 1978), p. 75.

5. Ann Weiss, *The Last Album: Eyes from the Ashes of Auschwitz-Birkenau* (New York and London, 2001), p. 14.

6. Jeffrey D. Feldman, 'An Etymology of Opinion: Yad Vashem, Authority, and the Shifting Aesthetic of Holocaust Museums', in Y. Doosry (ed.), *Representations of Auschwitz: 50 Years of Photographs, Paintings and Graphics* (Oświęcim, 1995), p. 125.

7. *The World at War*, no. 20, 'Genocide', BBC Television, 1975.

8. Author's interview with Zvi Oren, Ghetto Fighters' House (GFH), 2000.

9. Author's visit to US Holocaust Memorial Museum (USHMM), 2000.

10. Author's correspondence with USHMM historian, Ann Millin.

11. Norman G. Finkelstein, *The Holocaust Industry: Reflections on the Exploitation of Jewish Suffering* (London and New York, 2000), p. 3. Finkelstein defines 'The Holocaust' as an ideological representation of the Nazi holocaust, the historical event, making a distinction between the two.

Schlink, Bernhard, *The Reader* (London, 1997).

Schoenberner, Gerhard, *The Yellow Star: The Persecution of the Jews in Europe, 1933–1945* (London, 1978).

Schwarberg, Günther, *In the Ghetto of Warsaw: Heinrich Jöst's Photographs* (Göttingen, 2001).

Schwarzbart, Isaak Ignacy, *The Story of the Warsaw Ghetto Uprising. Its Meaning and Message* (New York, 1953).

Seabrook, Jeremy, 'My Life is in That Box' *Ten.8*, no. 34 (1989).

Sehn, Jan, *Oświęcim-Brzezinka Concentration Camp* (Warsaw, 1961).

— *Oboz Koncentracyjny Oświęcim-Brzezinka* (Warsaw, 1964).

Seidel, Gill, *The Holocaust Denial: Antisemitism, Racism and the New Right* (Leeds, 1986).

Seko, Kazimierz, 'Dymitr Baltermanc', *Fotografia*, vol. 1, no. 39 (Poland, 1986).

Sekula, Allan, 'Photography Between Labour and Capital', in B. H. D. Buchloh and R. Wilkie (eds), *Mining Photographs and Other Pictures 1948–1968* (Nova Scotia, 1983).

— *Photography Against the Grain: Essays and Photo Works 1973–1983* (Nova Scotia, 1984).

Shalom Foundation, *And I Still See Their Faces: Images of Polish Jews* (Warsaw, 1996).

Sharf, Andrew, 'The British Press and the Holocaust', in N. Eck and A. L. Kubovy (eds), *Yad Vashem Studies on the European Jewish Catastrophe and Resistance* (Jerusalem, 1963).

Shelhav, Yaacov, 'The Holocaust in the Consciousness of Our Generation', *Yad Vashem Bulletin*, no. 3 (July 1958).

Shneiderman, S. L. (ed.), *Warsaw Ghetto: A Diary by Mary Berg* (New York, 1945).

Simonov, Konstantin Mikhailovich, *The Death Factory Near Lublin* (London, 1944).

Sloan, Jacob (ed.), *Notes from the Warsaw Ghetto. The Journal of Emmanuel Ringelblum* (New York, 1958).

Smith, Frank Dabba, *My Secret Camera, Life in the Łódź Ghetto* (London, 2000).

Smolen, Kazimierz, *Auschwitz 1940–1945. Guide Book Through the Museum* (Oświęcim, 1961).

Sontag, Susan, *On Photography* (London, 1979).

Soviet Documents on Nazi Atrocities (London, 1942).

Spence, Jo, *Putting Myself in the Picture* (London, 1986).

Staeglich, Wilhelm, *Auschwitz: A Judge Looks at the Evidence* (Tübingen, 1990).

Stibbe, Matthew, *Nineteenth Century German Antisemitic Propagandists*, Holocaust Educational Trust Research Papers, vol. 2, no. 1 (2000–01).

Suchcitz, Andrzej, *Informator Studium Polski Podziemnej 1947–1997* (London, 1997).

Świebocka, Teresa (ed.), *Auschwitz: A History in Photographs* (Oświęcim, 1995).

— *The Architecture of Crime. The 'Central Camp Sauna' in Auschwitz II-Birkenau* (Oświęcim, 2001).

Sydnor Jnr, Charles W., *Soldiers of Destruction. The SS Death's Head Division 1933–1945* (New Jersey, 1977).

Szpilman, Władysław, *The Pianist: The Extraordinary Story of One Man's Survival in Warsaw, 1939–45* (London, 1999).

Tagg, John, *The Burden of Representation: Essays on Photographies and Histories* (London, 1988).

Taylor, John, *War Photography: Realism in the British Press* (London, 1991).

— *Body Horror, Photojournalism, Catastrophe and War* (Manchester, 1998).

Tetens, T. H., *The New Germany and the Old Nazis* (London, 1961).

Tower Hamlets Arts Project, *From Auschwitz and East London* (London 1983).

The Trial of Adolf Eichmann: Record of Proceedings in the District Court of Jerusalem, vol. I (Jerusalem, 1992).

Trial of the Major War Criminals Before the International Military Tribunal, 14 November 1945 – 1 October 1946, (42 vols) (Nuremberg, 1947–49).

Trials of War Criminals Before the Nuernberg Military Tribunals – Under Control Council Law Number 10, vol. x (Washington, DC, 1951).

United States Holocaust Memorial Museum, *Auschwitz: A Crime Against Mankind* (Washington, DC, 1991).

US Holocaust Memorial Council, *Remembering the Voices that were Silenced: Days of Remembrance* (Washington, DC, 1990).

Vishniac, Roman, *A Vanished World* (New York, 1983).

Voss, Frederick S., *Reporting the War: The Journalistic Coverage of World War II* (Washington, DC, 1994).

Walendy, Udo, *Forged War Crimes Malign the German Nation* (Hull, 1989).

War in Pictures, 6 vols (London, 1940–46).

War's Best Photographs, (London, 1946).

Watson, James R., *Between Auschwitz and Tradition, Postmodern Reflections on the Task of Thinking* (Amsterdam and Atlanta, GA, 1994).

Węgierski, Dominik, *September 1939* (London, 1940).

Weiss, Ann, *The Last Album: Eyes from the Ashes of Auschwitz-Birkenau* (New York and London, 2001).

Welch, David, *Propaganda and the German Cinema 1933–1945* (London, 2001).

We Shall Not Forgive: The Horrors of the German Invasion in Documents and Photographs (Moscow, 1942).

Werth, Alexander, *Russia at War 1941–1945* (London, 1964).

Wieczorek, Janusz and Stanisław Wroński, *To The Memory of the Heroic Defenders of the Ghetto: On the 35th Anniversary of the Outbreak of the Warsaw Ghetto Uprising* (Warsaw, 1979).

Wiesal, Marion (ed.), *To Give Them Light, the Legacy of Roman Vishniac* (New York, 1993).

Willett, John, *The New Sobriety: Art and Politics in the Weimar Period 1917–1933* (London, 1978).

Williams, Val, *Warworks, Women, Photography and the Iconography of War* (London, 1994).

Winkler, Allan M., *The Politics of Propaganda: The Office of War Information 1942–1945* (New Haven, CT and London, 1978).

Wirth, Andrzej, *The Stroop Report, The Jewish Quarter of Warsaw is No More* (London, 1980).

Wiśniewska, Anna and Czesław Rajca, *Majdanek: The Concentration Camp of Lublin* (Lublin, 1997).

Wolfe, Robert (ed.), *Captured German Documents and Related Records. A National Archives Conference*, vol. 3 (Ohio, 1974).

Wood, E. Thomas and Stanisław M. Jankowski, *Karski. How One Man Tried to Stop the Holocaust* (New York, 1994).

World Jewish Congress, *The Warsaw Ghetto Uprising and Its Historical Significance* (New York, 1963).

Wroński, Stanisław and Maria Zwolakowa *Polacy i Żydzi* (Warsaw, 1971).

Wrzoz-Glinka, Stanisław, *Cierpienie i Walka Narodu Polskiego Zdjęcia – Dokumenty* (Warsaw, 1958).

Yellow Spot: The Extermination of the Jews in Germany (London, 1936).

YIVO Institute for Jewish Research, *Life Struggle and Uprising in the Warsaw Ghetto* (New York, 1963).

Young, James E., *Writing and Rewriting the Holocaust: Narrative and the Consequences of Interpretation* (Bloomington, IN, 1988).

— *The Texture of Memory: Holocaust Memorials and Meaning* (New Haven, CT and London, 1993).

Zbrzeska, Teresa, 'Bringing History to Millions', *Pro Memoria 7* (Oświęcim, 1997).

Zelizer, Barbie, *Remembering to Forget: Holocaust Memory Through the Camera's Eye* (Chicago, IL and London, 1998).

— (ed.), *Visual Culture and the Holocaust* (London, 2001).

Zonabend, Nachman, *The Truth About the Saving of the Łódź Ghetto Archive* (Stockholm, 1991).

Zylberberg, M., *A Warsaw Diary 1939–1945* (London, 1969).

Index

An *italic* number indicates reference to a figure